Mastering Graphics Programming with Vulkan

Develop a modern rendering engine from first principles to state-of-the-art techniques

Marco Castorina

Gabriel Sassone

‹packt›

BIRMINGHAM—MUMBAI

Mastering Graphics Programming with Vulkan

Copyright © 2023 Packt Publishing

All rights reserved. No part of this book may be reproduced, stored in a retrieval system, or transmitted in any form or by any means, without the prior written permission of the publisher, except in the case of brief quotations embedded in critical articles or reviews.

Every effort has been made in the preparation of this book to ensure the accuracy of the information presented. However, the information contained in this book is sold without warranty, either express or implied. Neither the author(s), nor Packt Publishing or its dealers and distributors, will be held liable for any damages caused or alleged to have been caused directly or indirectly by this book.

Packt Publishing has endeavored to provide trademark information about all of the companies and products mentioned in this book by the appropriate use of capitals. However, Packt Publishing cannot guarantee the accuracy of this information.

Group Product Manager: Rohit Rajkumar

Publishing Product Manager: Nitin Nainani

Content Development Editor: Abhishek Jadhav

Technical Editor: Simran Ali

Copy Editor: Safis Editing

Project Coordinator: Aishwarya Mohan

Proofreader: Safis Editing

Indexer: Manju Arasan

Production Designer: Vijay Kamble

Marketing Coordinator: Nivedita Pandey

First published: January 2023

Production reference: 1130123

Published by Packt Publishing Ltd.

Livery Place

35 Livery Street

Birmingham

B3 2PB, UK.

ISBN 978-1-80324-479-2

www.packt.com

To my parents and my grandma, who taught me to work hard and never give up. To my kids, who remind me daily to look at things differently and always challenge my assumptions. And to my wife – without her support throughout the years, this book wouldn't exist.

– Marco Castorina

To my mum, dad, and sister who always believed in me and taught me how to strive to be better with an open mind and heart.

To my friend Enrico, for always being an inspiration in all the adventures of my life.

To Gianluca, Piero, Mauro, Roberto, Stefano, Riccardo, Emiliano, Stuart, Federico, Luca, and Stefano for being in my life and supporting me over the years.

To the Belluno crew, colleagues, and friends: Carlo Mangani, Fabio Pagetti, Mattia Poderi, Vittorio Conti, Flavio Bortot, and Luca Marchetti.

To all the Blacksand crew: Marco, Alessandro, Andrea, Gianluca, Alessandra, Elisa, Cinzia, and many more, who made me feel at home even when I was on the other side of the planet.

To all the colleagues that helped me on my journey: Tiziano Lena, Gabriele Barlocci, Alessandro Monopoli, Daniele Pieroni, Francesco Antolini, Andrea Pessino, Simone Kulczycki, Marco Vallario, Nicholas Rathbone, Peter Asberg, Dave Barrett, David Grijns, Christofer Sundberg, David Smethurst, Engin Cilasun, and Gennadiy Korol – you all taught me a lot.

To the awesome rendering community: Matt Pettineo, Natalya Tatarchuk, Inigo Quilez, Jorge Jimenez, Bart Wronski, Alan Wolfe, and many, many more.

And finally to everybody else that crossed my path: in one way or another, you changed my life.

– Gabriel Sassone

Acknowledgments

Like all published works, this book is the effort of many dedicated people. To Chayan Majumdar and Nitin Nainani, who first reached out to us about this project and helped us structure the book. To our editors Abhishek Jadhav and Aamir Ahmed, who helped us find our voice and made sure our content was clear and organized.

To our project managers, Ajesh Devavaram and Aishwarya Mohan, who kept us on track and were understanding when we needed more time. We would also like to thank our technical reviewer, who gave us invaluable feedback to make each chapter clearer and more accessible.

This book wouldn't exist if it weren't for the many dedicated graphics and rendering engineers all over the world who keep sharing their work and pushing the field forward. Many of those ideas have made it into this book and we hope we did them justice. The support of the graphics community has been invaluable and kept us motivated throughout the writing process.

I, Marco, would also like to thank AMD and 7th Sense, who have allowed me to work on this project in my spare time. Andy Poole at Samsung first helped me wade through the Vulkan specification. His insight and approach still help me on a daily basis. To Hugh McAtamney and Bryan Duggan from the Dublin Institute of Technology, who inspired me to pursue a career in graphics.

To Eike Anderson from Bournemouth University, who helped me to improve my technical writing and approach things from first principles. To Richard Brown and Alex Hughes at 7th Sense, as my discussions with them challenged me to push Vulkan to its limits and provided insight into improving my code architecture.

Finally, I couldn't have done it without Gabriel. His tremendous experience and continuous feedback supported me throughout this project. It was a joy working with him and I consider myself lucky that I can now call him a friend.

I, Gabriel, would like to thank The Multiplayer Group, who have allowed me to work on this project and were supportive of it.

To Matt Pettineo at ReadyAtDawn, for being my biggest inspiration in rendering and coding. Without his guidance and teachings, I would not have been able to tackle this project.

To Engin Cilasun, for being my rendering and engine design pal, teaching me a lot about how to think differently and challenging my assumptions to find new ways.

To Codemasters, ReadyAtDawn, Moon Studios, and Avalanche Studios for all the experience and teaching in my career.

Finally, to Marco, who gave me the possibility to work on this project. His deep knowledge and understanding of rendering and GPUs were paramount. His skill at solving complex problems and reading the Vulkan spec gave us the edge on the latest technology. I learned a lot from him and have deep gratitude toward him.

It was incredible working with him, and even better, having a new person to call a friend.

Contributors

About the authors

Marco Castorina first became familiar with Vulkan while working as a driver developer at Samsung. Later, he developed a 2D and 3D renderer in Vulkan from scratch for a leading media server company. He recently joined the games graphics performance team at AMD. In his spare time, he keeps up to date with the latest techniques in real-time graphics. He also likes cooking and playing guitar.

Gabriel Sassone is a rendering enthusiast currently working as a principal rendering engineer at The Multiplayer Group. Previously working for Avalanche Studios, where he first encountered Vulkan, they developed the Vulkan layer for the proprietary Apex Engine and its Google Stadia port. He previously worked at ReadyAtDawn, Codemasters, FrameStudios, and some other non-gaming tech companies. His spare time is filled with music and rendering, gaming, and outdoor activities.

About the reviewer

Victor Blanco Ruiz is an experienced programmer focused on graphics, low level programming, and game engine architecture. He has worked for big name international companies as an engine programmer, has worked on PUBG: Battlegrounds and ported multiple games to PSVR, PS4, and Nintendo Switch as a freelancer, as well as self-published the games DWVR and rRootage Reloaded. He is the author of the Vulkan learning website VkGuide.

Table of Contents

Preface   xv

Part 1: Foundations of a Modern Rendering Engine

1

Introducing the Raptor Engine and Hydra   3

Technical requirements	4	Understanding the gITF scene format	16
Windows	4	PBR in a nutshell	25
Linux	5	A word on GPU debugging	27
macOS	7	Summary	30
How to read this book	7	Further reading	30
Understanding the code structure	7		
Layers of code	8		

2

Improving Resources Management   31

Technical requirements	32	Compiling GLSL to SPIR-V	41
Unlocking and implementing bindless rendering	32	Understanding the SPIR-V output	42
		From SPIR-V to pipeline layout	45
Checking for support	32	Improving load times with a pipeline cache	51
Creating the descriptor pool	34		
Updating the descriptor set	36	Summary	54
Update to shader code	39	Further reading	55
Automating pipeline layout generation	40		

3

Unlocking Multi-Threading — 57

Technical requirements	58	Recording commands	
Task-based multi-threading using enkiTS	58	on multiple threads	76
Why task-based parallelism?	58	The allocation strategy	76
Using the enkiTS (Task-Scheduler) library	59	Command buffer recycling	77
		Primary versus secondary command buffers	77
Asynchronous loading	61	Drawing using primary command buffers	78
Creating the I/O thread and tasks	63	Drawing using secondary command buffers	79
Vulkan queues and the first parallel command generation	64	Spawning multiple tasks to record command buffers	81
The AsynchronousLoader class	69	Summary	82
		Further reading	83

4

Implementing a Frame Graph — 85

Technical requirements	85	Implementing topological sort	94
Understanding frame graphs	86	Driving rendering with the frame graph	102
Building a graph	86	Summary	106
A data-driven approach	88	Further reading	106
Implementing the frame graph	91		

5

Unlocking Async Compute — 107

Technical requirements	107	Adding a separate queue for async compute	114
Replacing multiple fences with a single timeline semaphore	107	Submitting work on separate queues	115
Enabling the timeline semaphore extension	109	Implementing cloth simulation using async compute	117
Creating a timeline semaphore	111		
Waiting for a timeline semaphore on the CPU	111	Benefits of using compute shaders	117
Using a timeline semaphore on the GPU	112		

Compute shaders overview	118	Summary	126
Writing compute shaders	120	Further reading	126

Part 2: GPU-Driven Rendering

6

GPU-Driven Rendering — 131

Technical requirements	132	Implementing mesh shaders	143
Breaking down large meshes into meshlets	132	GPU culling using compute	146
		Depth pyramid generation	147
Generating meshlets	135	Occlusion culling	149
Understanding task and mesh shaders	138	Summary	152
		Further reading	153
Implementing task shaders	140		

7

Rendering Many Lights with Clustered Deferred Rendering — 155

Technical requirements	155	Implementing light clusters	167
A brief history of clustered lighting	156	CPU lights assignment	168
		GPU light processing	174
Differences between forward and deferred techniques	157	Summary	176
		Further reading	176
Implementing a G-buffer	160		

8

Adding Shadows Using Mesh Shaders — 179

Technical requirements	179	Shadow mapping	180
A brief history of shadow techniques	180	Raytraced shadows	181
		Implementing shadow mapping using mesh shaders	181
Shadow volumes	180		

Overview	181	**Improving shadow memory with Vulkan's sparse resources**	**197**
Cubemap shadows	182		
A note about multiview rendering	184	Creating and allocating sparse textures	197
Per-light mesh instance culling	184	Choosing per-light shadow memory usage	200
Indirect draw commands generation	187	Rendering into a sparse shadow map	203
Shadow cubemap face culling	188	**Summary**	**206**
Meshlet shadow rendering – task shader	190	**Further reading**	**207**
Meshlet shadow rendering – mesh shader	193		
Shadow map sampling	194		

9

Implementing Variable Rate Shading — 209

Technical requirements	**209**	Taking advantage of specialization constants	216
Introducing variable rate shading	**209**	**Summary**	**219**
Determining the shading rate	210	**Further reading**	**219**
Integrating variable rate shading using Vulkan	**212**		

10

Adding Volumetric Fog — 221

Technical requirements	**222**	Calculating the lighting contribution	230
Introducing Volumetric Fog Rendering	**222**	Integrating scattering and extinction	232
		Applying Volumetric Fog to the scene	234
Volumetric Rendering	222	Adding filters	235
Volumetric Fog	224	Volumetric noise generation	238
Implementing Volumetric Fog Rendering	**228**	Blue noise	239
Data injection	228	**Summary**	**240**
		Further reading	**240**

Part 3: Advanced Rendering Techniques

11

Temporal Anti-Aliasing — 245

Technical requirements	247	Scene sampling	257
Overview	247	The history constraint	258
The simplest TAA implementation	249	Resolve	260
Jittering the camera	250	**Sharpening the image**	**262**
Choosing jittering sequences	251	Sharpness post-processing	262
Adding motion vectors	252	Negative mip bias	263
First implementation code	253	Unjitter texture UVs	263
Improving TAA	**254**	**Improving banding**	**264**
Reprojection	254	**Summary**	**265**
History sampling	256	**Further reading**	**265**

12

Getting Started with Ray Tracing — 267

Technical requirements	267	Defining and creating a ray tracing pipeline	276
Introduction to ray tracing in Vulkan	268	Summary	284
Building the BLAS and TLAS	270	Further reading	284

13

Revisiting Shadows with Ray Tracing — 287

Technical requirements	287	Computing visibility	292
Implementing simple ray-traced shadows	**288**	Computing filtered visibility	298
Improving ray-traced shadows	**289**	Using the filtered visibility	301
Motion vectors	290	**Summary**	**301**
Computing visibility variance	291	**Further reading**	**302**

14

Adding Dynamic Diffuse Global Illumination with Ray Tracing   303

Technical requirements	304	Ray-hit shader	312
Introduction to indirect lighting	304	Ray-miss shader	315
Introduction to Dynamic Diffuse Global Illumination (DDGI)	307	Updating probes irradiance and visibility shaders	315
Ray tracing for each probe	308	Indirect lighting sampling	320
Probes offsetting	308	Modifications to the calculate_lighting method	325
Probes irradiance and visibility updates	309	Probe offsets shader	326
Probes sampling	310	Summary	331
Implementing DDGI	311	Further reading	331
Ray-generation shader	311		

15

Adding Reflections with Ray Tracing   333

Technical requirements	333	Implementing a denoiser	340
How screen-space reflections work	334	Summary	347
Implementing ray-traced reflections	335	Further reading	348

Index   349

Other Books You May Enjoy   358

Preface

Vulkan is now an established and flexible multi-platform graphics API. It has been adopted in many industries, including game development, medical imaging, movie productions, and media playback.

Learning about Vulkan is a foundational step to understanding how a modern graphics API works, both on desktop and mobile.

In *Mastering Graphics Programming with Vulkan*, you will begin by developing the foundations of a rendering framework. You will learn how to leverage advanced Vulkan features to write a modern rendering engine. You will understand how to automate resource binding and dependencies. You will then take advantage of GPU-driven rendering to scale the size of your scenes and, finally, you will get familiar with ray tracing techniques that will improve the visual quality of your rendered image.

By the end of this book, you will have a thorough understanding of the inner workings of a modern rendering engine and the graphics techniques employed to achieve state-of-the-art results. The framework developed in this book will be the starting point for all your future experiments.

Who this book is for

This book is for professional or hobbyist graphics and game developers who would like to gain more in-depth knowledge about how to write a modern and performant rendering engine in Vulkan.

Users should be already familiar with basic concepts of graphics programming (that is, matrices and vectors) and have basic knowledge of Vulkan.

What this book covers

Chapter 1, *Introducing the Raptor Engine and Hydra*, introduces you to the structure of our framework by providing an overview of the main components. We will then see how to compile the code for Windows and Linux.

Chapter 2, *Improving Resources Management*, simplifies managing textures for rendering by moving our renderer to use bindless textures. We will also automate the pipeline layout generation by parsing the generated SPIR-V and demonstrate how to implement pipeline caching.

Chapter 3, *Unlocking Multi-Threading*, details the concept of task-based parallelism that will help us make use of multiple cores. We will leverage this technique to load resources asynchronously and record multiple command buffers in parallel.

Chapter 4, Implementing a Frame Graph, helps us develop the frame graph, a data structure that holds our render passes and how they depend on each other. We will leverage this data structure to automate resource barrier placement and improve memory usage with resource aliasing.

Chapter 5, Unlocking Async Compute, illustrates how to leverage the async compute queue in Vulkan. We introduce timeline semaphores, which make it easier to manage queue synchronization. Finally, we will implement a simple cloth simulation, which runs on a separate queue.

Chapter 6, GPU-Driven Rendering, moves our renderer from meshes to meshlets, which are small groups of triangles that are used to implement GPU culling. We will introduce mesh shaders and explain how they can be leveraged to implement modern culling techniques.

Chapter 7, Rendering Many Lights with Clustered Deferred Rendering, describes our G-buffer implementation before moving to clustered light rendering. We will demonstrate how to leverage screen tiles and depth binning for an efficient implementation.

Chapter 8, Adding Shadows Using Mesh Shaders, provides a brief history of shadow techniques and then proceeds to describe our chosen approach. We leverage our meshlets and mesh shaders support to efficiently render cubemap shadowmaps. We will also demonstrate how to use sparse resources to reduce memory usage.

Chapter 9, Implementing Variable Rate Shading, gives us an overview of variable rate shading and explains why it's useful. We will then describe how to use the Vulkan extension to add this technique to our renderer.

Chapter 10, Adding Volumetric Fog, implements a volumetric effect from first principles. We will then discuss spatial and temporal filtering to improve the quality of the final result.

Chapter 11, Temporal Anti-Aliasing, walks through a brief history of anti-aliasing techniques. We will then describe all the steps required to implement a robust temporal anti-aliasing solution.

Chapter 12, Getting Started with Ray Tracing, outlines the key concepts required to make use of the ray-tracing extension in Vulkan. We will then provide the implementation details for creating ray-tracing pipelines, shader-binding tables, and Acceleration Structures.

Chapter 13, Revisiting Shadows with Ray Tracing, offers up an alternative implementation of shadows that uses ray tracing. We will describe an algorithm that leverages dynamic ray count per light, paired with a spatial and temporal filter to produce stable results.

Chapter 14, Adding Dynamic Diffuse Global Illumination with Ray Tracing, involves adding global illumination to our scene. We will describe our use of ray tracing to generate probe data and provide a solution to minimize light leaking.

Chapter 15, Adding Reflections with Ray Tracing, briefly covers screen-space reflections and their shortcomings. We will then describe our implementation of ray-traced reflections. Finally, we will implement a denoiser to make the result usable for the final lighting computation.

To get the most out of this book

This book assumes the reader is familiar with the basic concepts of Vulkan or other modern rendering APIs such as DirectX 12 or Metal. You should be comfortable editing and compiling C or C++ code and GLSL shader code.

Software/hardware covered in the book	Operating system requirements
Vulkan 1.2	Windows or Linux

You will need a C++ compiler that supports C++17. The latest version of the Vulkan SDK also needs to be installed on the system. We provide a Visual Studio solution as well as CMake files to compile the project.

If you are using the digital version of this book, we advise you to type the code yourself or access the code from the book's GitHub repository (a link is available in the next section). Doing so will help you avoid any potential errors related to the copying and pasting of code.

For each chapter, we recommend you run the code and make sure you understand how it works. Each chapter builds on the concepts from the previous one and it is important you have internalized those concepts before moving on. We also suggest making your own changes to experiment with different approaches.

Download the example code files

You can download the example code files for this book from GitHub at `https://github.com/PacktPublishing/Mastering-Graphics-Programming-with-Vulkan`. If there's an update to the code, it will be updated in the GitHub repository.

We also have other code bundles from our rich catalog of books and videos available at `https://github.com/PacktPublishing/`. Check them out!

Download the color images

We also provide a PDF file that has color images of the screenshots and diagrams used in this book. You can download it here: `https://packt.link/ht2jV`.

Conventions used

There are a number of text conventions used throughout this book.

`Code in text`: Indicates code words in text, database table names, folder names, filenames, file extensions, pathnames, dummy URLs, user input, and Twitter handles. Here is an example: "For each resource type, we call the relative method on the `DescriptorSetCreation` object."

A block of code is set as follows:

```
export VULKAN_SDK=~/vulkan/1.2.198.1/x86_64
export PATH=$VULKAN_SDK/bin:$PATH
export LD_LIBRARY_PATH=$VULKAN_SDK/lib:$LD_LIBRARY_PATH
export VK_LAYER_PATH=$VULKAN_SDK/etc/vulkan/explicit_layer.d
```

When we wish to draw your attention to a particular part of a code block, the relevant lines or items are set in bold:

```
VkPhysicalDeviceFeatures2 device_features{ VK_STRUCTURE_TYPE_
PHYSICAL_DEVICE_FEATURES_2, &indexing_features };

    vkGetPhysicalDeviceFeatures2( vulkan_physical_device,
    &device_features );

    bindless_supported = indexing_features.
    descriptorBindingPartiallyBound && indexing_features.
    runtimeDescriptorArray;
```

Any command-line input or output is written as follows:

```
$ tar -xvf vulkansdk-linux-x86_64-1.2.198.1.tar.gz
```

Bold: Indicates a new term, an important word, or words that you see onscreen. For instance, words in menus or dialog boxes appear in **bold**. Here is an example: "We then start the application by clicking on **Launch**, and we will notice an overlay reporting the frame time and the number of frames rendered."

> Tips or important notes
> Appear like this.

Get in touch

Feedback from our readers is always welcome.

General feedback: If you have questions about any aspect of this book, email us at `customercare@packtpub.com` and mention the book title in the subject of your message.

Errata: Although we have taken every care to ensure the accuracy of our content, mistakes do happen. If you have found a mistake in this book, we would be grateful if you would report this to us. Please visit www.packtpub.com/support/errata and fill in the form.

Piracy: If you come across any illegal copies of our works in any form on the internet, we would be grateful if you would provide us with the location address or website name. Please contact us at copyright@packt.com with a link to the material.

If you are interested in becoming an author: If there is a topic that you have expertise in and you are interested in either writing or contributing to a book, please visit authors.packtpub.com.

Share Your Thoughts

Once you've read *Mastering Graphics Programming with Vulkan*, we'd love to hear your thoughts! Scan the QR code below to go straight to the Amazon review page for this book and share your feedback.

https://www.amazon.com/review/create-review/error?asin=1803244798

Your review is important to us and the tech community and will help us make sure we're delivering excellent quality content.

Download a free PDF copy of this book

Thanks for purchasing this book!

Do you like to read on the go but are unable to carry your print books everywhere?

Is your eBook purchase not compatible with the device of your choice?

Don't worry, now with every Packt book you get a DRM-free PDF version of that book at no cost.

Read anywhere, any place, on any device. Search, copy, and paste code from your favorite technical books directly into your application.

The perks don't stop there, you can get exclusive access to discounts, newsletters, and great free content in your inbox daily

Follow these simple steps to get the benefits:

1. Scan the QR code or visit the link below

   https://packt.link/free-ebook/9781803244792

2. Submit your proof of purchase
3. That's it! We'll send your free PDF and other benefits to your email directly

Part 1: Foundations of a Modern Rendering Engine

In this part, we will build a solid foundation for our rendering engine. We will cover the following chapters in this section:

- *Chapter 1, Introducing the Raptor Engine and Hydra*
- *Chapter 2, Improving Resources Management*
- *Chapter 3, Unlocking Multi-Threading*
- *Chapter 4, Implementing a Frame Graph*
- *Chapter 5, Unlocking Async Compute*

1
Introducing the Raptor Engine and Hydra

When we set out to write this book, we decided our goal was to start where a traditional Vulkan tutorial might end. There are plenty of great resources, both in print and on the web, that help beginners discover and understand the Vulkan API.

We decided to write this book as we felt there was a gap between these introductory tutorials and some of the more advanced material. Some of these topics might be covered in articles and blog posts, but we couldn't find a resource that organized them in a single and cohesive format.

While we assume some familiarity with Vulkan, in this chapter, we take the opportunity to go over some of the basic concepts that we will build upon throughout the remainder of the book. We will present the code organization and the classes and libraries that we use throughout the book.

In this chapter, we're going to cover the following main topics:

- How to read this book
- Understanding the code structure
- Understanding the glTF scene format
- Physically based rendering in a nutshell
- A word on GPU debugging

By the end of this chapter, you will be familiar with the Raptor Engine and the rendering framework we developed for this book. You will have also learned the structure of the glTF model format and the base concepts behind physically based rendering.

Technical requirements

You will need a GPU that supports at least Vulkan 1.1. At the time of writing, Vulkan 1.3 had just been announced and many vendors, such as AMD and Nvidia, have provided day-one support. We have kept the lower requirements to allow as many people as possible to follow along.

Some of the later chapters will make use of hardware features that might not be available on some of the older graphics cards. Wherever possible, we will provide an alternative software solution. If it's not feasible, we try to focus more on the generic aspects of the implementation and less on the API details.

The complete code for this chapter is available on GitHub at `https://github.com/PacktPublishing/Mastering-Graphics-Programming-with-Vulkan/tree/main/source/chapter1`.

Windows

The code has been tested on Windows with Visual Studio 2019 16.11 and the Vulkan SDK version 1.2.198.1 (this might change as we write the book).

To install the Vulkan SDK on Windows, you will need to download and run the following executable:

`https://sdk.lunarg.com/sdk/download/1.2.198.1/windows/VulkanSDK-1.2.198.1-Installer.exe`

After installing the Vulkan SDK, make sure you can run the `vulkaninfoSDK.exe` program in the `Bin` folder to confirm that the SDK has been installed correctly and that your graphics drivers support Vulkan.

Please check the official documentation (`https://vulkan.lunarg.com/doc/sdk/latest/windows/getting_started.html`) should you need further details on the installation process.

We have provided a Visual Studio solution that contains the full code for the book and that allows you to easily build the executable for each chapter.

Once the solution has been built, set the `Chapter1` project as the run target and run the program. Here's what you should be seeing:

Figure 1.1 – The rendering result

Linux

For Linux, we have used Visual Studio Code, GCC 9 or above, and CMake 3.22.1. The version of the Vulkan SDK matches the one on Windows. We tested both on Debian 11 and Ubuntu 20.04.

We have used CMake to support different build systems, but we have only tested with Makefile.

To install the Vulkan SDK, you will need to download this file: `https://sdk.lunarg.com/sdk/download/1.2.198.1/linux/vulkansdk-linux-x86_64-1.2.198.1.tar.gz`.

Assuming you have downloaded it in the `~/Downloads` folder, extract the package by running the following command:

```
$ tar -xvf vulkansdk-linux-x86_64-1.2.198.1.tar.gz
```

This will create the `1.2.198.1` top-level folder.

There are two options to make the SDK available to build the code:

- You can add the following environment variables to your ~/.bashrc file (or the main configuration file of your shell if you are not using Bash). Please note that you might have to create this file:

    ```
    export VULKAN_SDK=~/vulkan/1.2.198.1/x86_64
    export PATH=$VULKAN_SDK/bin:$PATH
    export LD_LIBRARY_PATH=$VULKAN_SDK/lib:
    $LD_LIBRARY_PATH
    export VK_LAYER_PATH=$VULKAN_SDK/etc/vulkan/
    explicit_layer.d
    ```

- The other option is to add the following to your ~/.bashrc file:

    ```
    source ~/Downloads/1.2.198.1/setup-env.sh
    ```

After you have edited the ~/.bashrc file, restart your Terminal. You should now be able to run vulkaninfo. If that's not the case, try to follow the previous steps again. Please refer to the official LunarG guide (https://vulkan.lunarg.com/doc/sdk/latest/linux/getting_started.html) should you need more details on the installation process.

To generate the build files, you need to run the following command:

```
$ cmake -B build -DCMAKE_BUILD_TYPE=Debug
```

If you'd like to create a release build, run the following command:

```
$ cmake -B build -DCMAKE_BUILD_TYPE=Release
```

This will create the build files in the build folder. You can, of course, use a different name for the folder.

To build the code for this chapter, run the following command:

```
$ cmake --build build --target chapter1 -- -j 4
```

The number after -j tells the compiler how many threads to use to compile the code in parallel. The recommended value is to use the number of cores your processor has.

After the build has completed, the Chapter1 executable has been created and is ready to run!

> **Note**
> Both Windows and Linux builds have been tested throughout the writing of the book by our technical reviewers and beta readers, but some issues might have gone unnoticed. If you have questions or if you would like to report an issue, please open a GitHub issue or reach out to us on Twitter: `@marco_castorina` and `@GabrielSassone`.

macOS

Vulkan is not natively available on macOS but is provided through a translation layer into Metal, the graphics API developed by Apple. This translation layer is provided by the Vulkan SDK with the MoltenVK library.

Because of this indirection, not all features and extensions are available on macOS. Given that we are going to make use of some advanced features such as ray tracing in this book, we didn't want to provide a partially working version of our code for macOS. For the time being, this platform is not supported.

How to read this book

We have organized the content of this book to gradually build on more advanced features. Advanced chapters in this book will rely on topics exposed earlier in the book. For this reason, we suggest that you read the book in order.

However, some of the later chapters on ray tracing could be read in any order as they cover topics that can be developed independently. If you are already familiar with the topic in one of the chapters, we still recommend that you skim through it as you might still find some valuable information.

Understanding the code structure

In this section, we will deep dive into the foundational code used throughout the book and we will explain the rationale behind some of the decisions we made.

When we started thinking about the code to be used, the objective was clear: there was the need for something lightweight, simple, and basic enough to give us the possibility to build upon it. A fully fledged library would have been too much.

Also, we needed something that we were familiar with to make the development process smoother and give us confidence.

There are different great libraries out there, such as Sokol (`https://github.com/floooh/sokol`) or BGFX (`https://github.com/bkaradzic/bgfx`), and a few more, but they all have some drawbacks that seemed problematic.

Sokol, for example, even though it is a great library, does not support the Vulkan API, and has an interface still based on older graphics APIs (such as OpenGL and D3D11).

BGFX is a more complete library, but it is a little too generic and feature-fledged to give us the possibility to build upon it.

After some research, we leaned toward the Hydra Engine – a library that Gabriel developed in the last couple of years as code to experiment with and write articles on rendering.

Here are some advantages of starting from the Hydra Engine (`https://github.com/JorenJoestar/DataDrivenRendering`) and evolving it into the Raptor Engine:

- Code familiarity
- Small and simple code base
- Vulkan-based API
- No advanced features, but strong building blocks

The Hydra Engine seemed perfect, being small but usable and familiar. From an API design perspective, it was a clear advantage compared to other libraries that both authors had used in the past.

Being designed from scratch by Gabriel, evolving the code through this book is done with the full knowledge of the underlying architecture.

Starting from the Hydra Engine, we changed some code to be more Vulkan-focused, and thus the Raptor Engine was born. In the following sections, we will have a brief look at the code architecture to familiarize you with the building blocks that will be used throughout all the chapters.

We will also look at the glTF data format used to import meshes, textures, and materials into the Raptor Engine.

Layers of code

The Raptor Engine is created with a layer-based mentality for code, in which a layer can interact only with lower ones.

This choice was made to simplify communication between layers and simplify the API design and the expected behavior for the final user.

There are three layers in Raptor:

- Foundation
- Graphics
- Application

The **foundation** and **application** layers are common to all chapters and can be found at `source/raptor`.

Each chapter has its own implementation of the **graphics** layer. This makes it easier to introduce new features in each chapter without having to worry about maintaining multiple code paths across all chapters. For instance, the code for the graphics layer for this chapter can be found at `source/chapter1/graphics`.

While developing the Raptor Engine, we enforced the communication direction based on the layer we were on, so that a layer could interact with the code within the same layer and the bottom layer only.

In this case, the foundation layer can interact only with the other code inside the layer, the graphics layer can interact with the foundation layer, and the application layer interacts with all the layers.

There will be possible situations where we need to have some communication from a bottom layer to an upper layer, and the solution to that is to create code in the upper layer to drive the communication between the lower layers.

For example, the `Camera` class is defined in the foundation layer, and it is a class that contains all the mathematical code to drive a rendering camera.

What if we need user input to move the camera, say with a mouse or gamepad?

Based on this decision, we created `GameCamera` in the application layer, which contains the input code, takes the user input, and modifies the camera as needed.

This upper layer bridging will be used in other areas of the code and will be explained when needed.

The following sections will give you an overview of the main layers and some of their fundamental code so that you will be familiar with all the available building blocks that will be used throughout the book.

Foundation layer

The foundation layer is a set of different classes that behave as fundamental bricks for everything needed in the framework.

The classes are very specialized and cover different types of needs, but they are required to build the rendering code written in this book. They range from data structures to file operations, logging, and string processing.

While similar data structures are provided by the C++ standard library, we have decided to write our own as we only need a subset of functionality in most cases. It also allows us to carefully control and track memory allocations.

We traded some comfort (that is, automatic release of memory on destruction) for more fine-tuned control over memory lifetime and better compile times. These all-important data structures are used for separate needs and will be used heavily in the graphics layer.

We will briefly go over each foundational block to help you get accustomed to them.

Memory management

Let's start with **memory management** (`source/raptor/foundation/memory.hpp`).

One key API decision made here is to have an explicit allocation model, so for any dynamically allocated memory, an allocator will be needed. This is reflected in all classes through the code base.

This foundational brick defines the main allocator API used by the different allocators that can be used throughout the code.

There is `HeapAllocator`, based on the `tlsf` allocator, a fixed-size linear allocator, a malloc-based allocator, a fixed-size stack allocator, and a fixed-size double stack allocator.

While we will not cover memory management techniques here, as it is less relevant to the purpose of this book, you can glimpse a more professional memory management mindset in the code base.

Arrays

Next, we will look at **arrays** (`source/raptor/foundation/array.hpp`).

Probably the most fundamental data structure of all software engineering, arrays are used to represent contiguous and dynamically allocated data, with an interface similar to the better-known `std::vector` (`https://en.cppreference.com/w/cpp/container/vector`).

The code is simpler compared to the **Standard Library** (`std`) implementation and requires an explicit allocator to be initialized.

The only notable difference from `std::vector` can be seen in the methods, such as `push_use()`, which grows the array and returns the newly allocated element to be filled, and the `delete_swap()` method, which removes an element and swaps it with the last element.

Hash maps

Hash maps (`source/raptor/foundation/hash_map.hpp`) are another fundamental data structure, as they boost search operation performance, and they are used extensively in the code base: every time there is the need to quickly find an object based on some simple search criteria (*search the texture by name*), then a hash map is the de facto standard data structure.

The sheer volume of information about hash maps is huge and out of the scope of this book, but recently a good all-round implementation of hash maps was documented and shared by Google inside their Abseil library (code available here: `https://github.com/abseil/abseil-cpp`).

The Abseil hash map is an evolution of the SwissTable hash map, storing some extra metadata per entry to quickly reject elements, using linear probing to insert elements, and finally, using Single Instruction Multiple Data (SIMD) instructions to quickly test more entries.

> **Important note**
>
> For a good overview of the ideas behind the Abseil hash map implementation, there are a couple of nice articles that can be read. They can be found here:
>
> **Article 1**: `https://gankra.github.io/blah/hashbrown-tldr/`
>
> **Article 2**: `https://blog.waffles.space/2018/12/07/deep-dive-into-hashbrown/`
>
> *Article 1* is a good overview of the topic and *Article 2* goes a little more in-depth about the implementation.

File operations

Next, we will look at **file operations** (`source/raptor/foundation/file.hpp`).

Another common set of operations performed in an engine is file handling, for example, to read a texture, a shader, or a text file from the hard drive.

These operations follow a similar pattern to the C file APIs, such as `file_open` being similar to the `fopen` function (`https://www.cplusplus.com/reference/cstdio/fopen/`).

In this set of functions, there are also the ones needed to create and delete a folder, or some utilities such as extrapolating the filename or the extension of a path.

For example, to create a texture, you need to first open the texture file in memory, then send it to the graphics layer to create a Vulkan representation of it to be properly usable by the GPU.

Serialization

Serialization (`source/raptor/foundation/blob_serialization.hpp`), the process of converting human-readable files to a binary counterpart, is also present here.

The topic is vast, and there is not as much information as it deserves, but a good starting point is the article `https://yave.handmade.network/blog/p/2723-how_media_molecule_does_serialization`, or `https://jorenjoestar.github.io/post/serialization_for_games`.

We will use serialization to process some human-readable files (mostly JSON files) into more custom files as they are needed.

The process is done to speed up loading files, as human-readable formats are great for expressing things and can be modified, but binary files can be created to suit the application's needs.

This is a fundamental step in any game-related technology, also called **asset baking**.

For the purpose of this code, we will use a minimal amount of serialization, but as with memory management, it is a topic to have in mind when designing any performant code.

Logging

Logging (`source/raptor/foundation/log.hpp`) is the process of writing some user-defined text to both help understand the flow of the code and debug the application.

It can be used to write the initialization steps of a system or to report some error with additional information so it can be used by the user.

Provided with the code is a simple logging service, providing the option of adding user-defined callbacks and intercepting any message.

An example of logging usage is the Vulkan debug layer, which will output any warning or error to the logging service when needed, giving the user instantaneous feedback on the application's behavior.

String processing

Next, we will look at **strings** (`source/raptor/foundation/string.hpp`).

Strings are arrays of characters used to store text. Within the Raptor Engine, the need to have clean control of memory and a simple interface added the need for custom-written string code.

The main class provided is the `StringBuffer` class, which lets the user allocate a maximum fixed amount of memory, and within that memory, perform typical string operations: concatenation, formatting, and substrings.

A second class provided is the `StringArray` class, which allows the user to efficiently store and track different strings inside a contiguous chunk of memory.

This is used, for example, when retrieving a list of files and folders. A final utility string class is the `StringView` class, used for read-only access to a string.

Time management

Next is **time management** (`source/raptor/foundation/time.hpp`).

When developing a custom engine, timing is very important, and having some functions to help calculate different timings is what the time management functions do.

For example, any application needs to calculate a time difference, used to advance time and calculations in various aspects, often known as **delta time**.

This will be manually calculated in the application layer, but it uses the time functions to do it. It can be also used to measure CPU performance, for example, to pinpoint slow code or gather statistics when performing some operations.

Timing methods conveniently allow the user to calculate time durations in different units, from seconds down to milliseconds.

Process execution

One last utility area is **process execution** (`source/raptor/foundation/process.hpp`) – defined as running any external program from within our own code.

In the Raptor Engine, one of the most important usages of external processes is the execution of Vulkan's shader compiler to convert GLSL shaders to SPIR-V format, as seen at `https://www.khronos.org/registry/SPIR-V/specs/1.0/SPIRV.html`. The Khronos specification is needed for shaders to be used by Vulkan.

We have been through all the different utilities building blocks (many seemingly unrelated) that cover the basics of a modern rendering engine.

These basics are not graphics related by themselves, but they are required to build a graphical application that gives the final user full control of what is happening and represents a watered-down mindset of what modern game engines do behind the scenes.

Next, we will introduce the graphics layer, where some of the foundational bricks can be seen in action and represent the most important part of the code base developed for this book.

Graphics layer

The most important architectural layer is the graphics layer, which will be the main focus of this book. Graphics will include all the Vulkan-related code and abstractions needed to draw anything on the screen using the GPU.

There is a caveat in the organization of the source code: having the book divided into different chapters and having one GitHub repository, there was the need to have a snapshot of the graphics code for each chapter; thus, graphics code will be duplicated and evolved in each chapter's code throughout the game.

We expect the code to grow in this folder as this book progresses after each chapter, and not only here, as we will develop shaders and use other data resources as well, but it is fundamental to know where we are starting from or where we were at a specific time in the book.

Once again, the API design comes from Hydra as follows:

- Graphics resources are created using a `creation` struct containing all the necessary parameters
- Resources are externally passed as handles, so they are easily copiable and safe to pass around

The main class in this layer is the `GpuDevice` class, which is responsible for the following:

- Vulkan API abstractions and usage
- Creation, destruction, and update of graphics resources
- Swapchain creation, destruction, resize, and update
- Command buffer requests and submission to the GPU

- GPU timestamps management
- GPU-CPU synchronization

We define graphics resources as anything residing on the GPU, such as the following:

- **Textures**: Images to read and write from
- **Buffers**: Arrays of homogeneous or heterogeneous data
- **Samplers**: Converters from raw GPU memory to anything needed from the shaders
- **Shaders**: SPIR-V compiled GPU executable code
- **Pipeline**: An almost complete snapshot of GPU state

The usage of graphics resources is the core of any type of rendering algorithm.

Therefore, `GpuDevice` (`source/chapter1/graphics/gpu_device.hpp`) is the gateway to creating rendering algorithms.

Here is a snippet of the `GpuDevice` interface for resources:

```
struct GpuDevice {
  BufferHandle create_buffer( const BufferCreation& bc );
  TextureHandle create_texture( const TextureCreation& tc
  );
  ...
  void destroy_buffer( BufferHandle& handle );
  void destroy_texture( TextureHandle& handle );
```

Here is an example of the creation and destruction to create `VertexBuffer`, taken from the Raptor ImGUI (`source/chapter1/graphics/raptor_imgui.hpp`) backend:

```
GpuDevice gpu;
// Create the main ImGUI vertex buffer
BufferCreation bc;
bc.set( VK_BUFFER_USAGE_VERTEX_BUFFER_BIT,
  ResourceUsageType::Dynamic, 65536 )
  .set_name( "VB_ImGui" );
BufferHandle imgui_vb = gpu.create(bc);
...
// Destroy the main ImGUI vertex buffer
gpu.destroy(imgui_vb);
```

In the Raptor Engine, graphics resources (`source/chapter1/graphics/gpu_resources.hpp`) have the same granularity as Vulkan but are enhanced to help the user write simpler and safer code.

Let's have a look at the `Buffer` class:

```
struct Buffer {
    VkBuffer                    vk_buffer;
    VmaAllocation               vma_allocation;
    VkDeviceMemory              vk_device_memory;
    VkDeviceSize                vk_device_size;
    VkBufferUsageFlags          type_flags      = 0;
    u32                         size            = 0;
    u32                         global_offset   = 0;
    BufferHandle                handle;
    BufferHandle                parent_buffer;

    const char* name            = nullptr;
}; // struct Buffer
```

As we can see, the `Buffer` struct contains quite a few extra pieces of information.

First of all, `VkBuffer` is the main Vulkan struct used by the API. Then there are some members related to memory allocations on the GPU, such as device memory and size.

Note that there is a utility class used in the Raptor Engine called **Virtual Memory Allocator** (**VMA**) (https://github.com/GPUOpen-LibrariesAndSDKs/VulkanMemoryAllocator), which is the de facto standard utility library to write Vulkan code.

Here, it is reflected in the `vma_allocation` member variable.

Furthermore, there are usage flags – size and offset, as well as global offsets – current buffer handle and parent handle (we will see their usage later in the book), as well as a human-readable string for easier debugging. This `Buffer` can be seen as the blueprint of how other abstractions are created in the Raptor Engine, and how they help the user to write simpler and safer code.

They still respect Vulkan's design and philosophy but can hide some implementation details that can be less important once the focus of the user is exploring rendering algorithms.

We had a brief overview of the graphics layer, the most important part of the code in this book. We will evolve its code after each chapter, and we will dwell deeper on design choices and implementation details throughout the book.

Next, there is the application layer, which works as the final step between the user and the application.

The application layer

The application layer is responsible for handling the actual application side of the engine – from window creation and update based on the operating system to gathering user input from the mouse and keyboard.

In the layer is also included a very handy backend for ImGui (`https://github.com/ocornut/imgui`), an amazing library to design the UI to enhance user interaction with the application so that it is much easier to control its behavior.

There is an application class that will be the blueprint for any demo application that will be created in the book so that the user can focus more on the graphics side of the application.

The foundation and application layers' code is in the `source/raptor` folder. This code will be almost constant throughout the book, but as we are writing mainly a graphics system, this is put in a shared folder between all the chapters.

In this section, we have explained the structure of the code and presented the three main layers of the Raptor Engine: foundation, graphics, and application. For each of these layers, we highlighted some of the main classes, how to use them, and the reasoning and inspiration behind the choices we have made.

In the next section, we are going to present the file format we selected to load 3D data from and how we have integrated it into the engine.

Understanding the glTF scene format

Many 3D file formats have been developed over the years, and for this book, we chose to use glTF. It has become increasingly popular in recent years; it has an open specification, and it supports a **physically based rendering** (**PBR**) model by default.

We chose this format because of its open specification and easy-to-understand structure. We can use several models provided by Khronos on GitHub to test our implementation and compare our results with other frameworks.

It is a JSON-based format and we built a custom parser for this book. The JSON data will be deserialized into a C++ class, which we are going to use to drive the rendering.

We now provide an overview of the main sections of the glTF format. At its root, we have a list of scenes, and each scene can have multiple nodes. You can see this in the following code:

```
"scene": 0,
"scenes": [
    {
        "nodes": [
            0,
```

```
            1,
            2,
            3,
            4,
            5
        ]
    }
],
```

Each node contains an index that is present in the mesh array:

```
"nodes": [
    {
        "mesh": 0,
        "name": "Hose_low"
    },
]
```

The data for the scene is stored in one or more buffers, and each section of the buffer is described by a buffer view:

```
"buffers": [
    {
        "uri": "FlightHelmet.bin",
        "byteLength": 3227148
    }
],
"bufferViews": [
    {
        "buffer": 0,
        "byteLength": 568332,
        "name": "bufferViewScalar"
    },
]
```

Each buffer view references the buffer that contains the actual data and its size. An accessor points into a buffer view by defining the type, offset, and size of the data:

```
"accessors": [
    {
        "bufferView": 1,
        "byteOffset": 125664,
        "componentType": 5126,
        "count": 10472,
        "type": "VEC3",
        "name": "accessorNormals"
    }
]
```

The `mesh` array contains a list of entries, and each entry is composed of one or more mesh primitives. A mesh primitive contains a list of attributes that point into the accessors array, the index of the indices accessor, and the index of the material:

```
"meshes": [
    {
        "primitives": [
            {
                "attributes": {
                    "POSITION": 1,
                    "TANGENT": 2,
                    "NORMAL": 3,
                    "TEXCOORD_0": 4
                },
                "indices": 0,
                "material": 0
            }
        ],
        "name": "Hose_low"
    }
]
```

The `materials` object defines which textures are used (diffuse color, normal map, roughness, and so on) and other parameters that control the rendering of the material:

```
"materials": [
    {
        "pbrMetallicRoughness": {
            "baseColorTexture": {
                "index": 2
            },
            "metallicRoughnessTexture": {
                "index": 1
            }
        },
        "normalTexture": {
            "index": 0
        },
        "occlusionTexture": {
            "index": 1
        },
        "doubleSided": true,
        "name": "HoseMat"
    }
]
```

Each texture is specified as a combination of an image and a sampler:

```
"textures": [
    {
        "sampler": 0,
        "source": 0,
        "name": "FlightHelmet_Materials_RubberWoodMat_Nor
                mal.png"
    },
],
"images": [
    {
        "uri": "FlightHelmet_Materials_RubberWoodMat_Nor
```

```
                    mal.png"
        },
    ],
    "samplers": [
        {
            "magFilter": 9729,
            "minFilter": 9987
        }
    ]
```

The glTF format can specify many other details, including animation data and cameras. Most of the models that we are using in this book don't make use of these features, but we will highlight them when that's the case.

The JSON data is deserialized into a C++ class, which is then used for rendering. We omitted glTF extensions in the resulting object as they are not used in this book. We are now going through a code example that shows how to read a glTF file using our parser. The first step is to load the file into a `glTF` object:

```
char gltf_file[512]{ };
memcpy( gltf_file, argv[ 1 ], strlen( argv[ 1 ] ) );
file_name_from_path( gltf_file );

glTF::glTF scene = gltf_load_file( gltf_file );
```

We now have a glTF model loaded into the `scene` variable.

The next step is to upload the buffers, textures, and samplers that are part of our model to the GPU for rendering. We start by processing textures and samplers:

```
Array<TextureResource> images;
images.init( allocator, scene.images_count );

for ( u32 image_index = 0; image_index
    < scene.images_count; ++image_index ) {
    glTF::Image& image = scene.images[ image_index ];
    TextureResource* tr = renderer.create_texture(
        image.uri.data, image.uri.data );

    images.push( *tr );
```

Understanding the glTF scene format

```
}

Array<SamplerResource> samplers;
samplers.init( allocator, scene.samplers_count );

for ( u32 sampler_index = 0; sampler_index
  < scene.samplers_count; ++sampler_index ) {
  glTF::Sampler& sampler = scene.samplers[ sampler_index ];

  SamplerCreation creation;
  creation.min_filter = sampler.min_filter == glTF::
      Sampler::Filter::LINEAR ? VK_FILTER_LINEAR :
          VK_FILTER_NEAREST;
  creation.mag_filter = sampler.mag_filter == glTF::
      Sampler::Filter::LINEAR ? VK_FILTER_LINEAR :
          VK_FILTER_NEAREST;

  SamplerResource* sr = renderer.create_sampler( creation
  );

  samplers.push( *sr );
}
```

Each resource is stored in an array. We go through each entry in the array and create the corresponding GPU resource. We then store the resources we just created in a separate array that will be used in the rendering loop.

Now let's see how we process the buffers and buffer views, as follows:

```
Array<void*> buffers_data;
buffers_data.init( allocator, scene.buffers_count );

for ( u32 buffer_index = 0; buffer_index
  < scene.buffers_count; ++buffer_index ) {
    glTF::Buffer& buffer = scene.buffers[ buffer_index ];

    FileReadResult buffer_data = file_read_binary(
        buffer.uri.data, allocator );
```

```
            buffers_data.push( buffer_data.data );
    }

    Array<BufferResource> buffers;
    buffers.init( allocator, scene.buffer_views_count );

    for ( u32 buffer_index = 0; buffer_index
      < scene.buffer_views_count; ++buffer_index ) {
        glTF::BufferView& buffer = scene.buffer_views[
            buffer_index ];

        u8* data = ( u8* )buffers_data[ buffer.buffer ] +
            buffer.byte_offset;

        VkBufferUsageFlags flags =
            VK_BUFFER_USAGE_VERTEX_BUFFER_BIT |
                VK_BUFFER_USAGE_INDEX_BUFFER_BIT;

        BufferResource* br = renderer.create_buffer( flags,
            ResourceUsageType::Immutable, buffer.byte_length,
                data, buffer.name.data );

        buffers.push( *br );
    }
```

First, we read the full buffer data into CPU memory. Then, we iterate through each buffer view and create its corresponding GPU resource. We store the newly created resource in an array that will be used in the rendering loop.

Finally, we read the mesh definition to create its corresponding draw data. The following code provides a sample for reading the position buffer. Please refer to the code in chapter1/main.cpp for the full implementation:

```
for ( u32 mesh_index = 0; mesh_index < scene.meshes_count;
  ++mesh_index ) {
    glTF::Mesh& mesh = scene.meshes[ mesh_index ];
```

```
    glTF::MeshPrimitive& mesh_primitive = mesh.primitives[
        0 ];

    glTF::Accessor& position_accessor = scene.accessors[
        gltf_get_attribute_accessor_index(
        mesh_primitive.attributes, mesh_primitive.
        attribute_count, "POSITION" ) ];
    glTF::BufferView& position_buffer_view =
        scene.buffer_views[ position_accessor.buffer_view
        ];
    BufferResource& position_buffer_gpu = buffers[
        position_accessor.buffer_view ];

    MeshDraw mesh_draw{ };
    mesh_draw.position_buffer = position_buffer_gpu.handle;
    mesh_draw.position_offset = position_accessor.
                                byte_offset;
}
```

We have grouped all the GPU resources needed to render a mesh into a `MeshDraw` data structure. We retrieve the buffers and textures as defined by the `Accessor` object and store them in a `MeshDraw` object to be used in the rendering loop.

In this chapter, we load a model at the beginning of the application, and it's not going to change. Thanks to this constraint, we can create all of our descriptor sets only once before we start rendering:

```
DescriptorSetCreation rl_creation{};
rl_creation.set_layout( cube_rll ).buffer( cube_cb, 0 );
rl_creation.texture_sampler( diffuse_texture_gpu.handle,
    diffuse_sampler_gpu.handle, 1 );
rl_creation.texture_sampler( roughness_texture_gpu.handle,
    roughness_sampler_gpu.handle, 2 );
rl_creation.texture_sampler( normal_texture_gpu.handle,
    normal_sampler_gpu.handle, 3 );
rl_creation.texture_sampler( occlusion_texture_gpu.handle,
    occlusion_sampler_gpu.handle, 4 );
 mesh_draw.descriptor_set = gpu.create_descriptor_set(
     rl_creation );
```

For each resource type, we call the relative method on the `DescriptorSetCreation` object. This object stores the data that is going to be used to create the descriptor set through the Vulkan API.

We have now defined all the objects we need for rendering. In our render loop, we simply have to iterate over all meshes, bind each mesh buffer and descriptor set, and call `draw`:

```
for ( u32 mesh_index = 0; mesh_index < mesh_draws.size;
  ++mesh_index ) {
    MeshDraw mesh_draw = mesh_draws[ mesh_index ];

    gpu_commands->bind_vertex_buffer( sort_key++,
        mesh_draw.position_buffer, 0,
            mesh_draw.position_offset );
    gpu_commands->bind_vertex_buffer( sort_key++,
        mesh_draw.tangent_buffer, 1,
            mesh_draw.tangent_offset );
    gpu_commands->bind_vertex_buffer( sort_key++,
        mesh_draw.normal_buffer, 2,
            mesh_draw.normal_offset );
    gpu_commands->bind_vertex_buffer( sort_key++,
        mesh_draw.texcoord_buffer, 3,
            mesh_draw.texcoord_offset );
    gpu_commands->bind_index_buffer( sort_key++,
        mesh_draw.index_buffer, mesh_draw.index_offset );
    gpu_commands->bind_descriptor_set( sort_key++,
        &mesh_draw.descriptor_set, 1, nullptr, 0 );

    gpu_commands->draw_indexed( sort_key++,
        TopologyType::Triangle, mesh_draw.count, 1, 0, 0,
            0 );
}
```

We are going to evolve this code over the course of the book, but it's already a great starting point for you to try and load a different model or to experiment with the shader code (more on this in the next section).

There are several tutorials online about the glTF format, some of which are linked in the *Further reading* section. The glTF spec is also a great source of details and is easy to follow. We recommend you refer to it if something about the format is not immediately clear from reading the book or the code.

In this section, we have analyzed the glTF format and we have presented examples of the JSON objects most relevant to our renderer. We then demonstrated how to use the glTF parser, which we added to our framework, and showed you how to upload geometry and texture data to the GPU. Finally, we have shown how to use this data to draw the meshes that make up a model.

In the next section, we explain how the data we just parsed and uploaded to the GPU is used to render our model using a physically-based rendering implementation.

PBR in a nutshell

PBR is at the heart of many rendering engines. It was originally developed for offline rendering, but thanks to the advances in hardware capabilities and research efforts by the graphics community, it can now be used for real-time rendering as well.

As the name implies, this technique aims at modeling the physical interactions of light and matter and, in some implementations, ensuring that the amount of energy in the system is preserved.

There are plenty of in-depth resources available that describe PBR in great detail. Nonetheless, we want to give a brief overview of our implementation for reference. We have followed the implementation presented in the glTF spec.

To compute the final color of our surface, we have to determine the diffuse and specular components. The amount of specular reflection in the real world is determined by the roughness of the surface. The smoother the surface, the greater the amount of light that is reflected. A mirror reflects (almost) all the light it receives.

The roughness of the surface is modeled through a texture. In the glTF format, this value is packed with the metalness and the occlusion values in a single texture to optimize resource use. We distinguish materials between conductors (or metallic) and dielectric (non-metallic) surfaces.

A metallic material has only a specular term, while a non-metallic material has both diffuse and specular terms. To model materials that have both metallic and non-metallic components, we use the metalness term to interpolate between the two.

An object made of wood will likely have a metalness of 0, plastic will have a mix of both metalness and roughness, and the body of a car will be dominated by the metallic component.

As we are modeling the real-world response of a material, we need a function that takes the view and light direction and returns the amount of light that is reflected. This function is called the **bi-directional distribution function** (BRDF).

We use the Trowbridge-Reitz/GGX distribution for the specular BRDF, and it is implemented as follows:

```
float NdotH = dot(N, H);
float alpha_squared = alpha * alpha;
float d_denom = ( NdotH * NdotH ) * ( alpha_squared - 1.0 )
```

```
    + 1.0;
float distribution = ( alpha_squared * heaviside( NdotH ) )
    / ( PI * d_denom * d_denom );

float NdotL = dot(N, L);
float NdotV = dot(N, V);
float HdotL = dot(H, L);
float HdotV = dot(H, V);

float visibility = ( heaviside( HdotL ) / ( abs( NdotL ) +
  sqrt( alpha_squared + ( 1.0 - alpha_squared ) *
  ( NdotL * NdotL ) ) ) * ( heaviside( HdotV ) /
  ( abs( NdotV ) + sqrt( alpha_squared +
  ( 1.0 - alpha_squared ) *
  ( NdotV * NdotV ) ) ) );

float specular_brdf = visibility * distribution;
```

First, we compute the distribution and visibility terms according to the formula presented in the glTF specification. Then, we multiply them to obtain the specular BRDF term.

There are other approximations that can be used, and we encourage you to experiment and replace ours with a different one!

We then compute the diffuse BDRF, as follows:

```
vec3 diffuse_brdf = (1 / PI) * base_colour.rgb;
```

We now introduce the Fresnel term. This determines the color of the reflection based on the viewing angle and the index of refraction of the material. Here is the implementation of the Schlick approximation, both for the metallic and dielectric components:

```
// f0 in the formula notation refers to the base colour
    here
vec3 conductor_fresnel = specular_brdf * ( base_colour.rgb
    + ( 1.0 - base_colour.rgb ) * pow( 1.0 - abs( HdotV ),
        5 ) );

// f0 in the formula notation refers to the value derived
    from ior = 1.5
```

```
float f0 = 0.04; // pow( ( 1 - ior ) / ( 1 + ior ), 2 )
float fr = f0 + ( 1 - f0 ) * pow(1 - abs( HdotV ), 5 );
vec3 fresnel_mix = mix( diffuse_brdf, vec3(
                        specular_brdf ), fr );
```

Here we compute the Fresnel term for both the conductor and the dielectric components according to the formula in the glTF specification.

Now that we have computed all the components of the model, we interpolate between them, based on the metalness of the material, as follows:

```
vec3 material_colour = mix( resnel_mix,
                        conductor_fresnel, metalness );
```

The occlusion term is not used as it only affects indirect light, which we haven't implemented yet.

We realize this is a very quick introduction, and we skipped over a lot of the theory that makes these approximations work. However, it should provide a good starting point for further study.

We have added links to some excellent resources in the *Further reading* section if you'd like to experiment and modify our base implementation.

In the next section, we are going to introduce a debugging tool that we rely on whenever we have a non-trivial rendering issue. It has helped us many times while writing this book!

A word on GPU debugging

No matter how much experience you have in graphics programming, there will come a time when you need to debug an issue. Understanding exactly what the GPU is doing when it executes your program is not as immediate as on the CPU. Thankfully, GPU debugging tools have come a long way to help us when our program doesn't behave as expected.

GPU vendors provide great tools to debug and profile your shaders: Nvidia has developed Nsight graphics, and AMD has a suite of tools that includes the Radeon GPU analyzer and Radeon GPU profiler.

For this book, we have primarily used RenderDoc (available at `https://renderdoc.org/`). It is a staple tool of the graphics programming community as it allows you to capture a frame and record all the Vulkan API calls that have been issued during that frame.

Introducing the Raptor Engine and Hydra

Using RenderDoc is really simple. You start by providing the path to your application, as follows:

Program	
Executable Path	C:\workspace\raptor_engine\build\source\chapter1\Debug\Chapter1.exe
Working Directory	C:\workspace\raptor_engine\build\source\chapter1\Debug
Command-line Arguments	C:/workspace/glTF_models/2.0/FlightHelmet/glTF/FlightHelmet.gltf
Environment Variables	

Figure 1.2 – Setting the application path in RenderDoc

You then start the application by clicking **Launch**, and you will notice an overlay reporting the frame time and the number of frames rendered. If you press *F12*, RenderDoc will record the current frame. You can now close your application, and the recorded frame will automatically load.

On the left, you have the list of API calls grouped in render passes. This view also lists the **event ID** (**EID**), which is a progressive number defined by RenderDoc. This is useful for comparing events across multiple frames:

EID	Name
	˅ Frame #608
0	Capture Start
5	=> vkQueueSubmit(1)[0]: vkBeginCommandBuffer(**Baked Command Buffer 1016**)
6-63	˅ Frame
7	vkCmdBeginRenderPass(C=Clear, D=Clear)
17	vkCmdDrawIndexed(59040, 1)
24	vkCmdDrawIndexed(72534, 1)
31	vkCmdDrawIndexed(24408, 1)
38	vkCmdDrawIndexed(60288, 1)
45	vkCmdDrawIndexed(65688, 1)
52	vkCmdDrawIndexed(2208, 1)
53-62	> ImGUI
65	vkCmdEndRenderPass(C=Store, D=Don't Care)
66	=> vkQueueSubmit(1)[0]: vkEndCommandBuffer(**Baked Command Buffer 1016**)
67	▶ vkQueuePresentKHR(**Swapchain Image 636**)

Figure 1.3 – The list of Vulkan API calls for the captured frame

On the right side of the application window, you have multiple tabs that allow you to inspect which textures are bound when a draw call is made, the buffer content, and the state of the pipeline.

The following figure shows the **Texture Viewer** tab. It shows the rendering output after a given draw and which input textures were bound:

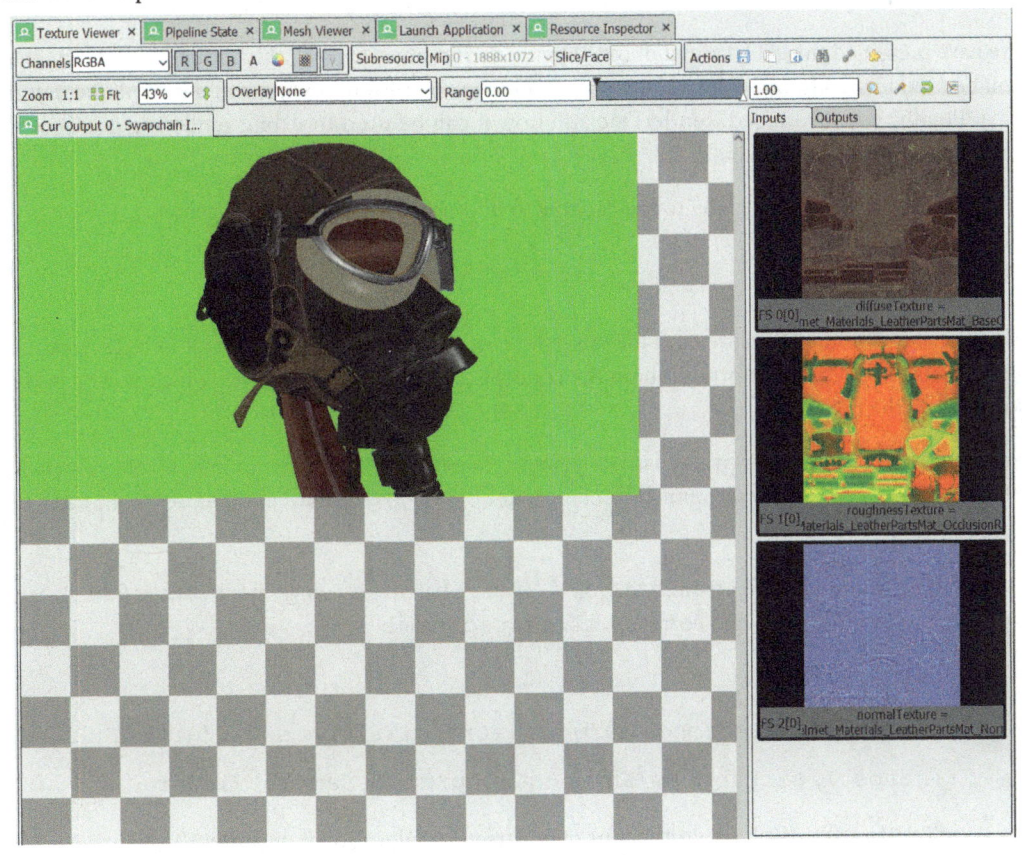

Figure 1.4 – RenderDoc texture viewer

If you right-click on a pixel in the **Texture Viewer** tab, you can inspect the history of that pixel to understand which draws affected it.

There is also a debug feature that allows you to step through the shader code and analyze intermediate values. Be careful when using this feature, as we have noticed that the values are not always accurate.

This was a quick overview of RenderDoc and its functionality. You have learned how to capture a frame in RenderDoc when running a graphics application. We presented a breakdown of the main panels, their functionality, and how to use them to understand how the final image is rendered.

We encourage you to run the code from this chapter under RenderDoc to better understand how the frame is built.

Summary

In this chapter, we laid the foundations for the rest of the book. By now, you should be familiar with how the code is structured and how to use it. We introduced the Raptor Engine, and we have provided an overview of the main classes and libraries that are going to be used throughout the book.

We have presented the glTF format of the 3D models and how we parse this format into objects that will be used for rendering. We gave a brief introduction to PBR modeling and our implementation of it. Finally, we introduced RenderDoc and how it can be used to debug rendering issues or to understand how a frame is built.

In the next chapter, we are going to look at how to improve our resource management!

Further reading

We have only skimmed the surface of the topics we have presented. Here, we provide links to resources you can use to get more information on the concepts exposed in this chapter, which will be useful throughout the book.

While we have written our own standard library replacement, there are other options if you are starting your own project. We highly recommend looking into https://github.com/electronicarts/EASTL, developed by EA.

- **The Vulkan specification**: https://www.khronos.org/registry/vulkan/specs/1.3-extensions/html/vkspec.html
- **The glTF format**:
    - https://www.khronos.org/registry/glTF/specs/2.0/glTF-2.0.html
    - https://github.com/KhronosGroup/glTF-Sample-Viewer
- **glTF libraries**: We have written our own parser for educational purposes. If you are starting your own project, we suggest evaluating these libraries:
    - https://github.com/jkuhlmann/cgltf
    - https://github.com/code4game/libgltf
    - https://github.com/syoyo/tinygltfloader
- **Resources on PBR**:
    - https://google.github.io/filament/Filament.html
    - https://blog.selfshadow.com/publications/s2012-shading-course/
    - https://pbr-book.org/

2
Improving Resources Management

In this chapter, we are going to improve resource management to make it easier to deal with materials that might have a varying number of textures. This technique is usually referred to as bindless, even though it's not entirely accurate. We are still going to bind a list of resources; however, we can access them by using an index rather than having to specify exactly which resources are going to be used during a particular draw.

The second improvement we are going to make is automating the generation of pipeline layouts. Large projects have hundreds or thousands of shaders, compiled with many different variations depending on the combinations of materials used by a particular application. If developers had to manually update their pipeline layout definitions every time a change is made, very few applications would make it to market. The implementation presented in this chapter relies on the information provided by the SPIR-V binary format.

Finally, we are going to add pipeline caching to our GPU device implementation. This solution improves the creation time of pipeline objects after the first run, and can significantly improve an application's loading times.

In summary, in this chapter, we're going to cover the following main topics:

- Unlocking and implementing bindless resources
- Automating pipeline layout generation
- Improving load times with a pipeline cache

By the end of this chapter, you will understand how to enable and use bindless resources in Vulkan. You will also be able to parse SPIR-V binary data to automatically generate pipeline layouts. Finally, you will be able to speed up the loading time of your application by using pipeline caching.

Technical requirements

The code for this chapter can be found at the following URL: `https://github.com/PacktPublishing/Mastering-Graphics-Programming-with-Vulkan/tree/main/source/chapter2`.

Unlocking and implementing bindless rendering

In the previous chapter, we had to manually bind the textures for each material. This also meant that if we wanted to support different types of materials requiring a different number of textures, we would have needed separate shaders and pipelines.

Vulkan provides a mechanism to bind an array of textures that can be used across multiple shaders. Each texture can then be accessed through an index. In the following sections, we are going to highlight the changes we have made to the GPU device implementation to enable this feature and describe how to use it.

In the following sections, we will first check that the extensions required to enable bindless resources are available on a given GPU. Then we will show the changes required to the descriptor pool creation and descriptor set update to make use of bindless resources. The last step will be to update our shaders to use indices in our texture array for rendering.

Checking for support

Most desktop GPUs, even if relatively old, should support the `VK_EXT_descriptor_indexing` extension, provided you have up-to-date drivers. It's still good practice to verify that the extension is available and, for a production implementation, provide an alternative code path that uses the standard binding model if the extension is not available.

To verify that your device supports this extension, you can use the following code, or you can run the `vulkaninfo` application provided by the Vulkan SDK. See *Chapter 1, Introducing the Raptor Engine and Hydra*, for how to install the SDK.

The first step then is to query the physical device to determine whether the GPU supports this extension. The following code section accomplishes this:

```
VkPhysicalDeviceDescriptorIndexingFeatures indexing
_features{ VK_STRUCTURE_TYPE_PHYSICAL_DEVICE_DESCRIPTOR
        _INDEXING_FEATURES, nullptr };
VkPhysicalDeviceFeatures2 device_features{
    VK_STRUCTURE_TYPE_PHYSICAL_DEVICE_FEATURES_2,
        &indexing_features };
```

```
vkGetPhysicalDeviceFeatures2( vulkan_physical_device,
                              &device_features );

bindless_supported = indexing_features.
                     descriptorBindingPartiallyBound &&
                     indexing_features.
                     runtimeDescriptorArray;
```

We have to populate the `VkPhysicalDeviceDescriptorIndexingFeatures` structure and chain it to the `VkPhysicalDeviceFeatures2` structure. The driver will then populate the `indexing_features` variable members when calling `vkGetPhysicalDeviceFeatures2`. To check that the descriptor indexing extension is supported, we verify that the `descriptorBindingPartiallyBound` and `runtimeDescriptorArray` values are `true`.

Once we have confirmed that the extension is supported, we can enable it when creating the device:

```
VkPhysicalDeviceFeatures2 physical_features2 = {
    VK_STRUCTURE_TYPE_PHYSICAL_DEVICE_FEATURES_2 };
vkGetPhysicalDeviceFeatures2( vulkan_physical_device,
                              &physical_features2 );

VkDeviceCreateInfo device_create_info = {};
// same code as chapter 1
device_create_info.pNext = &physical_features2;

if ( bindless_supported ) {
    physical_features2.pNext = &indexing_features;
}

vkCreateDevice( vulkan_physical_device,
                &device_create_info,
                vulkan_allocation_callbacks,
                &vulkan_device );
```

We have to chain the `indexing_features` variable to the `physical_features2` variable used when creating our device. The rest of the code is unchanged from *Chapter 1, Introducing the Raptor Engine and Hydra*.

Creating the descriptor pool

The next step is to create a descriptor pool from which we can allocate descriptor sets that support updating the content of a texture after it is bound:

```
VkDescriptorPoolSize pool_sizes_bindless[] =
{
    { VK_DESCRIPTOR_TYPE_COMBINED_IMAGE_SAMPLER,
      k_max_bindless_resources },
    { VK_DESCRIPTOR_TYPE_STORAGE_IMAGE,
      k_max_bindless_resources },
};

pool_info.flags = VK_DESCRIPTOR_POOL_CREATE_UPDATE
                    _AFTER_BIND_BIT_EXT;
pool_info.maxSets = k_max_bindless_resources * ArraySize(
                    pool_sizes_bindless );
pool_info.poolSizeCount = ( u32 )ArraySize(
                    pool_sizes_bindless );
pool_info.pPoolSizes = pool_sizes_bindless;
vkCreateDescriptorPool( vulkan_device, &pool_info,
                    vulkan_allocation_callbacks,
                    &vulkan_bindless_descriptor_pool);
```

The main difference with the code from *Chapter 1, Introducing the Raptor Engine and Hydra*, is the addition of the VK_DESCRIPTOR_POOL_CREATE_UPDATE_AFTER_BIND_BIT_EXT flag. This flag is needed to allow the creation of descriptor sets that can be updated after they have been bound.

Next, we have to define the descriptor set layout bindings:

```
const u32 pool_count = ( u32 )ArraySize(
                    pool_sizes_bindless );
VkDescriptorSetLayoutBinding vk_binding[ 4 ];

VkDescriptorSetLayoutBinding& image_sampler_binding =
    vk_binding[ 0 ];
image_sampler_binding.descriptorType = VK_DESCRIPTOR
                                        _TYPE_COMBINED
                                        _IMAGE_SAMPLER;
```

```
image_sampler_binding.descriptorCount =
    k_max_bindless_resources;
image_sampler_binding.binding = k_bindless_texture_binding;

VkDescriptorSetLayoutBinding& storage_image_binding =
    vk_binding[ 1 ];
storage_image_binding.descriptorType = VK_DESCRIPTOR
                                        _TYPE_STORAGE_IMAGE;
storage_image_binding.descriptorCount =
    k_max_bindless_resources;
storage_image_binding.binding = k_bindless_texture_binding
                                        + 1;
```

Notice that `descriptorCount` no longer has a value of 1 but has to accommodate the maximum number of textures we can use. We can now use this data to create a descriptor set layout:

```
VkDescriptorSetLayoutCreateInfo layout_info = {
    VK_STRUCTURE_TYPE_DESCRIPTOR_SET_LAYOUT_CREATE_INFO };
layout_info.bindingCount = pool_count;
layout_info.pBindings = vk_binding;
layout_info.flags = VK_DESCRIPTOR_SET_LAYOUT_CREATE
                    _UPDATE_AFTER_BIND_POOL_BIT_EXT;

VkDescriptorBindingFlags bindless_flags =
    VK_DESCRIPTOR_BINDING_PARTIALLY_BOUND_BIT_EXT |
        VK_DESCRIPTOR_BINDING_UPDATE_AFTER_BIND_BIT_EXT;
VkDescriptorBindingFlags binding_flags[ 4 ];

binding_flags[ 0 ] = bindless_flags;
binding_flags[ 1 ] = bindless_flags;

VkDescriptorSetLayoutBindingFlagsCreateInfoEXT
extended_info{
    VK_STRUCTURE_TYPE_DESCRIPTOR_SET_LAYOUT
        _BINDING_FLAGS_CREATE_INFO_EXT, nullptr };
extended_info.bindingCount = pool_count;
```

```
extended_info.pBindingFlags = binding_flags;

layout_info.pNext = &extended_info;

vkCreateDescriptorSetLayout( vulkan_device, &layout_info,
                             vulkan_allocation_callbacks,
                             &vulkan_bindless
                             _descriptor_layout );
```

The code is very similar to the version seen in the previous chapter; however, we have added the `bindless_flags` values to enable partial updates to the descriptor set. We also have to chain a `VkDescriptorSetLayoutBindingFlagsCreateInfoEXT` structure to the `layout_info` variable. Finally, we can create the descriptor set we are going to use for the lifetime of the application:

```
VkDescriptorSetAllocateInfo alloc_info{
    VK_STRUCTURE_TYPE_DESCRIPTOR_SET_ALLOCATE_INFO };
alloc_info.descriptorPool = vulkan_bindless
                            _descriptor_pool;
alloc_info.descriptorSetCount = 1;
alloc_info.pSetLayouts = &vulkan_bindless_descriptor
                         _layout;

vkAllocateDescriptorSets( vulkan_device, &alloc_info,
                          &vulkan_bindless_descriptor_set
                          );
```

We simply populate the `VkDescriptorSetAllocateInfo` structure with the values we have defined so far and call `vkAllocateDescriptorSets`.

Updating the descriptor set

We have done most of the heavy lifting at this point. When we call `GpuDevice::create_texture`, the newly created resource gets added to the `texture_to_update_bindless` array:

```
if ( gpu.bindless_supported ) {
    ResourceUpdate resource_update{
        ResourceDeletionType::Texture,
        texture->handle.index, gpu.current_frame };
```

```
        gpu.texture_to_update_bindless.push( resource_update );
}
```

It's also possible to associate a specific sampler to a given texture. For instance, when we load a texture for a given material, we add the following code:

```
gpu.link_texture_sampler( diffuse_texture_gpu.handle,
                         diffuse_sampler_gpu.handle );
```

This links the diffuse texture with its sampler. This information will be used in the next code section to determine whether we use a default sampler or the one we have just assigned to the texture.

Before the next frame is processed, we update the descriptor set we have created in the previous section with any new textures that have been uploaded:

```
for ( i32 it = texture_to_update_bindless.size - 1;
   it >= 0; it-- ) {
    ResourceUpdate& texture_to_update =
        texture_to_update_bindless[ it ];

    Texture* texture = access_texture( {
                       texture_to_update.handle } );
    VkWriteDescriptorSet& descriptor_write =
        bindless_descriptor_writes[ current_write_index ];
    descriptor_write = {
        VK_STRUCTURE_TYPE_WRITE_DESCRIPTOR_SET };
    descriptor_write.descriptorCount = 1;
    descriptor_write.dstArrayElement =
        texture_to_update.handle;
    descriptor_write.descriptorType =
        VK_DESCRIPTOR_TYPE_COMBINED_IMAGE_SAMPLER;
    descriptor_write.dstSet =
        vulkan_bindless_descriptor_set;
    descriptor_write.dstBinding =
        k_bindless_texture_binding;

    Sampler* vk_default_sampler = access_sampler(
                                  default_sampler );
    VkDescriptorImageInfo& descriptor_image_info =
```

Improving Resources Management

```
            bindless_image_info[ current_write_index ];

    if ( texture->sampler != nullptr ) {
        descriptor_image_info.sampler =
        texture->sampler->vk_sampler;
    }
    else {
        descriptor_image_info.sampler =
        vk_default_sampler->vk_sampler;
    }

    descriptor_image_info.imageView =
        texture->vk_format != VK_FORMAT_UNDEFINED ?
        texture->vk_image_view : vk_dummy_texture->
        vk_image_view;
    descriptor_image_info.imageLayout =
        VK_IMAGE_LAYOUT_SHADER_READ_ONLY_OPTIMAL;
    descriptor_write.pImageInfo = &descriptor_image_info;

    texture_to_update.current_frame = u32_max;

    texture_to_update_bindless.delete_swap( it );

    ++current_write_index;
}
```

The preceding code is quite similar to the previous version. We have highlighted the main differences: the sampler selection, as we mentioned in the previous paragraph, and the use of a dummy texture if a slot is empty. We still have to assign a texture to each slot, hence the use of a dummy texture if one is not specified. This is also useful for spotting any missing textures in your scene.

If you prefer to have a tightly packed array of textures, another option is to enable the `VK_DESCRIPTOR_BINDING_VARIABLE_DESCRIPTOR_COUNT_BIT_EXT` flag and chain a `VkDescriptorSetVariableDescriptorCountAllocateInfoEXT` structure when creating the descriptor set. We already have some preliminary code to enable this feature, and we encourage you to complete the implementation!

Update to shader code

The final piece of the puzzle to use bindless rendering is in the shader code, as it needs to be written in a different way.

The steps are similar for all shaders making use of bindless resources, and it would be beneficial to have them defined in a common header. Unfortunately, this is not fully supported by the **OpenGL Shading Language**, or **GLSL**.

We recommend automating this step as it can be easily added when compiling the shader in the engine code.

The first thing to do is to enable the nonuniform qualifier in the GLSL code:

```
#extension GL_EXT_nonuniform_qualifier : enable
```

This will enable the extension in the current shader, not globally; thus, it must be written in every shader.

The following code is the declaration of the proper bindless textures, with a catch:

```
layout ( set = 1, binding = 10 ) uniform sampler2D global_textures[];
layout ( set = 1, binding = 10 ) uniform sampler3D global_textures_3d[];
```

This is a known trick to alias the texture declarations to the same binding point. This allows us to have just one global bindless texture array, but all kinds of textures (one-dimensional, two-dimensional, three-dimensional, and their array counterparts) are supported in one go!

This simplifies the usage of bindless textures across the engine and the shaders.

Finally, to read the texture, the code in the shader has to be modified as follows:

```
texture(global_textures[nonuniformEXT(texture_index)],
        vTexcoord0)
```

Let's go in the following order:

1. First of all, we need the integer index coming from a constant. In this case, `texture_index` will contain the same number as the texture position in the bindless array.
2. Second, and this is the crucial change, we need to wrap the index with the `nonuniformEXT` qualifier (https://github.com/KhronosGroup/GLSL/blob/master/extensions/ext/GL_EXT_nonuniform_qualifier.txt); this will basically synchronize the programs between the different executions to properly read the texture index, in case the index is different across different threads of the same shader invocation.

This might sound complicated at first but think about it as a multithreading issue that needs synchronization to make sure the proper texture index is read in each thread and, as a result, the correct texture is used.

   3. Lastly, using the synchronized index we read from the `global_textures` array, we finally have the texture sample we wanted!

We have now added bindless textures support to the Raptor Engine! We started by checking whether the GPU supports this feature. Then we detailed the changes we made to the creation of the descriptor pool and descriptor set.

Finally, we have shown how the descriptor set is updated as new textures are uploaded to the GPU and the necessary shader modifications to make use of bindless textures. All the rendering from now on will use this feature; thus, this concept will become familiar.

Next, we are going to improve our engine capabilities by adding automatic pipeline generation by parsing shaders' binary data.

Automating pipeline layout generation

In this section, we are going to take advantage of the data provided by the SPIR-V binary format to extract the information needed to create a pipeline layout. SPIR-V is the **intermediate representation** (**IR**) that shader sources are compiled to before being passed to the GPU.

Compared to standard GLSL shader sources, which are plain text, SPIR-V is a binary format. This means it's a more compact format to use when distributing an application. More importantly, developers don't have to worry about their shaders getting compiled into a different set of high-level instructions depending on the GPU and driver their code is running on.

However, a SPIR-V binary does not contain the final instructions that will be executed by the GPU. Every GPU will take a SPIR-V blob and do a final compilation into GPU instructions. This step is still required because different GPUs and driver versions can produce different assemblies for the same SPIR-V binary.

Having SPIR-V as an intermediate step is still a great improvement. Shader code validation and parsing are done offline, and developers can compile their shaders together with their application code. This allows us to spot any syntax mistakes before trying to run the shader code.

Another benefit of having an intermediate representation is being able to compile shaders written in different languages to SPIR-V so that they can be used with Vulkan. It's possible, for instance, to compile a shader written in HLSL into SPIR-V and reuse it in a Vulkan renderer.

Before this option was available, developers either had to port the code manually or had to rely on tools that rewrote the shader from one language to another.

By now, you should be convinced of the advantages the introduction of SPIR-V has brought to developers and the Vulkan API.

In the following sections, we are going to use one of our shaders to show you how to compile it to SPIR-V and explain how to use the information in the binary data to automatically generate a pipeline layout.

Compiling GLSL to SPIR-V

We are going to use the vertex shader code that we developed in *Chapter 1, Introducing the Raptor Engine and Hydra*. Previously, we stored the shader code string in the main.cpp file and we didn't compile it to SPIR-V before passing it to the Vulkan API to create a pipeline.

Starting from this chapter, we are storing all shader code in the shaders folder of each chapter. For *Chapter 2, Improving Resources Management*, you will find two files: main.vert for the vertex shader and main.frag for the fragment shader. Here is the content of main.vert:

```glsl
#version 450

layout ( std140, binding = 0 ) uniform LocalConstants {
    mat4        model;
    mat4        view_projection;
    mat4        model_inverse;
    vec4        eye;
    vec4        light;
};

layout(location=0) in vec3 position;
layout(location=1) in vec4 tangent;
layout(location=2) in vec3 normal;
layout(location=3) in vec2 texCoord0;

layout (location = 0) out vec2 vTexcoord0;
layout (location = 1) out vec3 vNormal;
layout (location = 2) out vec4 vTangent;
layout (location = 3) out vec4 vPosition;

void main() {
    gl_Position = view_projection * model * vec4(position,
                                                 1);
```

```
        vPosition = model * vec4(position, 1.0);
        vTexcoord0 = texCoord0;
        vNormal = mat3(model_inverse) * normal;
        vTangent = tangent;
}
```

This code is quite standard for a vertex shader. We have four streams of data for position, tangent, normal, and texture coordinates. We have also defined a `LocalConstants` uniform buffer that stores the data common for all vertices. Finally, we have defined the `out` variables that are going to be passed to the fragment shader.

The Vulkan SDK provides the tools to compile GLSL to SPIR-V and to disassemble the generated SPIR-V into human-readable form. This can be useful to debug a shader that is not behaving as expected.

To compile our vertex shader, we run the following command:

```
glslangValidator -V main.vert -o main.vert.spv
```

This will produce a `main.vert.spv` file that contains the binary data. To view the contents of this file in a human-readable format, we run the following command:

```
spirv-dis main.vert.spv
```

This command will print the disassembled SPIR-V on the Terminal. We are now going to examine the relevant sections of the output.

Understanding the SPIR-V output

Starting from the top of the output, the following is the first set of information we are provided with:

```
       OpCapability Shader
%1 =   OpExtInstImport "GLSL.std.450"
       OpMemoryModel Logical GLSL450
       OpEntryPoint Vertex %main "main" %_ %position
       %vPosition %vTexcoord0 %texCoord0 %vNormal %normal
       %vTangent %tangent
       OpSource GLSL 450
       OpName %main "main"
```

This preamble defines the version of GLSL that was used to write the shader. The `OpEntryPoint` directive references the main function and lists the inputs and outputs for the shader. The convention is for variables to be prefixed by %, and it's possible to forward declare a variable that is defined later.

The next section defines the output variables that are available in this shader:

```
OpName %gl_PerVertex "gl_PerVertex"
OpMemberName %gl_PerVertex 0 "gl_Position"
OpMemberName %gl_PerVertex 1 "gl_PointSize"
OpMemberName %gl_PerVertex 2 "gl_ClipDistance"
OpMemberName %gl_PerVertex 3 "gl_CullDistance"
OpName %_ ""
```

These are variables that are automatically injected by the compiler and are defined by the GLSL specification. We can see we have a `gl_PerVertex` structure, which in turn has four members: `gl_Position`, `gl_PointSize`, `gl_ClipDistance`, and `gl_CullDistance`. There is also an unnamed variable defined as `%_`. We're going to discover soon what it refers to.

We now move on to the structures we have defined:

```
OpName %LocalConstants "LocalConstants"
OpMemberName %LocalConstants 0 "model"
OpMemberName %LocalConstants 1 "view_projection"
OpMemberName %LocalConstants 2 "model_inverse"
OpMemberName %LocalConstants 3 "eye"
OpMemberName %LocalConstants 4 "light"
OpName %__0 ""
```

Here, we have the entries for our `LocalConstants` uniform buffer, its members, and their position within the struct. We see again an unnamed `%__0` variable. We'll get to it shortly. SPIR-V allows you to define member decorations to provide additional information that is useful to determine the data layout and location within the struct:

```
OpMemberDecorate %LocalConstants 0 ColMajor
OpMemberDecorate %LocalConstants 0 Offset 0
OpMemberDecorate %LocalConstants 0 MatrixStride 16
OpMemberDecorate %LocalConstants 1 ColMajor
OpMemberDecorate %LocalConstants 1 Offset 64
OpMemberDecorate %LocalConstants 1 MatrixStride 16
OpMemberDecorate %LocalConstants 2 ColMajor
OpMemberDecorate %LocalConstants 2 Offset 128
OpMemberDecorate %LocalConstants 2 MatrixStride 16
OpMemberDecorate %LocalConstants 3 Offset 192
```

```
OpMemberDecorate %LocalConstants 4 Offset 208
OpDecorate %LocalConstants Block
```

From these entries, we can start to have some insights as to the type of each member of the struct. For instance, we can identify the first three entries as being matrices. The last one only has an offset.

The offset value is the most relevant value for our purposes as it allows us to know where exactly each member starts. This is crucial when transferring data from the CPU to the GPU, as the alignment rules for each member could be different.

The next two lines define the descriptor set and binding for our struct:

```
OpDecorate %__0 DescriptorSet 0
OpDecorate %__0 Binding 0
```

As you can see, these decorations refer to the unnamed %__0 variable. We have now reached the section where the variable types are defined:

```
%float = OpTypeFloat 32
%v4float = OpTypeVector %float 4
%uint = OpTypeInt 32 0
%uint_1 = OpConstant %uint 1
%_arr_float_uint_1 = OpTypeArray %float %uint_1
%gl_PerVertex = OpTypeStruct %v4float %float
                %_arr_float_uint_1 %_arr_float_uint_1
%_ptr_Output_gl_PerVertex = OpTypePointer Output
                            %gl_PerVertex
%_ = OpVariable %_ptr_Output_gl_PerVertex Output
```

For each variable, we have its type and, depending on the type, additional information that is relevant to it. For instance, the %float variable is of type 32-bit float; the %v4float variable is of type vector, and it contains 4 %float values.

This corresponds to vec4 in GLSL. We then have a constant definition for an unsigned value of 1 and a fixed-sized array of the float type and length of 1.

The definition of the %gl_PerVertex variable follows. It is of the struct type and, as we have seen previously, it has four members. Their types are vec4 for gl_Position, float for gl_PointSize, and float[1] for gl_ClipDistance and gl_CullDistance.

The SPIR-V specs require that each variable that can be read or written to is referred to by a pointer. And that's exactly what we see with %_ptr_Output_gl_PerVertex: it's a pointer to the gl_PerVertex struct. Finally, we can see the type for the unnamed %_ variable is a pointer to the gl_PerVertex struct.

Finally, we have the type definitions for our own uniform data:

```
%LocalConstants = OpTypeStruct %mat4v4float %mat4v4float
                    %mat4v4float %v4float %v4float
%_ptr_Uniform_LocalConstants = OpTypePointer Uniform
                    %LocalConstants
%__0 = OpVariable %_ptr_Uniform_LocalConstants
       Uniform
```

As before, we can see that `%LocalConstants` is a struct with five members, three of the `mat4` type and two of the `vec4` type. We then have the type definition of the pointer to our uniform struct and finally, the `%__0` variable of this type. Notice that this variable has the `Uniform` attribute. This means it is read-only and we will make use of this information later to determine the type of descriptor to add to the pipeline layout.

The rest of the disassembly contains the input and output variable definitions. Their definition follows the same structure as the variables we have seen so far, so we are not going to analyze them all here.

The disassembly also contains the instructions for the body of the shader. While it is interesting to see how the GLSL code is translated into SPIR-V instructions, this detail is not relevant to the pipeline creation, and we are not going to cover it here.

Next, we are going to show how we can leverage all of this data to automate pipeline creation.

From SPIR-V to pipeline layout

Khronos already provides functionality to parse SPIR-V data to create a pipeline layout. You can find the implementation at `https://github.com/KhronosGroup/SPIRV-Reflect`. For this book, we decided to write a simplified version of the parser that we believe is easier to follow as we are interested only in a small subset of entries.

You can find the implementation in `source\chapter2\graphics\spirv_parser.cpp`. Let's see how to use this API and how it works under the hood:

```
spirv::ParseResult parse_result{ };
spirv::parse_binary( ( u32* )spv_vert_data,
                    spv_vert_data_size, name_buffer,
                    &parse_result );
spirv::parse_binary( ( u32* )spv_frag_data,
```

```
                        spv_frag_data_size, name_buffer,
                        &parse_result );
```

Here, we assume that the binary data for the vertex and fragment shader has already been read into the `spv_vert_data` and `spv_frag_data` variables. We have to define an empty `spirv::ParseResult` structure that will contain the result of the parsing. Its definition is quite simple:

```
struct ParseResult {
    u32 set_count;
    DescriptorSetLayoutCreation sets[MAX_SET_COUNT];
};
```

It contains the number of sets that we identified from the binary data and the list of entries for each set.

The first step of the parsing is to make sure that we are reading valid SPIR-V data:

```
u32 spv_word_count = safe_cast<u32>( data_size / 4 );

u32 magic_number = data[ 0 ];
RASSERT( magic_number == 0x07230203 );

u32 id_bound = data[3];
```

We first compute the number of 32-bit words that are included in the binary. Then we verify that the first four bytes match the magic number that identifies a SPIR-V binary. Finally, we retrieve the number of IDs that are defined in the binary.

Next, we loop over all the words in the binary to retrieve the information we need. Each ID definition starts with the Op type and the number of words that it is composed of:

```
SpvOp op = ( SpvOp )( data[ word_index ] & 0xFF );
u16 word_count = ( u16 )( data[ word_index ] >> 16 );
```

The Op type is stored in the bottom 16 bits of the word, and the word count is in the top 16 bits. Next, we parse the data for the Op types we are interested in. We are not going to cover all Op types in this section, as the structure is the same for all types. We suggest you refer to the SPIR-V specification (linked in the *Further reading* section) for more details on each Op type.

We start with the type of shader we are currently parsing:

```
case ( SpvOpEntryPoint ):
{
```

```
        SpvExecutionModel model = ( SpvExecutionModel )data[
                                    word_index + 1 ];

        stage = parse_execution_model( model );

        break;
    }
```

We extract the execution model, translate it into a `VkShaderStageFlags` value, and store it in the `stage` variable.

Next, we parse the descriptor set index and binding:

```
    case ( SpvOpDecorate ):
    {
        u32 id_index = data[ word_index + 1 ];

        Id& id= ids[ id_index ];

        SpvDecoration decoration = ( SpvDecoration )data[
                                    word_index + 2 ];
        switch ( decoration )
        {
            case ( SpvDecorationBinding ):
            {
                id.binding = data[ word_index + 3 ];
                break;
            }

            case ( SpvDecorationDescriptorSet ):
            {
                id.set = data[ word_index + 3 ];
                break;
            }
        }

        break;
    }
```

First, we retrieve the index of the ID. As we mentioned previously, variables can be forward declared, and we might have to update the values for the same ID multiple times. Next, we retrieve the value of the decoration. We are only interested in the descriptor set index (`SpvDecorationDescriptorSet`) and binding (`SpvDecorationBinding`) and we store their values in the entry for this ID.

We follow with an example of a variable type:

```
case ( SpvOpTypeVector ):
{
    u32 id_index = data[ word_index + 1 ];

    Id& id = ids[ id_index ];
    id.op = op;
    id.type_index = data[ word_index + 2 ];
    id.count = data[ word_index + 3 ];

    break;
}
```

As we saw in the disassembly, a vector is defined by its entry type and count. We store them in the `type_index` and `count` members of the ID struct. Here, we also see how an ID can refer to another one if needed. The `type_index` member stores the index to another entry in the `ids` array and can be used later to retrieve additional type information.

Next, we have a sampler definition:

```
case ( SpvOpTypeSampler ):
{
    u32 id_index = data[ word_index + 1 ];
    RASSERT( id_index < id_bound );

    Id& id = ids[ id_index ];
    id.op = op;

    break;
}
```

We only need to store the Op type for this entry. Finally, we have the entry for a variable type:

```
case ( SpvOpVariable ):
{
```

```
        u32 id_index = data[ word_index + 2 ];

    Id& id= ids[ id_index ];
    id.op = op;
    id.type_index = data[ word_index + 1 ];
    id.storage_class = ( SpvStorageClass )data[
                            word_index + 3 ];

    break;
}
```

The relevant information for this entry is `type_index`, which will always refer to an entry of `pointer` type and the storage class. The storage class tells us which entries are variables that we are interested in and which ones we can skip.

And that is exactly what the next part of the code is doing. Once we finish parsing all IDs, we loop over each ID entry and identify the ones we are interested in. We first identify all variables:

```
for ( u32 id_index = 0; id_index < ids.size; ++id_index ) {
    Id& id= ids[ id_index ];

    if ( id.op == SpvOpVariable ) {
```

Next, we use the variable storage class to determine whether it is a uniform variable:

```
switch ( id.storage_class ) {
    case ( SpvStorageClassUniform ):
    case ( SpvStorageClassUniformConstant ):
    {
```

We are only interested in the `Uniform` and `UniformConstant` variables. We then retrieve the `uniform` type. Remember, there is a double indirection to retrieve the actual type of a variable: first, we get the `pointer` type, and from the `pointer` type, we get to the real type of the variable. We have highlighted the code that does this:

```
Id& uniform_type = ids[ ids[ id.type_index ].type_index ];

DescriptorSetLayoutCreation& setLayout =
parse_result->sets[ id.set ];
```

```
setLayout.set_set_index( id.set );

DescriptorSetLayoutCreation::Binding binding{ };
binding.start = id.binding;
binding.count = 1;
```

After retrieving the type, we get the `DescriptorSetLayoutCreation` entry for the set this variable is part of. We then create a new `binding` entry and store the `binding` value. We always assume a count of 1 for each resource.

In this last step, we determine the resource type for this binding and add its entry to the set layout:

```
switch ( uniform_type.op ) {
    case (SpvOpTypeStruct):
    {
        binding.type = VK_DESCRIPTOR_TYPE_UNIFORM_BUFFER;
        binding.name = uniform_type.name.text;
        break;
    }

    case (SpvOpTypeSampledImage):
    {
        binding.type = VK_DESCRIPTOR_TYPE_COMBINED
        _IMAGE_SAMPLER;
        binding.name = id.name.text;
        break;
    }
}

setLayout.add_binding_at_index( binding, id.binding );
```

We use the `Op` type to determine the type of resource we have found. So far, we are only interested in `Struct` for uniform buffers and `SampledImage` for textures. We are going to add support for more types when needed for the remainder of the book.

While it's possible to distinguish between uniform buffers and storage buffers, the binary data cannot determine whether a buffer is dynamic or not. In our implementation, the application code needs to specify this detail.

An alternative would be to use a naming convention (prefixing dynamic buffers with `dyn_`, for instance) so that dynamic buffers can be automatically identified.

This concludes our introduction to the SPIR-V binary format. It might take a couple of readings to fully understand how it works, but don't worry, it certainly took us a few iterations to fully understand it!

Knowing how to parse SPIR-V data is an important tool to automate other aspects of graphics development. It can be used, for instance, to automate the generation of C++ headers to keep CPU and GPU structs in sync. We encourage you to expand our implementation to add support for the features you might need!

In this section, we have explained how to compile a shader source into SPIR-V. We have shown how the SPIR-V binary format is organized and how to parse this data to help us automatically create a pipeline layout.

In the next and final section of this chapter, we are going to add pipeline caching to our GPU device implementation.

Improving load times with a pipeline cache

Each time we create a graphics pipeline and, to a lesser extent, a compute pipeline, the driver has to analyze and compile the shaders we have provided. It also has to inspect the state we have defined in the creation structure and translate it into instructions to program the different units of the GPU. This process is quite expensive, and it's one of the reasons why, in Vulkan we have to define most of the pipeline state upfront.

In this section, we are going to add pipeline caching to our GPU device implementation to improve loading times. If your application has to create thousands of pipelines, it can incur a significant startup time or, for a game, long loading times between levels.

The technique described in this section will help to reduce the time spent creating pipelines. The first change you will notice is that the `GpuDevice::create_pipeline` method accepts a new optional parameter that defines the path of a pipeline cache file:

```
GpuDevice::create_pipeline( const PipelineCreation&
                            creation, const char*
                            cache_path )
```

We then need to define the `VkPipelineCache` structure:

```
VkPipelineCache pipeline_cache = VK_NULL_HANDLE;
VkPipelineCacheCreateInfo pipeline_cache_create_info {
    VK_STRUCTURE_TYPE_PIPELINE_CACHE_CREATE_INFO };
```

Improving Resources Management

The next step is to check whether the pipeline cache file already exists. If it does, we load the file data and add it to the pipeline cache creation:

```
FileReadResult read_result = file_read_binary( cache_path,
                                               allocator );

pipeline_cache_create_info.initialDataSize =
   read_result.size;
pipeline_cache_create_info.pInitialData = read_result.data;
```

If the file doesn't exist, we don't have to make any further changes to the creation structure. We can now call vkCreatePipelineCache:

```
vkCreatePipelineCache( vulkan_device,
                       &pipeline_cache_create_info,
                       vulkan_allocation_callbacks,
                       &pipeline_cache );
```

This will return a handle to a VkPipelineCache object that we are going to use when creating the pipeline object:

```
vkCreateGraphicsPipelines( vulkan_device, pipeline_cache,
                           1, &pipeline_info,
                           vulkan_allocation_callbacks,
                           &pipeline->vk_pipeline );
```

We can do the same for compute pipelines:

```
vkCreateComputePipelines( vulkan_device, pipeline_cache, 1,
                          &pipeline_info,
                          vulkan_allocation_callbacks,
                          &pipeline->vk_pipeline );
```

If we have loaded a pipeline cache file, the driver will use the data to accelerate the pipeline creation. If, on the other hand, this is the first time we are creating the given pipeline, we can now query and store the pipeline cache data for later reuse:

```
sizet cache_data_size = 0;
vkGetPipelineCacheData( vulkan_device, pipeline_cache,
                        &cache_data_size, nullptr );
```

```
void* cache_data = allocator->allocate( cache_data_size, 64 );
vkGetPipelineCacheData( vulkan_device, pipeline_cache,
                        &cache_data_size, cache_data );

file_write_binary( cache_path, cache_data, cache_data_size );
```

We first call `vkGetPipelineCacheData` with `nullptr` for the data member to retrieve the cache data size. We then allocate the memory that is needed to store the cache data and call `vkGetPipelineCacheData` again, this time with a pointer to the memory where the cache data will be stored. Finally, we write this data to the file specified when `GpuDevice::create_pipeline` was called.

We are now done with the pipeline cache data structure, and it can be destroyed:

```
vkDestroyPipelineCache( vulkan_device, pipeline_cache,
                        vulkan_allocation_callbacks );
```

Before we conclude, we want to mention a shortcoming of pipeline caching. The data in the cache is controlled by each vendor driver implementation. When a new driver version is released, the data format of the cache might change and become incompatible with the data previously stored in the cache file. Having a cache file, in this case, might provide no benefit as the driver cannot make use of it.

For this reason, each driver has to prefix the cache data with the following header:

```
struct VkPipelineCacheHeaderVersionOne {
    uint32_t                      headerSize;
    VkPipelineCacheHeaderVersion  headerVersion;
    uint32_t                      vendorID;
    uint32_t                      deviceID;
    uint8_t                       pipeline
                                  CacheUUID[VK_UUID_SIZE];
}
```

When we load the cache data from disk, we can compare the values in the header against the values returned by the driver and GPU we are running on:

```
VkPipelineCacheHeaderVersionOne* cache_header =
    (VkPipelineCacheHeaderVersionOne*)read_result.data;

if ( cache_header->deviceID == vulkan_physical
     _properties.deviceID && cache_header->vendorID ==
```

```
            vulkan_physical_properties.vendorID &&
            memcmp( cache_header->pipelineCacheUUID,
            vulkan_physical_properties.pipelineCacheUUID,
            VK_UUID_SIZE ) == 0 ) {
        pipeline_cache_create_info.initialDataSize =
        read_result.size;
        pipeline_cache_create_info.pInitialData =
        read_result.data;
    }
    else
    {
        cache_exists = false;
    }
```

If the values in the header match the ones of the device we are running on, we use the cache data as before. If they don't, we act as if the cache didn't exist and store a new version after the pipeline has been created.

In this section, we have demonstrated how to leverage pipeline caching to speed up pipeline creation at runtime. We have highlighted the changes made to our GPU device implementation to make use of this feature and how it has been used in this chapter's code.

Summary

In this chapter, we improved our GPU device implementation to make it easier to manage a large number of textures with bindless resources. We explained which extensions are needed and detailed which changes are required when creating a descriptor set layout to allow the use of bindless resources. We then showed the changes needed when creating a descriptor set to update the array of textures in use.

We then added automatic pipeline layout generation by parsing the SPIR-V binaries generated by the `glslang` compiler for our shaders. We provided an overview of the SPIR-V binary data format and explained how to parse it to extract the resources bound to a shader, and how to use this information to create a pipeline layout.

Finally, we enhanced our pipeline creation API by adding pipeline caching to improve the load times of our applications after the first run. We presented the Vulkan APIs that are needed to either generate or load the pipeline cache data. We also explained some of the limitations of pipeline caching and how to deal with them.

All the techniques presented in this chapter have the common goal of making it easier to deal with large projects and reduce manual code changes to a minimum when making changes to our shaders or materials.

We will continue to scale our engine in the next chapter by adding multithreading to record multiple command buffers or to submit multiple workloads in parallel to the GPU.

Further reading

We have covered only a small subset of the SPIR-V specification. If you would like to expand our parser implementation for your needs, we highly recommend consulting the official specification: `https://www.khronos.org/registry/SPIR-V/specs/unified1/SPIRV.html`.

We wrote a custom SPIR-V parser for this chapter, primarily for educational purposes. For your own project, we recommend using the existing reflection library from Khronos: `https://github.com/KhronosGroup/SPIRV-Reflect`.

It provides the functionality described in this chapter to deduce the pipeline layout for a shader binary and many other features.

3
Unlocking Multi-Threading

In this chapter, we will talk about adding multi-threading to the Raptor Engine.

This requires both a big change in the underlying architecture and some Vulkan-specific changes and synchronization work so that the different cores of the CPU and the GPU can cooperate in the most correct and the fastest way.

Multi-threading rendering is a topic covered many times over the years and a feature that most game engines have needed since the era of multi-core architectures exploded. Consoles such as the PlayStation 2 and the Sega Saturn already offered multi-threading support, and later generations continued the trend by providing an increasing number of cores that developers could take advantage of.

The first trace of multi-threading rendering in a game engine is as far back as 2008 when Christer Ericson wrote a blog post (`https://realtimecollisiondetection.net/blog/?p=86`) and showed that it was possible to parallelize and optimize the generation of commands used to render objects on the screen.

Older APIs such as OpenGL and DirectX (up until version 11) did not have proper multi-threading support, especially because they were big state machines with a global context tracking down each change after each command. Still, the command generation across different objects could take a few milliseconds, so multi-threading was already a big save in performance.

Luckily for us, Vulkan fully supports multi-threading command buffers natively, especially with the creation of the `VkCommandBuffer` class, from an architectural perspective of the Vulkan API.

The Raptor Engine, up until now, was a single-threaded application and thus required some architectural changes to fully support multi-threading. In this chapter, we will see those changes, learn how to use a task-based multi-threading library called enkiTS, and then unlock both asynchronous resource loading and multi-threading command recording.

In this chapter, we will cover the following topics:

- How to use a task-based multi-threading library
- How to asynchronously load resources
- How to draw in parallel threads

By the end of the chapter, we will know how to run concurrent tasks both for loading resources and drawing objects on the screen. By learning how to reason with a task-based multi-threading system, we will be able to perform other parallel tasks in future chapters as well.

Technical requirements

The code for this chapter can be found at the following URL: `https://github.com/PacktPublishing/Mastering-Graphics-Programming-with-Vulkan/tree/main/source/chapter3`.

Task-based multi-threading using enkiTS

To achieve parallelism, we need to understand some basic concepts and choices that led to the architecture developed in this chapter. First, we should note that when we talk about parallelism in software engineering, we mean the act of executing chunks of code at the same time.

This is possible because modern hardware has different units that can be operated independently, and operating systems have dedicated execution units called **threads**.

A common way to achieve parallelism is to reason with tasks – small independent execution units that can run on any thread.

Why task-based parallelism?

Multi-threading is not a new subject, and since the early years of it being added to various game engines, there have been different ways of implementing it. Game engines are pieces of software that use all of the hardware available in the most efficient way, thus paving the way for more optimized software architectures.

Therefore, we'll take some ideas from game engines and gaming-related presentations. The initial implementations started by adding a thread with a single job to do – something specific, such as rendering a single thread, an asynchronous **input/output** (**I/O**) thread, and so on.

This helped add more granularity to what could be done in parallel, and it was perfect for the older CPUs (having two cores only), but it soon became limiting.

There was the need to use cores in a more agnostic way so that any type of job could be done by almost any core and to improve performance. This gave way to the emergence of two new architectures: **task-based** and **fiber-based** architectures.

Task-based parallelism is achieved by feeding multiple threads with different tasks and orchestrating them through dependencies. Tasks are inherently platform agnostic and cannot be interrupted, leading to a more straightforward capability to schedule and organize code to be executed with them.

On the other hand, fibers are software constructs similar to tasks, but they rely heavily on the scheduler to interrupt their flow and resume when needed. This main difference makes it hard to write a proper fiber system and normally leads to a lot of subtle errors.

For the simplicity of using tasks over fibers and the bigger availability of libraries implementing task-based parallelism, the enkiTS library was chosen to handle everything. For those curious about more in-depth explanations, there are a couple of great presentations about these architectures.

A great example of a task-based engine is the one behind the Destiny franchise (with an in-depth architecture you can view at `https://www.gdcvault.com/play/1021926/Destiny-s-Multithreaded-Rendering`), while a fiber-based one is used by the game studio Naughty Dog for their games (there is a presentation about it at `https://www.gdcvault.com/play/1022186/Parallelizing-the-Naughty-Dog-Engine`).

Using the enkiTS (Task-Scheduler) library

Task-based multi-threading is based on the concept of a task, defined as a *unit of independent work that can be executed on any core of a CPU*.

To do that, there is a need for a scheduler to coordinate different tasks and take care of the possible dependencies between them. Another interesting aspect of a task is that it could have one or more dependencies so that it could be scheduled to run only after certain tasks finish their execution.

This means that tasks can be submitted to the scheduler at any time, and with proper dependencies, we create a graph-based execution of the engine. If done properly, each core can be utilized fully and results in optimal performance to the engine.

The scheduler is the brain behind all the tasks: it checks dependencies and priorities, and schedules or removes tasks based on need, and it is a new system added to the Raptor Engine.

When initializing the scheduler, the library spawns a number of threads, each waiting to execute a task. When adding tasks to the scheduler, they are inserted into a queue. When the scheduler is told to execute pending tasks, each thread gets the next available task from the queue – according to dependency and priority – and executes it.

It's important to note that running tasks can spawn other tasks. These tasks will be added to the thread's local queue, but they are up for grabs if another thread is idle. This implementation is called a **work-stealing queue**.

Initializing the scheduler is as simple as creating a configuration and calling the `Initialize` method:

```
enki::TaskSchedulerConfig config;
config.numTaskThreadsToCreate = 4;

enki::TaskScheduler task_scheduler;
task_scheduler.Initialize( config );
```

With this code, we are telling the task scheduler to spawn four threads that it will use to perform its duties. enkiTS uses the `TaskSet` class as a unit of work, and it uses both inheritance and lambda functions to drive the execution of tasks in the scheduler:

```
Struct ParallelTaskSet : enki::ItaskSet {
    void ExecuteRange( enki::TaskSetPartition range_,
                       uint32_t threadnum_ ) override {
        // do something here, can issue tasks with
            task_scheduler
    }
};

int main(int argc, const char * argv[]) {
    enki::TaskScheduler task_scheduler;
    task_scheduler.Initialize( config );

    ParallelTaskSet task; // default constructor has a set
                          size of 1
    task_scheduler.AddTaskSetToPipe( &task );

    // wait for task set (running tasks if they exist)
    // since we've just added it and it has no range we'll
        likely run it.
    Task_scheduler.WaitforTask( &task );
    return 0;
}
```

In this simple snippet, we see how to create an empty `TaskSet` (as the name implies, a set of tasks) that defines how a task will execute the code, leaving the scheduler with the job of deciding how many of the tasks will be needed and which thread will be used.

A more streamlined version of the previous code uses lambda functions:

```
enki::TaskSet task( 1, [](enki::TaskSetPartition range_,
   uint32_t threadnum_  ) {
         // do something here
   } );
task_scheduler.AddTaskSetToPipe( &task );
```

This version can be easier when reading the code as it does break the flow less, but it is functionally equivalent to the previous one.

Another feature of the enkiTS scheduler is the possibility to add pinned tasks – special tasks that will be bound to a thread and will always be executed there. We will see the use of pinned tasks in the next section to perform asynchronous I/O operations.

In this section, we talked briefly about the different types of multi-threading so that we could express the reason for choosing to use task-based multi-threading. We then showed some simple examples of the enkiTS library and its usage, adding multi-threading capabilities to the Raptor Engine.

In the next section, we will finally see a real use case in the engine, which is the asynchronous loading of resources.

Asynchronous loading

The loading of resources is one of the (if not *the*) slowest operations that can be done in any framework. This is because the files to be loaded are big, and they can come from different sources, such as optical units (DVD and Blu-ray), hard drives, and even the network.

It is another great topic, but the most important concept to understand is the inherent speed necessary to read the memory:

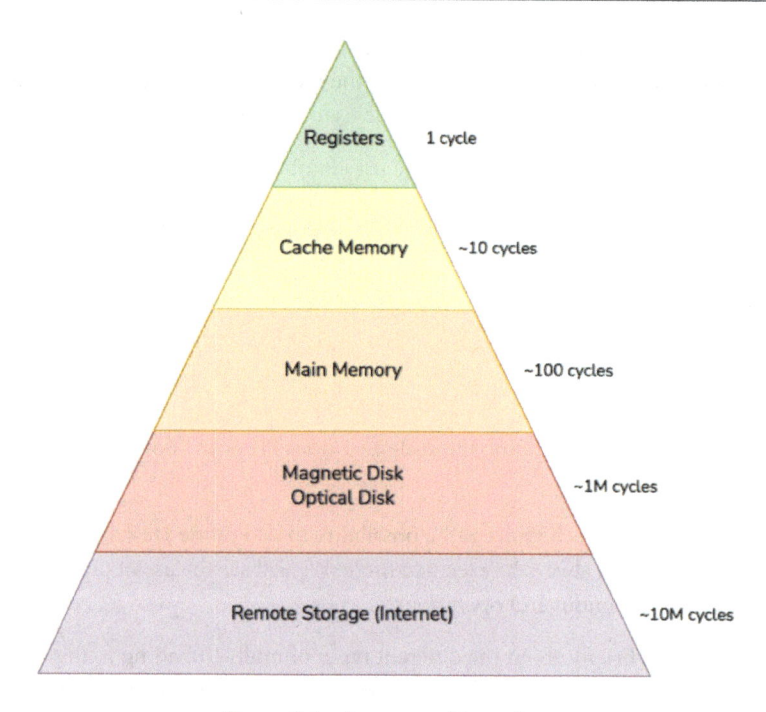

Figure 3.1 – A memory hierarchy

As shown in the preceding diagram, the fastest memory is the registers memory. After registers follows the cache, with different levels and access speeds: both registers and caches are directly in the processing unit (both the CPU and GPU have registers and caches, even with different underlying architectures).

Main memory refers to the RAM, which is the area that is normally populated with the data used by the application. It is slower than the cache, but it is the target of the loading operations as the only one directly accessible from the code. Then there are magnetic disks (hard drives) and optical drives – much slower but with greater capacity. They normally contain the asset data that will be loaded into the main memory.

The final memory is in remote storage, such as from some servers, and it is the slowest. We will not deal with that here, but it can be used when working on applications that have some form of online service, such as multiplayer games.

With the objective of optimizing the read access in an application, we want to transfer all the needed data into the main memory, as we can't interact with caches and registers. To hide the slow speed of magnetic and optical disks, one of the most important things that can be done is to parallelize the loading of any resource coming from any medium so that the fluidity of the application is not slowed down.

The most common way of doing it, and one example of the thread-specialization architecture we talked briefly about before, is to have a separate thread that handles just the loading of resources and interacts with other systems to update the used resources in the engine.

In the following sections, we will talk about how to set up enkiTS and create tasks for parallelizing the Raptor Engine, as well as talk about Vulkan queues, which are necessary for parallel command submission. Finally, we will dwell on the actual code used for asynchronous loading.

Creating the I/O thread and tasks

In the enkiTS library, there is a feature called **pinned-task** that associates a task to a specific thread so that it is continuously running there unless stopped by the user or a higher priority task is scheduled on that thread.

To simplify things, we will add a new thread and avoid it being used by the application. This thread will be mostly idle, so the context switch should be low:

```
config.numTaskThreadsToCreate = 4;
```

We then create a pinned task and associate it with a thread ID:

```
// Create IO threads at the end
RunPinnedTaskLoopTask run_pinned_task;
run_pinned_task.threadNum = task_scheduler.
                            GetNumTaskThreads() - 1;
task_scheduler.AddPinnedTask( &run_pinned_task );
```

At this point, we can create the actual task responsible for asynchronous loading, associating it with the same thread as the pinned task:

```
// Send async load task to external thread
AsynchronousLoadTask async_load_task;
async_load_task.threadNum = run_pinned_task.threadNum;
task_scheduler.AddPinnedTask( &async_load_task );
```

The final piece of the puzzle is the actual code for these two tasks. First, let us have a look at the first pinned task:

```
struct RunPinnedTaskLoopTask : enki::IPinnedTask {
    void Execute() override {
        while ( task_scheduler->GetIsRunning() && execute )
        {
            task_scheduler->WaitForNewPinnedTasks();
            // this thread will 'sleep' until there are new
                pinned tasks
            task_scheduler->RunPinnedTasks();
```

```
            }
        }

        enki::TaskScheduler*task_scheduler;
        bool execute = true;
}; // struct RunPinnedTaskLoopTask
```

This task will wait for any other pinned task and run them when possible. We have added an `execute` flag to stop the execution when needed, for example, when exiting the application, but it could be used in general to suspend it in other situations (such as when the application is minimized).

The other task is the one executing the asynchronous loading using the `AsynchronousLoader` class:

```
struct AsynchronousLoadTask : enki::IPinnedTask {
    void Execute() override {
        while ( execute ) {
            async_loader->update();
        }
    }
    AsynchronousLoader*async_loader;
    enki::TaskScheduler*task_scheduler;
    bool execute = true;
}; // struct AsynchronousLoadTask
```

The idea behind this task is to always be active and wait for requests for resource loading. The `while` loop ensures that the root pinned task never schedules other tasks on this thread, locking it to I/O as intended.

Before moving on to look at the `AsynchronousLoader` class, we need to look at an important concept in Vulkan, namely queues, and why they are a great addition for asynchronous loading.

Vulkan queues and the first parallel command generation

The concept of a *queue* – which can be defined as the entry point to submit commands recorded in `VkCommandBuffers` to the GPU – is an addition to Vulkan compared to OpenGL and needs to be taken care of.

Submission using a queue is a single-threaded operation, and a costly operation that becomes a synchronization point between CPU and GPU to be aware of. Normally, there is the main queue to which the engine submits command buffers before presenting the frame. This will send the work to the GPU and create the rendered image intended.

Asynchronous loading 65

But where there is one queue, there can be more. To enhance parallel execution, we can instead create different *queues* – and use them in different threads instead of the main one.

A more in-depth look at queues can be found at `https://github.com/KhronosGroup/Vulkan-Guide/blob/master/chapters/queues.adoc`, but what we need to know is that each queue can submit certain types of commands, visible through a queue's flag:

- `VK_QUEUE_GRAPHICS_BIT` can submit all `vkCmdDraw` commands
- `VK_QUEUE_COMPUTE` can submit all `vkCmdDispatch` and `vkCmdTraceRays` (used for ray tracing)
- `VK_QUEUE_TRANSFER` can submit copy commands, such as `vkCmdCopyBuffer`, `vkCmdCopyBufferToImage`, and `vkCmdCopyImageToBuffer`

Each available queue is exposed through a queue family. Each queue family can have multiple capabilities and can expose multiple queues. Here is an example to clarify:

```
{
    "VkQueueFamilyProperties": {
        "queueFlags": [
            "VK_QUEUE_GRAPHICS_BIT",
            "VK_QUEUE_COMPUTE_BIT",
            "VK_QUEUE_TRANSFER_BIT",
            "VK_QUEUE_SPARSE_BINDING_BIT"
        ],
        "queueCount": 1,
    }
},
{
    "VkQueueFamilyProperties": {
        "queueFlags": [
            "VK_QUEUE_COMPUTE_BIT",
            "VK_QUEUE_TRANSFER_BIT",
            "VK_QUEUE_SPARSE_BINDING_BIT"
        ],
        "queueCount": 2,
    }
},
{
```

```
            "VkQueueFamilyProperties": {
                "queueFlags": [
                    "VK_QUEUE_TRANSFER_BIT",
                    "VK_QUEUE_SPARSE_BINDING_BIT"
                ],
                "queueCount": 2,
            }
        }
```

The first queue exposes all capabilities, and we only have one of them. The next queue can be used for compute and transfer, and the third one for transfer (we'll ignore the sparse feature for now). We have two queues for each of these families.

It is guaranteed that on a GPU there will always be at least one queue that can submit all types of commands, and that will be our main queue.

In some GPUs, though, there can be specialized queues that have only the VK_QUEUE_TRANSFER flag activated, which means that they can use **direct memory access** (**DMA**) to speed up the transfer of data between the CPU and the GPU.

One last thing: the Vulkan logical device is responsible for creating and destroying queues – an operation normally done at the startup/shutdown of the application. Let us briefly see the code to query the support for different queues:

```
u32 queue_family_count = 0;
    vkGetPhysicalDeviceQueueFamilyProperties(
    vulkan_physical_device, &queue_family_count, nullptr );

    VkQueueFamilyProperties*queue_families = (
        VkQueueFamilyProperties* )ralloca( sizeof(
            VkQueueFamilyProperties ) * queue_family_count,
            temp_allocator );
    vkGetPhysicalDeviceQueueFamilyProperties(
        vulkan_physical_device, &queue_family_count,
            queue_families );

    u32 main_queue_index = u32_max, transfer_queue_index =
    u32_max;
    for ( u32 fi = 0; fi < queue_family_count; ++fi) {
        VkQueueFamilyProperties queue_family =
```

Asynchronous loading

```
            queue_families[ fi ];

    if ( queue_family.queueCount == 0 ) {
        continue;
    }
    // Search for main queue that should be able to do
        all work (graphics, compute and transfer)
    if ( (queue_family.queueFlags & (
        VK_QUEUE_GRAPHICS_BIT | VK_QUEUE_COMPUTE_BIT |
        VK_QUEUE_TRANSFER_BIT )) == (
        VK_QUEUE_GRAPHICS_BIT | VK_QUEUE_COMPUTE_BIT |
        VK_QUEUE_TRANSFER_BIT ) ) {
            main_queue_index = fi;
    }
    // Search for transfer queue
    if ( ( queue_family.queueFlags &
        VK_QUEUE_COMPUTE_BIT ) == 0 &&
        (queue_family.queueFlags &
        VK_QUEUE_TRANSFER_BIT) ) {
        transfer_queue_index = fi;
    }
}
```

As can be seen in the preceding code, we get the list of all queues for the selected GPU, and we check the different bits that identify the types of commands that can be executed there.

In our case, we will save the *main queue* and the *transfer queue*, if it is present on the GPU, and we will save the indices of the *queues* to retrieve the VkQueue after the device creation. Some devices don't expose a separate transfer queue. In this case, we will use the main queue to perform transfer operations, and we need to make sure that access to the queue is correctly synchronized for upload and graphics submissions.

Let's see how to create the *queues*:

```
// Queue creation
VkDeviceQueueCreateInfo queue_info[ 2 ] = {};
VkDeviceQueueCreateInfo& main_queue = queue_info[ 0 ];
main_queue.sType = VK_STRUCTURE_TYPE_DEVICE_QUEUE
                    _CREATE_INFO;
```

```
main_queue.queueFamilyIndex = main_queue_index;
main_queue.queueCount = 1;
main_queue.pQueuePriorities = queue_priority;

if ( vulkan_transfer_queue_family < queue_family_count ) {
    VkDeviceQueueCreateInfo& transfer_queue_info =
        queue_info[ 1 ];
    transfer_queue_info.sType = VK_STRUCTURE_TYPE
                                 _DEVICE_QUEUE_CREATE_INFO;
    transfer_queue_info.queueFamilyIndex = transfer_queue
                                            _index;
transfer_queue_info.queueCount = 1;
transfer_queue_info.pQueuePriorities = queue_priority;
}
VkDeviceCreateInfo device_create_info {
    VK_STRUCTURE_TYPE_DEVICE_CREATE_INFO };
device_create_info.queueCreateInfoCount = vulkan_transfer
    _queue_family < queue_family_count ? 2 : 1;
device_create_info.pQueueCreateInfos = queue_info;
...
result = vkCreateDevice( vulkan_physical_device,
                         &device_create_info,
                         vulkan_allocation_callbacks,
                         &vulkan_device );
```

As already mentioned, `vkCreateDevice` is the command that creates *queues* by adding pQueueCreateInfos in the VkDeviceCreateInfo struct.

Once the device is created, we can query for all the queues as follows:

```
// Queue retrieval
// Get main queue
vkGetDeviceQueue( vulkan_device, main_queue_index, 0,
                 &vulkan_main_queue );
// Get transfer queue if present
if ( vulkan_transfer_queue_family < queue_family_count ) {
    vkGetDeviceQueue( vulkan_device, transfer_queue_index,
```

```
                    0, &vulkan_transfer_queue );
}
```

At this point, we have both the main and the transfer queues ready to be used to submit work in parallel.

We had a look at how to submit parallel work to copy memory over the GPU without blocking either the GPU or the CPU, and we created a specific class to do that, `AsynchronousLoader`, which we will cover in the next section.

The AsynchronousLoader class

Here, we'll finally see the code for the class that implements asynchronous loading.

The `AsynchronousLoader` class has the following responsibilities:

- Process load from file requests
- Process GPU upload transfers
- Manage a staging buffer to handle a copy of the data
- Enqueue the command buffers with copy commands
- Signal to the renderer that a texture has finished a transfer

Before focusing on the code that uploads data to the GPU, there is some Vulkan-specific code that is important to understand, relative to command pools, transfer queues, and using a staging buffer.

Creating command pools for the transfer queue

In order to submit commands to the transfer queue, we need to create command pools that are linked to that queue:

```
for ( u32 i = 0; i < GpuDevice::k_max_frames; ++i ) {
VkCommandPoolCreateInfo cmd_pool_info = {
    VK_STRUCTURE_TYPE_COMMAND_POOL_CREATE_INFO, nullptr };
cmd_pool_info.queueFamilyIndex = gpu->vulkan
                                 _transfer_queue_family;
cmd_pool_info.flags = VK_COMMAND_POOL_CREATE_RESET
                      _COMMAND_BUFFER_BIT;
vkCreateCommandPool( gpu->vulkan_device, &cmd_pool_info,
                     gpu->vulkan_allocation_callbacks,
                     &command_pools[i]);
}
```

The important part is `queueFamilyIndex`, to link `CommandPool` to the transfer queue so that every command buffer allocated from this pool can be properly submitted to the transfer queue.

Next, we will simply allocate the command buffers linked to the newly created pools:

```
for ( u32 i = 0; i < GpuDevice::k_max_frames; ++i) {
    VkCommandBufferAllocateInfo cmd = {
        VK_STRUCTURE_TYPE_COMMAND_BUFFER_ALLOCATE_INFO,
            nullptr };
        cmd.commandPool = command_pools[i];
cmd.level = VK_COMMAND_BUFFER_LEVEL_PRIMARY;
cmd.commandBufferCount = 1;
vkAllocateCommandBuffers( renderer->gpu->vulkan_device,
                          &cmd, &command_buffers[i].
                          vk_command_buffer );
```

With this setup, we are now ready to submit commands to the transfer queue using the command buffers.

Next, we will have a look at the staging buffer – an addition to ensure that the transfer to the GPU is the fastest possible from the CPU.

Creating the staging buffer

To optimally transfer data between the CPU and the GPU, there is the need to create an area of memory that can be used as a source to issue commands related to copying data to the GPU.

To achieve this, we will create a staging buffer, a persistent buffer that will serve this purpose. We will see both the Raptor wrapper and the Vulkan-specific code to create a persistent staging buffer.

In the following code, we will allocate a persistently mapped buffer of 64 MB:

```
BufferCreation bc;
bc.reset().set( VK_BUFFER_USAGE_TRANSFER_SRC_BIT,
                ResourceUsageType::Stream, rmega( 64 )
                ).set_name( "staging_buffer" ).
                set_persistent( true );
BufferHandle staging_buffer_handle = gpu->create_buffer
                                     ( bc );
```

This translates to the following code:

```
VkBufferCreateInfo buffer_info{
    VK_STRUCTURE_TYPE_BUFFER_CREATE_INFO };
```

Asynchronous loading

```
buffer_info.usage = VK_BUFFER_USAGE_TRANSFER_SRC_BIT;
buffer_info.size = 64 * 1024 * 1024; // 64 MB

VmaAllocationCreateInfo allocation_create_info{};
allocation_create_info.flags = VMA_ALLOCATION_CREATE
 _STRATEGY_BEST_FIT_BIT | VMA_ALLOCATION_CREATE_MAPPED_BIT;
VmaAllocationInfo allocation_info{};
check( vmaCreateBuffer( vma_allocator, &buffer_info,
        &allocation_create_info, &buffer->vk_buffer,
        &buffer->vma_allocation, &allocation_info ) );
```

This buffer will be the source of the memory transfers, and the VMA_ALLOCATION_CREATE_MAPPED_BIT flag ensures that it will always be mapped.

We can retrieve and use the pointer to the allocated data from the allocation_info structure, filled by vmaCreateBuffer:

```
buffer->mapped_data = static_cast<u8*>(allocation_info.
                                       pMappedData);
```

We can now use the staging buffer for any operation to send data to the GPU, and if ever there is the need for a bigger allocation, we could recreate a new staging buffer with a bigger size.

Next, we need to see the code to create a semaphore and a fence used to submit and synchronize the CPU and GPU execution of commands.

Creating semaphores and fences for GPU synchronization

The code here is straightforward; the only important part is the creation of a signaled fence because it will let the code start to process uploads:

```
VkSemaphoreCreateInfo semaphore_info{
    VK_STRUCTURE_TYPE_SEMAPHORE_CREATE_INFO };
vkCreateSemaphore( gpu->vulkan_device, &semaphore_info,
                   gpu->vulkan_allocation_callbacks,
                   &transfer_complete_semaphore );

VkFenceCreateInfo fence_info{
    VK_STRUCTURE_TYPE_FENCE_CREATE_INFO };
fence_info.flags = VK_FENCE_CREATE_SIGNALED_BIT;
vkCreateFence( gpu->vulkan_device, &fence_info,
```

```
                    gpu->vulkan_allocation_callbacks,
                    &transfer_fence );
```

Finally, we have now arrived at processing the requests.

Processing a file request

File requests are not specifically Vulkan-related, but it is useful to see how they are done.

We use the STB image library (https://github.com/nothings/stb) to load the texture into memory and then simply add the loaded memory and the associated texture to create an upload request. This will be responsible for copying the data from the memory to the GPU using the transfer queue:

```
FileLoadRequest load_request = file_load_requests.back();
// Process request
int x, y, comp;
u8* texture_data = stbi_load( load_request.path, &x, &y,
                              &comp, 4 );
// Signal the loader that an upload data is ready to be
   transferred to the GPU
UploadRequest& upload_request = upload_requests.push_use();
upload_request.data = texture_data;
upload_request.texture = load_request.texture;
```

Next, we will see how to process an upload request.

Processing an upload request

This is the part that finally uploads the data to the GPU. First, we need to ensure that the fence is signaled to proceed, which is why we created it already signaled.

If it is signaled, we can reset it so we can let the API signal it when the submission is done:

```
// Wait for transfer fence to be finished
if ( vkGetFenceStatus( gpu->vulkan_device, transfer_fence )
     != VK_SUCCESS ) {
return;
}
// Reset if file requests are present.
vkResetFences( gpu->vulkan_device, 1, &transfer_fence );
```

We then proceed to take a request, allocate memory from the staging buffer, and use a command buffer to upload the GPU:

```
// Get last request
UploadRequest request = upload_requests.back();
const sizet aligned_image_size = memory_align(
                                 texture->width *
                                 texture->height *
                                 k_texture_channels,
                                 k_texture_alignment );
// Request place in buffer
const sizet current_offset = staging_buffer_offset +
                             aligned_image_size;

CommandBuffer* cb = &command_buffers[ gpu->current_frame ;
cb->begin();
cb->upload_texture_data( texture->handle, request.data,
                         staging_buffer->handle,
                         current_offset );
free( request.data );
cb->end();
```

The upload_texture_data method is the one that takes care of uploading data and adding the needed barriers. This can be tricky, so we've included the code to show how it can be done.

First, we need to copy the data to the staging buffer:

```
// Copy buffer_data to staging buffer
memcpy( staging_buffer->mapped_data +
        staging_buffer_offset, texture_data,
        static_cast< size_t >( image_size ) );
```

Then we can prepare a copy, in this case, from the staging buffer to an image. Here, it is important to specify the offset into the staging buffer:

```
VkBufferImageCopy region = {};
region.bufferOffset = staging_buffer_offset;
region.bufferRowLength = 0;
region.bufferImageHeight = 0;
```

We then proceed with adding a precopy memory barrier to perform a layout transition and specify that the data is using the transfer queue.

This uses the code suggested in the synchronization examples provided by the Khronos Group (https://github.com/KhronosGroup/Vulkan-Docs/wiki/Synchronization-Examples).

Once again, we show the raw Vulkan code that is simplified with some utility functions, highlighting the important lines:

```
// Pre copy memory barrier to perform layout transition
VkImageMemoryBarrier preCopyMemoryBarrier;
...
.srcAccessMask = 0,
.dstAccessMask = VK_ACCESS_TRANSFER_WRITE_BIT,
.oldLayout = VK_IMAGE_LAYOUT_UNDEFINED,
.newLayout = VK_IMAGE_LAYOUT_TRANSFER_DST_OPTIMAL,
.srcQueueFamilyIndex = VK_QUEUE_FAMILY_IGNORED,
.dstQueueFamilyIndex = VK_QUEUE_FAMILY_IGNORED,
.image = image,
.subresourceRange = ... };
...
```

The texture is now ready to be copied to the GPU:

```
// Copy from the staging buffer to the image
vkCmdCopyBufferToImage( vk_command_buffer,
                        staging_buffer->vk_buffer,
                        texture->vk_image,
                        VK_IMAGE_LAYOUT_TRANSFER_DST
                        _OPTIMAL, 1, &region );
```

The texture is now on the GPU, but it is still not usable from the main queue.

That is why we need another memory barrier that will also transfer ownership:

```
// Post copy memory barrier
VkImageMemoryBarrier postCopyTransferMemoryBarrier = {
...
.srcAccessMask = VK_ACCESS_TRANFER_WRITE_BIT,
.dstAccessMask = 0,
.oldLayout = VK_IMAGE_LAYOUT_TRANSFER_DST_OPTIMAL,
```

```
.newLayout = VK_IMAGE_LAYOUT_SHADER_READ_ONLY_OPTIMAL,
.srcQueueFamilyIndex = transferQueueFamilyIndex,
.dstQueueFamilyIndex = graphicsQueueFamilyIndex,
.image = image,
.subresourceRange = ... };
```

Once the ownership is transferred, a final barrier is needed to ensure that the transfer is complete and the texture can be read from the shaders, but this will be done by the renderer because it needs to use the main queue.

Signaling the renderer of the finished transfer

The signaling is implemented by simply adding the texture to a mutexed list of textures to update so that it is thread safe.

At this point, we need to perform a final barrier for each transferred texture. We opted to add these barriers after all the rendering is done and before the present step, but it could also be done at the beginning of the frame.

As stated before, one last barrier is needed to signal that the newly updated image is ready to be read by shaders and that all the writing operations are done:

```
VkImageMemoryBarrier postCopyGraphicsMemoryBarrier = {
...
.srcAccessMask = 0,
.dstAccessMask = VK_ACCESS_SHADER_READ_BIT,
.oldLayout = VK_IMAGE_LAYOUT_TRANSFER_DST_OPTIMAL,
.newLayout = VK_IMAGE_LAYOUT_SHADER_READ_ONLY_OPTIMAL,
.srcQueueFamilyIndex = transferQueueFamilyIndex,
.dstQueueFamilyIndex = graphicsQueueFamilyIndex,
.image = image,
.subresourceRange = ... };
```

We are now ready to use the texture on the GPU in our shaders, and the asynchronous loading is working. A very similar path is created for uploading buffers and thus will be omitted from the book but present in the code.

In this section, we saw how to unlock the asynchronous loading of resources to the GPU by using a transfer queue and different command buffers. We also showed how to manage ownership transfer between queues. Then, we finally saw the first steps in setting up tasks with the task scheduler, which is used to add multi-threading capabilities to the Raptor Engine.

In the next section, we will use the acquired knowledge to add the parallel recording of commands to draw objects on the screen.

Recording commands on multiple threads

To record commands using multiple threads, it is necessary to use different command buffers, at least one on each thread, to record the commands and then submit them to the main queue. To be more precise, in Vulkan, any kind of pool needs to be externally synchronized by the user; thus, the best option is to have an association between a thread and a pool.

In the case of command buffers, they are allocated from the associated pool and commands registered in it. Pools can be `CommandPools`, `DescriptorSetPools`, and `QueryPools` (for time and occlusion queries), and once associated with a thread, they can be used freely inside that thread of execution.

The execution order of the command buffers is based on the order of the array submitted to the main queue – thus, from a Vulkan perspective, sorting can be performed on a command buffer level.

We will see how important the allocation strategy for command buffers is and how easy it is to draw in parallel once the allocation is in place. We will also talk about the different types of command buffers, a unique feature of Vulkan.

The allocation strategy

The success in recording commands in parallel is achieved by taking into consideration both thread access and frame access. When creating command pools, not only does each thread need a unique pool to allocate command buffers and commands from, but it also needs to not be in flight in the GPU.

A simple allocation strategy is to decide the maximum number of threads (we will call them `T`) that will record commands and the max number of frames (we will call them `F`) that can be in flight, then allocate command pools that are `F * T`.

For each task that wants to render, using the pair frame-thread ID, we will guarantee that no pool will be either in flight or used by another thread.

This is a very conservative approach and can lead to unbalanced command generations, but it can be a great starting point and, in our case, enough to provide support for parallel rendering to the Raptor Engine.

In addition, we will allocate a maximum of five empty command buffers, two primary and three secondary, so that more tasks can execute chunks of rendering in parallel.

The class responsible for this is the `CommandBufferManager` class, accessible from the device, and it gives the user the possibility to request a command buffer through the `get_command_buffer` method.

In the next section, we will see the difference between primary and secondary command buffers, which are necessary to decide the granularity of the tasks to draw the frame in parallel.

Command buffer recycling

Linked to the allocation strategy is the recycling of the buffers. When a buffer has been executed, it can be reused to record new commands instead of always allocating new ones.

Thanks to the allocation strategy we chose, we associate a fixed amount of CommandPools to each frame, and thus to reuse the command buffers, we will reset its corresponding CommandPool instead of manually freeing buffers: this has been proven to be much more efficient on CPU time.

Note that we are not freeing the memory associated with the buffer, but we give CommandPool the freedom to reuse the total memory allocated between the command buffers that will be recorded, and it will reset all the states of all its command buffers to their initial state.

At the beginning of each frame, we call a simple method to reset pools:

```
void CommandBufferManager::reset_pools( u32 frame_index ) {
    for ( u32 i = 0; i < num_pools_per_frame; i++ ) {
        const u32 pool_index = pool_from_indices(
                                frame_index, i );
        vkResetCommandPool( gpu->vulkan_device,
                            vulkan_command_pools[
                            pool_index ], 0 );
    }
}
```

There is a utility method to calculate the pool index, based on the thread and frame.

After the reset of the pools, we can reuse the command buffers to record commands without needing to explicitly do so for each command.

We can finally have a look at the different types of command buffers.

Primary versus secondary command buffers

The Vulkan API has a unique difference in what command buffers can do: a command buffer can either be primary or secondary.

Primary command buffers are the most used ones and can perform any of the commands – drawing, compute, or copy commands, but their granularity is pretty coarse – at least one render pass must be used, and no pass can be further parallelized.

Secondary command buffers are much more limited – they can actually only execute draw commands within a render pass – but they can be used to parallelize the rendering of render passes that contain many draw calls (such as a G-Buffer render pass).

It is paramount then to make an informed decision about the granularity of the tasks, and especially important is to understand when to record using a primary or secondary buffer.

In *Chapter 4, Implementing a Frame Graph*, we will see how a graph of the frame can give enough information to decide which command buffer type to use and how many objects and render passes should be used in a task.

In the next section, we will see how to use both primary and secondary command buffers.

Drawing using primary command buffers

Drawing using primary command buffers is the most common way of using Vulkan and also the simplest. A primary command buffer, as already stated before, can execute any kind of command with no limitation, and it is the only one that can be submitted to a queue to be executed on the GPU.

Creating a primary command buffer is simply a matter of using `VK_COMMAND_BUFFER_LEVEL_PRIMARY` in the `VkCommandBufferAllocateInfo` structure passed to the `vkAllocateCommandBuffers` function.

Once created, at any time, we can begin the commands recording (with the `vkBeginCommandBuffer` function), bind passes and pipelines, and issue draw commands, copy commands, and compute ones.

Once the recording is finished, the `vkEndCommandBuffer` function must be used to signal the end of recording and prepare the buffer to be ready to be submitted to a queue:

```
VkSubmitInfo submit_info = {
    VK_STRUCTURE_TYPE_SUBMIT_INFO };
submit_info.commandBufferCount = num_queued_command
                                 _buffers;
submit_info.pCommandBuffers = enqueued_command_buffers;
...
vkQueueSubmit( vulkan_main_queue, 1, &submit_info,
         *render_complete_fence );
```

To record commands in parallel, there are only two conditions that must be respected by the recording threads:

- Simultaneous recording on the same `CommandPool` is forbidden
- Commands relative to `RenderPass` can only be executed in one thread

What happens if a pass (such as a Forward or G-Buffer typical pass) contains a lot of draw-calls, thus requiring parallel rendering? This is where secondary command buffers can be useful.

Drawing using secondary command buffers

Secondary command buffers have a very specific set of conditions to be used – they can record commands relative to only one render pass.

That is why it is important to allow the user to record more than one secondary command buffer: it could be possible that more than one pass needs per-pass parallelism, and thus more than one secondary command buffer is needed.

Secondary buffers always need a primary buffer and can't be submitted directly to any queue: they must be copied into the primary buffer and inherit only `RenderPass` and `FrameBuffers` set when beginning to record commands.

Let's have a look at the different steps involving the usage of secondary command buffers. First, we need to have a primary command buffer that needs to set up a render pass and frame buffer to be rendered into, as this is absolutely necessary because no secondary command buffer can be submitted to a queue or set `RenderPass` or `FrameBuffer`.

Those will be the only states inherited from the primary command buffer, thus, even when beginning to record commands, viewport and stencil states must be set again.

Let's start by showing a primary command buffer setup:

```
VkClearValue clearValues[2];
VkRenderPassBeginInfo renderPassBeginInfo {};
renderPassBeginInfo.renderPass = renderPass;
renderPassBeginInfo.framebuffer = frameBuffer;

vkBeginCommandBuffer(primaryCommandBuffer, &cmdBufInfo);
```

When beginning a render pass that will be split among one or more secondary command buffers, we need to add the VK_SUBPASS_CONTENTS_SECONDARY_COMMAND_BUFFERS flag:

```
vkCmdBeginRenderPass(primaryCommandBuffer,
&renderPassBeginInfo, VK_SUBPASS_CONTENTS_SECONDARY_COMMAND_
BUFFERS);
```

We can then pass the `inheritanceInfo` struct to the secondary buffer:

```
VkCommandBufferInheritanceInfo inheritanceInfo {};
inheritanceInfo.renderPass = renderPass;
inheritanceInfo.framebuffer = frameBuffer;
```

And then we can begin the secondary command buffer:

```
VkCommandBufferBeginInfo commandBufferBeginInfo {};
commandBufferBeginInfo.flags =
VK_COMMAND_BUFFER_USAGE_RENDER_PASS_CONTINUE_BIT;
commandBufferBeginInfo.pInheritanceInfo = &inheritanceInfo;
VkBeginCommandBuffer(secondaryCommandBuffer,
                     &commandBufferBeginInfo);
```

The secondary command buffer is now ready to start issuing drawing commands:

```
vkCmdSetViewport(secondaryCommandBuffers.background, 0, 1,
                 &viewport);
vkCmdSetScissor(secondaryCommandBuffers.background, 0, 1,
                &scissor);
vkCmdBindPipeline(secondaryCommandBuffers.background,
                  VK_PIPELINE_BIND_POINT_GRAPHICS,
                  pipelines.starsphere);
VkDrawIndexed(...)
```

Note that the scissor and viewport must always be set at the beginning, as no state is inherited outside of the bound render pass and frame buffer.

Once we have finished recording the commands, we can call the `VkEndCommandBuffer` function and put the buffer into a copiable state in the primary command buffer. To copy the secondary command buffers into the primary one, there is a specific function, `vkCmdExecuteCommands`, that needs to be called:

```
vkCmdExecuteCommands(primaryCommandBuffer,
                     commandBuffers.size(),
                     commandBuffers.data());
```

This function accepts an array of secondary command buffers that will be sequentially copied into the primary one.

To ensure a correct ordering of the commands recorded, not guaranteed by multi-threading (as threads can finish in any order), we can give each command buffer an execution index, put them all into an array, sort them, and then use this sorted array in the `vkCmdExecuteCommands` function.

At this point, the primary command buffer can record other commands or be submitted to the queue, as it contains all the commands copied from the secondary command buffers.

Spawning multiple tasks to record command buffers

The last step is to create multiple tasks to record command buffers in parallel. We have decided to group multiple meshes per command buffer as an example, but usually, you would record separate command buffers per render pass.

Let's take a look at the code:

```
SecondaryDrawTask secondary_tasks[ parallel_recordings ]{ };

u32 start = 0;
for ( u32 secondary_index = 0;
      secondary_index < parallel_recordings;
      ++secondary_index ) {
    SecondaryDrawTask& task = secondary_tasks[
                                    secondary_index ];

    task.init( scene, renderer, gpu_commands, start,
               start + draws_per_secondary );
    start += draws_per_secondary;

    task_scheduler->AddTaskSetToPipe( &task );
}
```

We add a task to the scheduler for each mesh group. Each task will record a command buffer for a range of meshes.

Once we have added all the tasks, we have to wait until they complete before adding the secondary command buffers for execution on the main command buffer:

```
for ( u32 secondary_index = 0;
      secondary_index < parallel_recordings;
      ++secondary_index ) {
    SecondaryDrawTask& task = secondary_tasks[
```

```
                         secondary_index ];
    task_scheduler->WaitforTask( &task );

    vkCmdExecuteCommands( gpu_commands->vk_command_buffer,
                          1, &task.cb->vk_command_buffer );
}
```

We suggest reading the code for this chapter for more details on the implementation.

In this section, we have described how to record multiple command buffers in parallel to optimize this operation on the CPU. We have detailed our allocation strategy for command buffers and how they can be reused across frames.

We have highlighted the differences between primary and secondary buffers and how they are used in our renderer. Finally, we have demonstrated how to record multiple command buffers in parallel.

In the next chapter, we are going to introduce the frame graph, a system that allows us to define multiple render passes and that can take advantage of the task system we have described to record the command buffer for each render pass in parallel.

Summary

In this chapter, we learned about the concept of task-based parallelism and saw how using a library such as enkiTS can quickly add multi-threading capabilities to the Raptor Engine.

We then learned how to add support for loading data from files to the GPU using an asynchronous loader. We also focused on Vulkan-related code to have a second queue of execution that can run in parallel to the one responsible for drawing. We saw the difference between primary and secondary command buffers.

We talked about the importance of the buffer's allocation strategy to ensure safety when recording commands in parallel, especially taking into consideration command reuse between frames.

Finally, we showed step by step how to use both types of command buffers, and this should be enough to add the desired level of parallelism to any application that decides to use Vulkan as its graphics API.

In the next chapter, we will work on a data structure called **Frame Graph**, which will give us enough information to automate some of the recording processes, including barriers, and will ease the decision making about the granularity of the tasks that will perform parallel rendering.

Further reading

Task-based systems have been in use for many years. `https://www.gdcvault.com/play/1012321/Task-based-Multithreading-How-to` provides a good overview.

Many articles can be found that cover work-stealing queues at `https://blog.molecular-matters.com/2015/09/08/job-system-2-0-lock-free-work-stealing-part-2-a-specialized-allocator/` and are a good starting point on the subject.

The PlayStation 3 and Xbox 360 use the Cell processor from IBM to provide more performance to developers through multiple cores. In particular, the PlayStation 3 has several **synergistic processor units** (**SPUs**) that developers can use to offload work from the main processor.

There are many presentations and articles that detail many clever ways developers have used these processors, for example, `https://www.gdcvault.com/play/1331/The-PlayStation-3-s-SPU` and `https://gdcvault.com/play/1014356/Practical-Occlusion-Culling-on`.

4
Implementing a Frame Graph

In this chapter, we are introducing **frame graphs**, a new system to control the rendering steps for a given frame. As the name implies, we are going to organize the steps (passes) required to render a frame in a **Directed Acyclic Graph** (DAG). This will allow us to determine the order of execution of each pass and which passes can be executed in parallel.

Having a graph also provides us with many other benefits, such as the following:

- It allows us to automate the creation and management of render passes and frame buffers, as each pass defines the input resources it will read from and which resources it will write to.

- It helps us reduce the memory required for a frame with a technique called **memory aliasing**. We can determine how long a resource will be in use by analyzing the graph. After the resource is no longer needed, we can reuse its memory for a new resource.

- Finally, we'll be able to let the graph manage the insertion of memory barriers and layout transitions during its execution. Each input and output resource defines how it will be used (texture versus attachment, for instance), and we can infer its next layout with this information.

In summary, in this chapter, we're going to cover the following main topics:

- Understanding the structure of a frame graph and the details of our implementations
- Implementing a topological sort to make sure the passes execute in the right order
- Using the graph to drive rendering and automate resource management and layout transitions

Technical requirements

The code for this chapter can be found at the following URL: `https://github.com/PacktPublishing/Mastering-Graphics-Programming-with-Vulkan/tree/main/source/chapter4`.

Understanding frame graphs

So far, the rendering in the Raptor Engine has consisted of one pass only. While this approach has served us well for the topics we have covered, it won't scale for some of the later chapters. More importantly, it wouldn't be representative of how modern rendering engines organize their work. Some games and engines implement hundreds of passes, and having to manually manage them can become tedious and error-prone.

Thus, we decided this was a good time in the book to introduce a frame graph. In this section, we are going to present the structure of our graph and the main interfaces to manipulate it in the code.

Let's start with the basic concepts of a graph.

Building a graph

Before we present our solution and implementation for the frame graph, we would like to provide some of the building blocks that we are going to use throughout the chapter. If you're familiar with frame graphs, or graphs in general, feel free to skim through this section.

A graph is defined by two elements: **nodes** (or vertices) and **edges**. Each node can be connected to one or more nodes, and each connection is defined by an edge.

Figure 4.1 – An edge from node A to B

In the introduction of this chapter, we mentioned that a frame graph is a DAG. It's important that our frame graph has these properties as otherwise, we wouldn't be able to execute it:

- **Directed**: This means that the edges have a direction. If, for instance, we define an edge to go from node *A* to node *B*, we can't use the same edge to go from *B* to *A*. We would need a different edge to go from *B* to *A*.

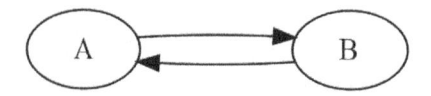

Figure 4.2 – Connecting A to B and B to A in a directed graph

- **Acyclic**: This means that there can't be any cycles in the graph. A cycle is introduced when we can go back to a given node after following the path from one of its children. If this happens, our frame graph will enter an infinite loop.

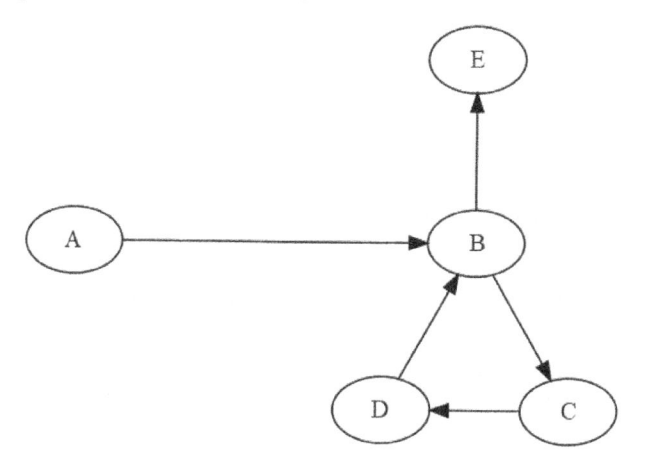

Figure 4.3 – An example of a graph containing a cycle

In the case of a frame graph, each node represents a rendering pass: depth prepass, g-buffer, lighting, and so on. We don't define the edges explicitly. Instead, each node will define a number of outputs and, if needed, a number of inputs. An edge is then implied when the output of a given pass is used as input in another pass.

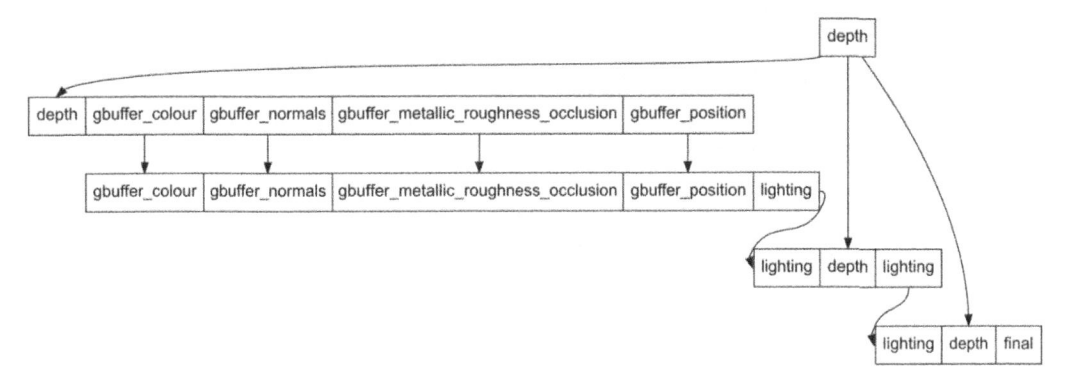

Figure 4.4 – An example of a full frame graph

These two concepts, nodes and edges, are all that is needed to understand a frame graph. Next, we are going to present how we decided to encode this data structure.

A data-driven approach

Some engines only provide a code interface to build a frame graph, while others let developers specify the graph in a human-readable format – JSON for example – so that making changes to the graph doesn't necessarily require code changes.

After some consideration, we have decided to define our graph in JSON and implement a parser to instantiate the classes required. There are a few reasons we opted for this approach:

- It allows us to make some changes to the graph without having to recompile the code. If, for instance, we want to change the size or format of a render target, all we have to do is make the change in the JSON definition of the graph and rerun the program.
- We can also reorganize the graph and remove some of its nodes without making changes to the code.
- It's easier to understand the flow of the graph. Depending on the implementation, the definition of the graph in code could be spread across different code locations or even different files. This makes it harder to determine the graph structure.
- It's easier for non-technical contributors to make changes. The graph definition could also be done through a visual tool and translated into JSON. The same approach wouldn't be feasible if the graph definition was done purely in code.

We can now have a look at a node in our frame graph:

```
{
    "inputs":
    [
        {
            "type": "attachment",
            "name": "depth"
        }
    ],
    "name": "gbuffer_pass",
    "outputs":
    [
        {
            "type": "attachment",
            "name": "gbuffer_colour",
            "format": "VK_FORMAT_B8G8R8A8_UNORM",
            "resolution": [ 1280, 800 ],
```

```
            "op": "VK_ATTACHMENT_LOAD_OP_CLEAR"
        },
        {
            "type": "attachment",
            "name": "gbuffer_normals",
            "format": "VK_FORMAT_R16G16B16A16_SFLOAT",
            "resolution": [ 1280, 800 ],
            "op": "VK_ATTACHMENT_LOAD_OP_CLEAR"
        },
        ...
    ]
}
```

A node is defined by three variables:

- name: This helps us identify the node during execution, and it also gives us a meaningful name for other elements, for instance, the render pass associated with this node.
- inputs: This lists the inputs for this node. These are resources that have been produced by another node. Note that it would be an error to define an input that has not been produced by another node in the graph. The only exceptions are external resources, which are managed outside the render graph, and the user will have to provide them to the graph at runtime.
- outputs: These are the resources produced by a given node.

We have defined four different types of resources depending on their use:

- attachment: The list of attachments is used to determine the render pass and framebuffer composition of a given node. As you noticed in the previous example, attachments can be defined both for inputs and outputs. This is needed to continue working on a resource in multiple nodes. After we run a depth prepass, for instance, we want to load the depth data and use it during the g-buffer pass to avoid shading pixels for objects that are hidden behind other objects.
- texture: This type is used to distinguish images from attachments. An attachment has to be part of the definition of the render pass and framebuffer for a node, while a texture is read during the pass and is part of a shader data definition.

    This distinction is also important to determine which images need to be transitioned to a different layout and require an image barrier. We'll cover this in more detail later in the chapter.

    We don't need to specify the size and format of the texture here, as we had already done so when we first defined the resource as an output.

- `buffer`: This type represents a storage buffer that we can write to or read from. As with textures, we will need to insert memory barriers to ensure the writes from a previous pass are completed before accessing the buffer data in another pass.
- `reference`: This type is used exclusively to ensure the right edges between nodes are computed without creating a new resource.

All types are quite intuitive, but we feel that the reference type deserves an example to better understand why we need this type:

```
{
    "inputs":
    [
        {
            "type": "attachment",
            "name": "lighting"
        },
        {
            "type": "attachment",
            "name": "depth"
        }
    ],
    "name": "transparent_pass",
    "outputs":
    [
        {
            "type": "reference",
            "name": "lighting"
        }
    ]
}
```

In this case, lighting is an input resource of the `attachment` type. When processing the graph, we will correctly link the node that produced the lighting resource to this node. However, we also need to make sure that the next node that makes use of the lighting resource creates a connection to this node, as otherwise, the node ordering would be incorrect.

For this reason, we add a reference to the lighting resource in the output of the transparent pass. We can't use the `attachment` type here as otherwise, we would double count the lighting resource in the creation of the render pass and framebuffer.

Now that you have a good understanding of the frame graph structure, it's time to look at some code!

Implementing the frame graph

In this section, we are going to define the data structures that are going to be used throughout the chapter, namely resources and nodes. Next, we are going to parse the JSON definition of the graph to create resources and nodes that will be used for subsequent steps.

Let's start with the definition of our data structures.

Resources

Resources define an input or an output of a node. They determine the use of the resource for a given node and, as we will explain later, they are used to define edges between the frame graph nodes. A resource is structured as follows:

```
struct FrameGraphResource {
    FrameGraphResourceType type;
    FrameGraphResourceInfo resource_info;

    FrameGraphNodeHandle producer;
    FrameGraphResourceHandle output_handle;

    i32 ref_count = 0;

    const char* name = nullptr;
};
```

A resource can be either an input or an output of a node. It's worth going through each field in the following list:

- `type`: Defines whether we are dealing with an image or a buffer.
- `resource_info`: Contains the details about the resource (such as size, format, and so on) based on `type`.
- `producer`: Stores a reference to the node that outputs a resource. This will be used to determine the edges of the graph.
- `output_handle`: Stores the parent resource. It will become clearer later why we need this field.
- `ref_count`: Will be used when computing which resources can be aliased. Aliasing is a technique that allows multiple resources to share the same memory. We will provide more details on how this works later in this chapter.

- **name**: Contains the name of the resource as defined in JSON. This is useful for debugging and also to retrieve the resource by name.

Next, we are going to look at a graph node:

```
struct FrameGraphNode {
    RenderPassHandle render_pass;
    FramebufferHandle framebuffer;

    FrameGraphRenderPass* graph_render_pass;

    Array<FrameGraphResourceHandle> inputs;
    Array<FrameGraphResourceHandle> outputs;

    Array<FrameGraphNodeHandle> edges;

    const char* name = nullptr;
};
```

A node stores the list of inputs it will use during execution and the outputs it will produce. Each input and output is a different instance of `FrameGraphResource`. The `output_handle` field is used to link an input to its output resource. We need separate resources because their type might differ; an image might be used as an output attachment and then used as an input texture. This is an important detail that will be used to automate memory barrier placement.

A node also stores a list of the nodes it is connected to, its name, the framebuffer, and the render pass created according to the definition of its inputs and outputs. Like resources, a node also stores its name as defined on JSON.

Finally, a node contains a pointer to the rendering implementation. We'll discuss later how we link a node to its rendering pass.

These are the main data structures used to define our frame graph. We have also created a `FrameGraphBuilder` helper class that will be used by the `FrameGraph` class. The `FrameGraphBuilder` helper class contains the functionality to create nodes and resources.

Let's see how these building blocks are used to define our frame graph!

Parsing the graph

Now that we have defined the data structures that make our graph, we need to parse the JSON definition of the graph to fill those structures and create our frame graph definition. Here are the steps that need to be executed to parse the frame graph:

1. We start by initializing a `FrameGraphBuilder` and `FrameGraph` class:

    ```
    FrameGraphBuilder frame_graph_builder;
    frame_graph_builder.init( &gpu );

    FrameGraph frame_graph;
    frame_graph.init( &frame_graph_builder );
    ```

2. Next, we call the `parse` method to read the JSON definition of the graph and create the resources and nodes for it:

    ```
    frame_graph.parse( frame_graph_path,
                       &scratch_allocator );
    ```

3. Once we have our graph definition, we have our compile step:

    ```
    frame_graph.compile();
    ```

    This step is where the magic happens. We analyze the graph to compute the edges between nodes, create the framebuffer and render passes for each class, and determine which resources can be aliased. We are going to explain each of these steps in detail in the next section.

4. Once we have compiled our graph, we need to register our rendering passes:

    ```
    frame_graph->builder->register_render_pass(
        "depth_pre_pass", &depth_pre_pass );
    frame_graph->builder->register_render_pass(
        "gbuffer_pass", &gbuffer_pass );
    frame_graph->builder->register_render_pass(
        "lighting_pass", &light_pass );
    frame_graph->builder->register_render_pass(
        "transparent_pass", &transparent_pass );
    frame_graph->builder->register_render_pass(
        "depth_of_field_pass", &dof_pass );
    ```

    This allows us to test different implementations for each pass by simply swapping which class we register for a given pass. It's even possible to swap these passes at runtime.

5. Finally, we are ready to render our scene:

   ```
   frame_graph->render( gpu_commands, scene );
   ```

We are now going to look at the `compile` and `render` methods in detail.

Implementing topological sort

As we mentioned in the preceding section, the most interesting aspects of the frame graph implementation are inside the `compile` method. We have abbreviated some of the code for clarity in the following sections.

Please refer to the GitHub link mentioned in the *Technical requirements* section of the chapter for the full implementation.

Here is a breakdown of the algorithm that we use to compute the edges between nodes:

1. The first step we perform is to create the edges between nodes:

   ```
   for ( u32 r = 0; r < node->inputs.size; ++r ) {
       FrameGraphResource* resource = frame_graph->
           get_resource( node->inputs[ r ].index );

       u32 output_index = frame_graph->find_resource(
           hash_calculate( resource->name ) );

       FrameGraphResource* output_resource = frame_graph
           ->get_resource( output_index );
   ```

   We accomplish this by iterating through each input and retrieving the corresponding output resource. Note that internally, the graph stores the outputs in a map keyed by name.

2. Next, we save the details of the output in the input resource. This way we have direct access to this data in the input as well:

   ```
   resource->producer = output_resource->producer;
   resource->resource_info = output_resource->
                              resource_info;
   resource->output_handle = output_resource->
                              output_handle;
   ```

3. Finally, we create an edge between the node that produces this input and the node we are currently processing:

   ```
   FrameGraphNode* parent_node = ( FrameGraphNode*)
                                 frame_graph->
                                 get_node(
                                 resource->
                                 producer.index );

   parent_node->edges.push( frame_graph->nodes[
                            node_index ] );
   }
   ```

At the end of this loop, each node will contain the list of nodes it is connected to. While we currently don't do this, at this stage, it would be possible to remove nodes that have no edges from the graph.

Now that we have computed the connection between nodes, we can sort them in topological order. At the end of this step, we will obtain the list of nodes ordered to ensure that nodes that produce an output come before the nodes that make use of that output.

Here is a breakdown of the sorting algorithm where we have highlighted the most relevant sections of the code:

1. The `sorted_node` array will contain the sorted nodes in reverse order:

   ```
   Array<FrameGraphNodeHandle> sorted_nodes;
   sorted_nodes.init( &local_allocator, nodes.size );
   ```

2. The `visited` array will be used to mark which nodes we have already processed. We need to keep track of this information to avoid infinite loops:

   ```
   Array<u8> visited;
   visited.init( &local_allocator, nodes.size, nodes.size
   );
   memset( visited.data, 0, sizeof( bool ) * nodes.size );
   ```

3. Finally, the `stack` array is used to keep track of which nodes we still have to process. We need this data structure as our implementation doesn't make use of recursion:

   ```
   Array<FrameGraphNodeHandle> stack;
   stack.init( &local_allocator, nodes.size );
   ```

4. The graph is traversed by using **depth-first search** (**DFS**). The code that follows performs exactly this task:

```
for ( u32 n = 0; n < nodes.size; ++n ) {
    stack.push( nodes[ n ] );
```

5. We iterate through each node and add it to the stack. We do this to ensure we process all the nodes in the graph:

```
while ( stack.size > 0 ) {
    FrameGraphNodeHandle node_handle =
        stack.back();
```

6. We then have a second loop that will be active until we have processed all nodes that are connected to the node we just added to the stack:

```
if (visited[ node_handle.index ] == 2) {
    stack.pop();

    continue;
}
```

If a node has already been visited and added to the list of sorted nodes, we simply remove it from the stack and continue processing other nodes. Traditional graph processing implementations don't have this step.

We had to add it as a node might produce multiple outputs. These outputs, in turn, might link to multiple nodes, and we don't want to add the producing node multiple times to the sorted node list.

7. If the node we are currently processing has already been visited and we got to it in the stack, it means we processed all of its children, and it can be added to the list of sorted nodes. As mentioned in the following code, we also mark it as added so that we won't add it multiple times to the list:

```
if ( visited[ node_handle.index ]   == 1) {
    visited[ node_handle.index ] = 2; // added

    sorted_nodes.push( node_handle );

    stack.pop();
```

Understanding frame graphs

```
            continue;
        }
```

8. When we first get to a node, we mark it as `visited`. As mentioned in the following code block, this is needed to make sure we don't process the same node multiple times:

    ```
    visited[ node_handle.index ] = 1; // visited
    ```

9. If the node we are processing has no edges, we continue to iterate:

    ```
    FrameGraphNode* node = ( FrameGraphNode* )
                            builder->node_cache.
                            nodes.access_resource
                            ( node_handle.index
                            );

    // Leaf node
    if ( node->edges.size == 0 ) {
        continue;
    }
    ```

10. On the other hand, if the node is connected to other nodes, we add them to the stack for processing and then iterate again. If this is the first time you've seen an iterative implementation of graph traversal, it might not be immediately clear how it relates to the recursive implementation. We suggest going through the code a few times until you understand it; it's a powerful technique that will come in handy at times!

    ```
    for ( u32 r = 0; r < node->edges.size; ++r ) {
        FrameGraphNodeHandle child_handle =
            node->edges[ r ];

        if ( !visited[ child_handle.index ] ) {
            stack.push( child_handle );
        }
    }
    ```

11. The final step is to iterate through the sorted nodes array and add them to the graph nodes in reverse order:

```
for ( i32 i = sorted_nodes.size - 1; i >= 0; --i ) {
    nodes.push( sorted_nodes[ i ] );
}
```

We have now completed the topological sorting of the graph! With the nodes sorted, we can now proceed to analyze the graph to identify which resources can be aliased.

Computing resource aliasing

Large frame graphs must deal with hundreds of nodes and resources. The lifetime of these resources might not span the full graph, and this gives us an opportunity to reuse memory for resources that are no longer needed. This technique is called **memory aliasing**, as multiple resources can point to the same memory allocation.

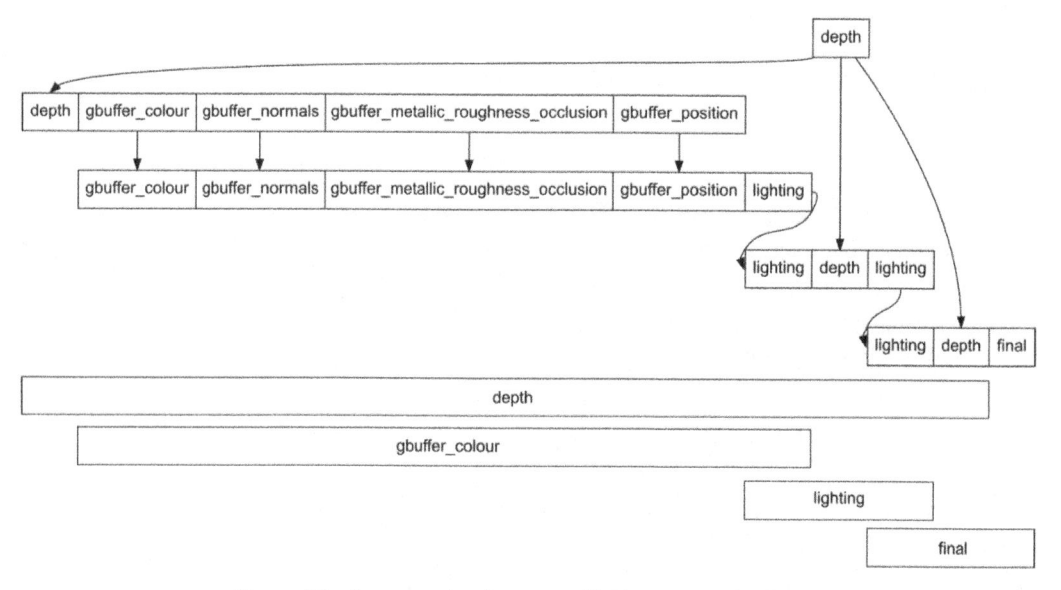

Figure 4.5 – An example of resource lifetime across the frame

In this example, we can see that the `gbuffer_colour` resource is not needed for the full frame, and its memory can be reused, for instance, for the `final` resource.

We first need to determine the first and last nodes that use a given resource. Once we have the information, we can determine whether a given node can reuse existing memory for its resources. The code that follows implements this technique.

Understanding frame graphs

We start by allocating a few helper arrays:

```
sizet resource_count = builder->resource_cache.resources.
                    used_indices;
Array<FrameGraphNodeHandle> allocations;
allocations.init( &local_allocator, resource_count,
                resource_count );
for ( u32 i = 0; i < resource_count; ++i) {
    allocations[ i ].index = k_invalid_index;
}

Array<FrameGraphNodeHandle> deallocations;
deallocations.init( &local_allocator, resource_count,
                  resource_count );
for ( u32 i = 0; i < resource_count; ++i) {
    deallocations[ i ].index = k_invalid_index;
}

Array<TextureHandle> free_list;
free_list.init( &local_allocator, resource_count );
```

They are not strictly needed by the algorithm, but they are helpful for debugging and ensuring our implementation doesn't have a bug. The `allocations` array will track on which node a given resource was allocated.

Similarly, the `deallocations` array contains the node at which a given resource can be deallocated. Finally, `free_list` will contain the resources that have been freed and can be reused.

Next, we are going to look at the algorithm that tracks the allocations and deallocations of resources:

```
for ( u32 i = 0; i < nodes.size; ++i ) {
    FrameGraphNode* node = ( FrameGraphNode* )builder->
                        node_cache.nodes.access
                        _resource( nodes[ i ].index );

    for ( u32 j = 0; j < node->inputs.size; ++j ) {
        FrameGraphResource* input_resource =
            builder->resource_cache.resources.get(
                node->inputs[ j ].index );
```

```cpp
                FrameGraphResource* resource =
                    builder->resource_cache.resources.get(
                        input_resource->output_handle.index );

                resource->ref_count++;
            }
        }
```

First, we loop through all the input resources and increase their reference count each time they are used as input. We also mark which node allocates the resource in the `allocations` array:

```cpp
for ( u32 i = 0; i < nodes.size; ++i ) {
    FrameGraphNode* node = builder->get_node(
                            nodes[ i ].index );

    for ( u32 j = 0; j < node->outputs.size; ++j ) {
        u32 resource_index = node->outputs[ j ].index;
        FrameGraphResource* resource =
            builder->resource_cache.resources.get(
                resource_index );
```

The next step is to iterate through all the nodes and their outputs. The code that follows is responsible for performing the memory allocations:

```cpp
if ( !resource->resource_info.external &&
  allocations[ resource_index ].index ==
  k_invalid_index ) {
        allocations[ resource_index ] = nodes[ i ];

if ( resource->type ==
  FrameGraphResourceType_Attachment ) {
        FrameGraphResourceInfo& info =
            resource->resource_info;

                if ( free_list.size > 0 ) {
                    TextureHandle alias_texture =
                        free_list.back();
```

```
                    free_list.pop();

                    TextureCreation texture_creation{ };

                    TextureHandle handle =
                        builder->device->create_texture(
                            texture_creation );

                    info.texture.texture = handle;
                } else {
                    TextureCreation texture_creation{ };

                    TextureHandle handle =
                        builder->device->create_texture(
                            texture_creation );

                    info.texture.texture = handle;
                }
            }
        }
    }
```

For each output resource, we first check whether there are any available resources that can be reused. If so, we pass the free resource to the `TextureCreation` structure. Internally, `GpuDevice` will use the memory from this resource and bind it to the newly created resource. If no free resources are available, we proceed by creating a new resource.

The last part of the loop takes care of determining which resources can be freed and added to the free list:

```
        for ( u32 j = 0; j < node->inputs.size; ++j ) {
            FrameGraphResource* input_resource =
                builder->resource_cache.resources.get(
                    node->inputs[ j ].index );

            u32 resource_index = input_resource->
                                    output_handle.index;
            FrameGraphResource* resource =
                builder->resource_cache.resources.get(
```

```
                    resource_index );

            resource->ref_count--;

  if ( !resource->resource_info.external &&
    resource->ref_count == 0 ) {
      deallocations[ resource_index ] = nodes[ i ];

  if ( resource->type ==
    FrameGraphResourceType_Attachment ||
    resource->type ==
    FrameGraphResourceType_Texture ) {
      free_list.push( resource->resource_info.
      texture.texture );
          }
        }
      }
}
```

We iterate over the inputs one final time and decrease the reference count of each resource. If the reference count reaches 0, it means this is the last node that uses the resource. We save the node in the `deallocations` array and add the resource to the free list, ready to be used for the next node we are going to process.

This concludes the implementation of the graph analysis. The resources we have created are used to create the `framebuffer` object, at which point the graph is ready for rendering!

We are going to cover the execution of the graph in the next section.

Driving rendering with the frame graph

After the graph has been analyzed, we have all the details we need for rendering. The following code is responsible for executing each node and ensuring all the resources are in the correct state for use by that node:

```
for ( u32 n = 0; n < nodes.size; ++n ) {
    FrameGraphNode*node = builder->get_node( nodes
                          [ n ].index );

    gpu_commands->clear( 0.3, 0.3, 0.3, 1 );
```

```
        gpu_commands->clear_depth_stencil( 1.0f, 0 );

for ( u32 i = 0; i < node->inputs.size; ++i ) {
   FrameGraphResource* resource =
   builder->get_resource( node->inputs[ i ].index
   );

if ( resource->type ==
   FrameGraphResourceType_Texture ) {
      Texture* texture =
      gpu_commands->device->access_texture(
      resource->resource_info.texture.texture
      );

util_add_image_barrier( gpu_commands->
    vk_command_buffer, texture->vk_image,
    RESOURCE_STATE_RENDER_TARGET,
    RESOURCE_STATE_PIXEL_SHADER_RESOURCE,
    0, 1, resource->resource_info.
    texture.format ==
    VK_FORMAT_D32_SFLOAT );
        } else if ( resource->type ==
                    FrameGraphResourceType_Attachment ) {
            Texture*texture = gpu_commands->device->
                              access_texture( resource->
                              resource_info.texture.texture
                              ); }
}
```

We first iterate through all the inputs of a node. If the resource is a texture, we insert a barrier to transition that resource from an attachment layout (for use in a render pass) to a shader stage layout (for use in a fragment shader).

This step is important to make sure any previous writes have completed before we access this resource for reading:

```
        for ( u32 o = 0; o < node->outputs.size; ++o ) {
            FrameGraphResource* resource =
```

```
            builder->resource_cache.resources.get(
                node->outputs[ o ].index );

        if ( resource->type ==
             FrameGraphResourceType_Attachment ) {
            Texture* texture =
                gpu_commands->device->access_texture(
                    resource->resource_info.texture.texture
                );

            width = texture->width;
            height = texture->height;

            if ( texture->vk_format == VK_FORMAT_D32_SFLOAT ) {
                util_add_image_barrier(
                gpu_commands->vk_command_buffer,
                texture->vk_image, RESOURCE_STATE_UNDEFINED,
                RESOURCE_STATE_DEPTH_WRITE, 0, 1, resource->
                resource_info.texture.format ==
                VK_FORMAT_D32_SFLOAT );
            } else {
                util_add_image_barrier( gpu_commands->
                vk_command_buffer, texture->vk_image,
                RESOURCE_STATE_UNDEFINED,
                RESOURCE_STATE_RENDER_TARGET, 0, 1,
                resource->resource_info.texture.format ==
                VK_FORMAT_D32_SFLOAT );
            }
        }
    }
}
```

Next, we iterate over the outputs of the node. Once again, we need to make sure the resource is in the correct state to be used as an attachment in the render pass. After this step, our resources are ready for rendering.

The render targets of each node could all have different resolutions. The following code ensures that our scissor and viewport sizes are correct:

```
Rect2DInt scissor{ 0, 0, ( u16 )width, ( u16 )height };
gpu_commands->set_scissor( &scissor );

Viewport viewport{ };
viewport.rect = { 0, 0, ( u16 )width, ( u16 )height };
viewport.min_depth = 0.0f;
viewport.max_depth = 1.0f;

gpu_commands->set_viewport( &viewport );
```

Once the viewport and scissor are set correctly, we call the `pre_render` method on each node. This allows each node to perform any operations that must happen outside a render pass. For instance, the render pass for the depth-of-field effect takes the input texture and computes the MIP maps for that resource:

```
node->graph_render_pass->pre_render( gpu_commands,
                                     render_scene );
```

Finally, we bind the render pass for this node, call the `render` method of the rendering pass that we registered for this node, and end the loop by ending the render pass:

```
gpu_commands->bind_pass( node->render_pass, node->
                         framebuffer, false );

node->graph_render_pass->render( gpu_commands,
                                 render_scene );

gpu_commands->end_current_render_pass();
}
```

This concludes the code overview for this chapter! We have covered a lot of ground; this is a good time for a brief recap: we started with the definition of the main data structures used by our frame graph implementation. Next, we explained how the graph is parsed to compute the edges between nodes by using inputs and outputs.

Once this step is completed, we can sort the nodes in topological order to ensure they are executed in the correct order. We then create the resources needed to execute the graph and make use of memory aliasing to optimize memory usage. Finally, we iterate over each node for rendering, making sure that all resources are in the correct state for that node.

There are some features that we haven't implemented and that could improve the functionality and robustness of our frame graph. For example, we should ensure there are no loops in the graph and that an input isn't being produced by the same node it's being used in.

For the memory aliasing implementation, we use a greedy approach and simply pick the first free resource that can accommodate a new resource. This can lead to fragmentation and suboptimal use of memory.

We encourage you to experiment with the code and improve on it!

Summary

In this chapter, we implemented a frame graph to improve the management of rendering passes and make it easier to expand our rendering pipeline in future chapters. We started by covering the basic concepts, nodes and edges, that define a graph.

Next, we gave an overview of the structure of our graph and how it's encoded in JSON format. We also mentioned why we went for this approach as opposed to defining the graph fully in code.

In the last part, we detailed how the graph is processed and made ready for execution. We gave an overview of the main data structures used for the graph, and covered how the graph is parsed to create nodes and resources, and how edges are computed. Next, we explained the topological sorting of nodes, which ensures they are executed in the correct order. We followed that with the memory allocation strategy, which allows us to reuse memory from resources that are no longer needed at given nodes. Finally, we provided an overview of the rendering loop and how we ensure that resources are in the correct state for rendering.

In the next chapter, we are going to take advantage of the techniques we have developed in the last two chapters. We are going to leverage multithreading and our frame graph implementation to demonstrate how to use compute and graphics pipelines in parallel for cloth simulation.

Further reading

Our implementation has been heavily inspired by the implementation of a frame graph in the Frostbite engine, and we recommend watching this presentation: `https://www.gdcvault.com/play/1024045/FrameGraph-Extensible-Rendering-Architecture-in`.

Many other engines implement a frame graph to organize and optimize their rendering pipeline. We encourage you to look at other implementations and find the solution that best fits your needs!

5
Unlocking Async Compute

In this chapter, we are going to improve our renderer by allowing compute work to be done in parallel with graphics tasks. So far, we have been recording and submitting all of our work to a single queue. We can still submit compute tasks to this queue to be executed alongside graphics work: in this chapter, for instance, we have started using a compute shader for the fullscreen lighting rendering pass. We don't need a separate queue in this case as we want to reduce the amount of synchronization between separate queues.

However, it might be beneficial to run other compute workloads on a separate queue and allow the GPU to fully utilize its compute units. In this chapter, we are going to implement a simple cloth simulation using compute shaders that will run on a separate compute queue. To unlock this new functionality, we will need to make some changes to our engine.

In this chapter, we're going to cover the following main topics:

- Using a single timeline semaphore to avoid multiple fences
- Adding a separate queue for async compute
- Implementing cloth simulation using async compute

Technical requirements

The code for this chapter can be found at the following URL: `https://github.com/PacktPublishing/Mastering-Graphics-Programming-with-Vulkan/tree/main/source/chapter5`

Replacing multiple fences with a single timeline semaphore

In this section, we are going to explain how fences and semaphores are currently used in our renderer and how to reduce the number of objects we must use by taking advantage of timeline semaphores.

Our engine already supports rendering multiple frames in parallel using fences. Fences must be used to ensure the GPU has finished using resources for a given frame. This is accomplished by waiting on the CPU before submitting a new batch of commands to the GPU.

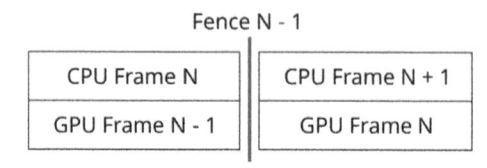

Fence N - 1
CPU Frame N	CPU Frame N + 1
GPU Frame N - 1	GPU Frame N

Figure 5.1 – The CPU is working on the current frame while the GPU is rendering the previous frame

There is a downside, however; we need to create a fence for each frame in flight. This means we will have to manage at least two fences for double buffering and three if we want to support triple buffering.

We also need multiple semaphores to ensure the GPU waits for certain operations to complete before moving on. For instance, we need to signal a semaphore once rendering is complete and pass that same semaphore to the present command. This is needed to guarantee that rendering is complete before we try to present the swap chain image.

The following diagram illustrates two scenarios; in the first one, no semaphore is present, and the swapchain image could be presented to the screen while rendering is still in progress.

In the second scenario, we have added a semaphore that is signaled in the render submission and is waited on before presenting. This ensures the correct behavior of the application. If we didn't have this semaphore, we would risk presenting an image that is still being rendered and displaying corrupted data.

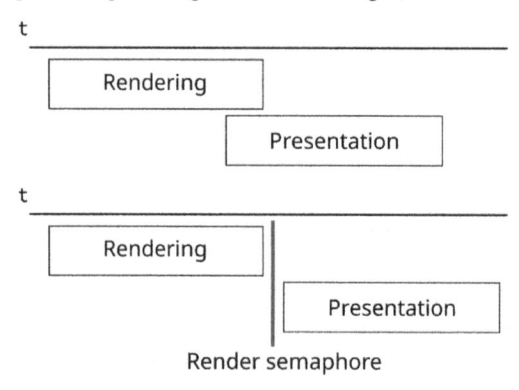

Figure 5.2 – Two scenarios illustrating the need for a semaphore between rendering and presentation

The situation worsens when we start to consider multiple queues. In this chapter, we are going to add a separate compute queue. This means that we will need to add more fences to wait on the CPU for compute work to complete. We will also need new semaphores to synchronize the compute and graphics queue to ensure the data produced by the compute queue is ready to be used by the graphics queue.

Even if we weren't using a compute queue, we might want to break our rendering work into multiple submissions. Each submission would need its own signal and wait for semaphores according to the dependencies of each workload. This can get out of hand quickly for large scenes that have tens, possibly hundreds, of submissions.

Luckily for us, there is a solution. If we think about it, the fence and the semaphore hold the same information; they get signaled once a submission is complete. What if there was a way to use a single object both on the CPU and the GPU? This exact functionality is provided by a timeline semaphore.

As the name suggests, a timeline semaphore holds a monotonically increasing value. We can define what value we want the semaphore to be signaled with and what value we want to wait for. This object can be waited on by both the GPU and the CPU, greatly reducing the number of objects needed to implement correct synchronization.

We are now going to show how to use timeline semaphores in Vulkan.

Enabling the timeline semaphore extension

The timeline semaphore feature has been promoted to core in Vulkan 1.2. However, it's not a mandatory extension, so we first need to query for support before using it. This is done, as usual, by enumerating the extension the device exposes and looking for the extension name:

```
vkEnumerateDeviceExtensionProperties(
    vulkan_physical_device, nullptr,
        &device_extension_count, extensions );
for ( size_t i = 0; i < device_extension_count; i++ ) {
    if ( !strcmp( extensions[ i ].extensionName,
        VK_KHR_TIMELINE_SEMAPHORE_EXTENSION_NAME ) ) {
            timeline_semaphore_extension_present = true;
            continue;
        }
}
```

If the extension is present, we need to populate an additional structure that will be used at device creation, as shown in the following code:

```
VkPhysicalDeviceFeatures2 physical_features2 {
VK_STRUCTURE_TYPE_PHYSICAL_DEVICE_FEATURES_2 };
void* current_pnext = nullptr;
```

```
VkPhysicalDeviceTimelineSemaphoreFeatures timeline_sempahore_
features{ VK_STRUCTURE_TYPE_PHYSICAL_DEVICE_TIMELINE_SEMAPHORE_
FEATURES };
if ( timeline_semaphore_extension_present ) {
    timeline_sempahore_features.pNext = current_pnext;
    current_pnext = &timeline_sempahore_features;
}

physical_features2.pNext = current_pnext;
vkGetPhysicalDeviceFeatures2( vulkan_physical_device,
    &physical_features2 );
```

We also need to add the extension name to the list of enabled extensions:

```
if ( timeline_semaphore_extension_present ) {
    device_extensions.push(
        VK_KHR_TIMELINE_SEMAPHORE_EXTENSION_NAME );
}
```

Finally, we use the data we just retrieved when creating the device:

```
VkDeviceCreateInfo device_create_info {
    VK_STRUCTURE_TYPE_DEVICE_CREATE_INFO };
device_create_info.enabledExtensionCount =
    device_extensions.size;
device_create_info.ppEnabledExtensionNames =
    device_extensions.data;
device_create_info.pNext = &physical_features2;

vkCreateDevice( vulkan_physical_device,
    &device_create_info, vulkan_allocation_callbacks,
        &vulkan_device );
```

We are now ready to use a timeline semaphore in our code! We will see how to create a timeline semaphore in the next section.

Creating a timeline semaphore

Creating a timeline semaphore is quite simple. We start by defining the standard creation structure:

```
VkSemaphoreCreateInfo semaphore_info{
    VK_STRUCTURE_TYPE_SEMAPHORE_CREATE_INFO };
```

We then need to pass an extra structure to tell the API that we want to create a timeline semaphore:

```
VkSemaphoreTypeCreateInfo semaphore_type_info{
    VK_STRUCTURE_TYPE_SEMAPHORE_TYPE_CREATE_INFO };
semaphore_type_info.semaphoreType =
    VK_SEMAPHORE_TYPE_TIMELINE;
semaphore_info.pNext = &semaphore_type_info;
Finally, we call the create function:
vkCreateSemaphore( vulkan_device, &semaphore_info,
    vulkan_allocation_callbacks, &vulkan_timeline_semaphore );
```

This is it! We now have a timeline semaphore that can be used in our renderer. In the next section, we will look at a few examples of how to use this type of semaphore.

Waiting for a timeline semaphore on the CPU

As mentioned previously, we can wait for a timeline semaphore to be signaled on the CPU. The following code does just that:

```
u64 timeline_value = …;

VkSemaphoreWaitInfo semaphore_wait_info{
    VK_STRUCTURE_TYPE_SEMAPHORE_WAIT_INFO };
semaphore_wait_info.semaphoreCount = 1;
semaphore_wait_info.pSemaphores =
    &vulkan_timeline_semaphore;
semaphore_wait_info.pValues = &timeline_value;

vkWaitSemaphores( vulkan_device, &semaphore_wait_info,
                  timeout );
```

As you probably noticed, it's possible to wait for multiple semaphores at once and specify a different value for each semaphore. This could be useful, for instance, when rendering to multiple windows, and each window uses a different semaphore. The `VkSemaphoreWaitInfo` structure also has a `flags` field.

Using the `VK_SEMAPHORE_WAIT_ANY_BIT` value in this field will terminate the wait as soon as one of the semaphores reaches the value we are waiting for. Otherwise, the wait will terminate only when all semaphores have reached their respective value.

The last important aspect of the preceding code is the timeout value. This value is specified in nanoseconds. If, after the given time, the wait condition is not satisfied, the call will return `VK_TIMEOUT`. We usually set the timeout to infinity, as we absolutely need the semaphore to be signaled.

However, there is a risk that the wait call might never return, for instance, if the combination of wait and signal values leads to a deadlock on the GPU. An alternative approach would be to set the timeout to a relatively large value – 1 second, for example. If the wait is not completed within this time span, there is likely an issue with our submission, and we can communicate the error to the user.

In this section, we have shown how to wait for a timeline semaphore on the CPU. In the next section, we are going to cover how to use a timeline semaphore on the GPU.

Using a timeline semaphore on the GPU

In this section, we are going to show how to update a timeline semaphore value and how to wait for a given value on the GPU.

> **Note**
> Before we begin, we'd like to point out that we are using the `VK_KHR_synchronization2` extension. This extension simplifies writing code for barriers and semaphores. Please refer to the full code to see how this is implemented using the old APIs.

We start by defining the list of semaphores we want to wait for:

```
VkSemaphoreSubmitInfoKHR wait_semaphores[]{
    { VK_STRUCTURE_TYPE_SEMAPHORE_SUBMIT_INFO_KHR, nullptr,
      vulkan_image_acquired_semaphore, 0,
      VK_PIPELINE_STAGE_2_COLOR_ATTACHMENT_OUTPUT_BIT_KHR,
      0 },
    { VK_STRUCTURE_TYPE_SEMAPHORE_SUBMIT_INFO_KHR, nullptr,
      vulkan_timeline_semaphore, absolute_frame - (
      k_max_frames - 1 ),
      VK_PIPELINE_STAGE_2_TOP_OF_PIPE_BIT_KHR , 0 }
};
```

This list can contain both standard semaphores and timeline semaphores. For standard semaphores, the `signal` value is ignored.

Similarly, we need to define a list of semaphores to wait on:

```
VkSemaphoreSubmitInfoKHR signal_semaphores[]{
    { VK_STRUCTURE_TYPE_SEMAPHORE_SUBMIT_INFO_KHR, nullptr,
      *render_complete_semaphore, 0,
      VK_PIPELINE_STAGE_2_COLOR_ATTACHMENT_OUTPUT_BIT_KHR,
      0 },
    { VK_STRUCTURE_TYPE_SEMAPHORE_SUBMIT_INFO_KHR, nullptr,
      vulkan_timeline_semaphore, absolute_frame + 1,
      VK_PIPELINE_STAGE_2_COLOR_ATTACHMENT_OUTPUT_BIT_KHR
      , 0 }
};
```

As before, we can use different semaphore types and the signal value is ignored for standard semaphores. It's important the signal value for a timeline semaphore is always increased. If we were to submit the same value twice or a smaller value, we would get a validation error.

We also need to be careful with the values we use for waiting and signaling. If we were to wait for a value that is set within the same submission, we would deadlock the GPU. As a rule of thumb, always try to use a value that is guaranteed to have been set by a previous submission. The validation layers will also help you catch this type of error.

The last step is to pass the two lists to the submit info structure:

```
VkSubmitInfo2KHR submit_info{
    VK_STRUCTURE_TYPE_SUBMIT_INFO_2_KHR };
submit_info.waitSemaphoreInfoCount = 2;
submit_info.pWaitSemaphoreInfos = wait_semaphores;
submit_info.commandBufferInfoCount =
    num_queued_command_buffers;
submit_info.pCommandBufferInfos = command_buffer_info;
submit_info.signalSemaphoreInfoCount = 2;
submit_info.pSignalSemaphoreInfos = signal_semaphores;

queue_submit2( vulkan_main_queue, 1, &submit_info,
    VK_NULL_HANDLE );
```

As you probably noticed, we can now wait for and signal the same timeline semaphore in a submission. We also no longer need a fence. This greatly simplifies the code and reduces the number of synchronization objects needed.

In this section, we have shown how to enable the extension to use timeline semaphores and how to create and use them to wait on the CPU. Finally, we have shown how to wait and signal timeline semaphores on the GPU.

In the next section, we are going to use this newly acquired knowledge to add a separate queue for async compute work.

Adding a separate queue for async compute

In this section, we are going to illustrate how to use separate queues for graphics and compute work to make full use of our GPU. Modern GPUs have many generic compute units that can be used both for graphics and compute work. Depending on the workload for a given frame (shader complexity, screen resolution, dependencies between rendering passes, and so on), it's possible that the GPU might not be fully utilized.

Moving some of the computation done on the CPU to the GPU using compute shaders can increase performance and lead to better GPU utilization. This is possible because the GPU scheduler can determine if any of the compute units are idle and assign work to them to overlap existing work:

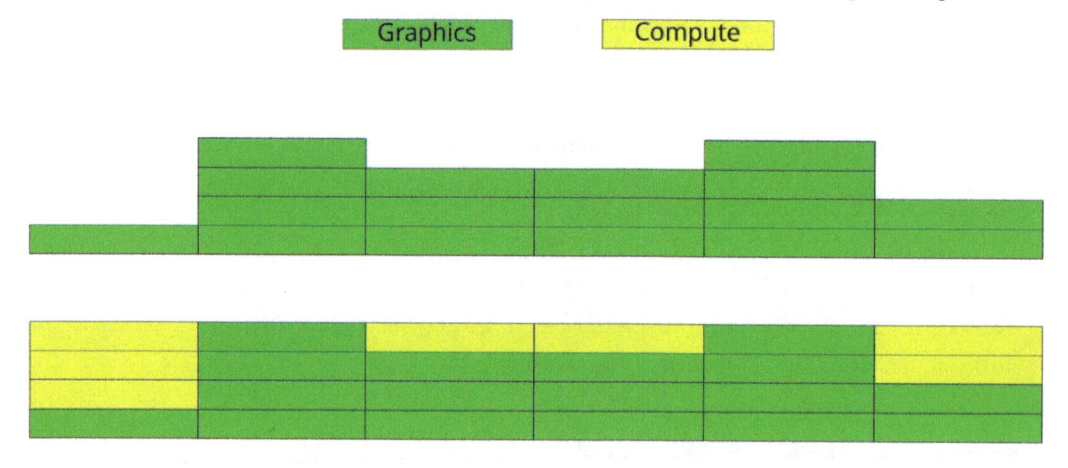

Figure 5.3 – Top: graphics workload is not fully utilizing the GPU; Bottom: compute workload can take advantage of unused resources for optimal GPU utilization

In the remainder of this section, we are going to demonstrate how to use the timeline semaphore introduced in the previous section to synchronize access to data between the two queues.

Submitting work on separate queues

We have already set up multiple queues in *Chapter 3, Unlocking Multi-Threading*. We now need to ensure that access to data from two queues is correctly synchronized; otherwise, we might access data that is out of date or, worse, data that hasn't been initialized yet.

The first step in this process is to create a separate command buffer. A different command buffer must be used for compute work, as the same command buffer can't be submitted to different queues. This is easily achieved by requesting a new command buffer from our `GpuDevice` implementation:

```
CommandBuffer* cb = gpu.get_command_buffer( 0,
gpu.current_frame, true );
```

Next, we need to create a new timeline semaphore to be used by the compute queue. This is the same code we have shown in the previous section, and we won't be duplicating it here.

We then need to increment the value of our timeline semaphore with each compute submission:

```
bool has_wait_semaphore = last_compute_semaphore_value > 0;

VkSemaphoreSubmitInfoKHR wait_semaphores[] {
    { VK_STRUCTURE_TYPE_SEMAPHORE_SUBMIT_INFO_KHR, nullptr,
      vulkan_compute_semaphore,
      last_compute_semaphore_value,
      VK_PIPELINE_STAGE_2_COMPUTE_SHADER_BIT_KHR, 0 }
};

last_compute_semaphore_value++;

VkSemaphoreSubmitInfoKHR signal_semaphores[] {
    { VK_STRUCTURE_TYPE_SEMAPHORE_SUBMIT_INFO_KHR, nullptr,
      vulkan_compute_semaphore,
      last_compute_semaphore_value,
      VK_PIPELINE_STAGE_2_COMPUTE_SHADER_BIT_KHR, 0 },
};
```

This code is similar to the code we showed before in relation to submitting timeline semaphores. The main difference is the wait stage, which must now be VK_PIPELINE_STAGE_2_COMPUTE_SHADER_BIT_KHR. Now that we have the list of wait and signal semaphores, they are ready to be used for our submission:

```
VkCommandBufferSubmitInfoKHR command_buffer_info{
    VK_STRUCTURE_TYPE_COMMAND_BUFFER_SUBMIT_INFO_KHR };
command_buffer_info.commandBuffer =
    command_buffer->vk_command_buffer;

VkSubmitInfo2KHR submit_info{
    VK_STRUCTURE_TYPE_SUBMIT_INFO_2_KHR };
submit_info.waitSemaphoreInfoCount =
    has_wait_semaphore ? 1 : 0;
submit_info.pWaitSemaphoreInfos = wait_semaphores;
submit_info.commandBufferInfoCount = 1;
submit_info.signalSemaphoreInfoCount = 1;
submit_info.pSignalSemaphoreInfos = signal_semaphores;

queue_submit2( vulkan_compute_queue, 1, &submit_info,
    VK_NULL_HANDLE );
```

Again, this should be familiar code. We want to highlight that we only add the wait semaphore after the first submission. If we were to wait for the semaphore on the first submission, we would deadlock the GPU, as the semaphore will never be signaled. Luckily, the validation layers will highlight this problem, and it can be easily corrected.

Now that we have submitted our compute workload, we need to make sure the graphics queue waits until the data is ready. We can achieve this by adding the compute semaphore to the list of wait semaphores when submitting the graphics queue. We are going to highlight only the new code:

```
bool wait_for_compute_semaphore = (
    last_compute_semaphore_value > 0 ) && has_async_work;
VkSemaphoreSubmitInfoKHR wait_semaphores[]{
    { VK_STRUCTURE_TYPE_SEMAPHORE_SUBMIT_INFO_KHR, nullptr,
      vulkan_image_acquired_semaphore, 0,
      VK_PIPELINE_STAGE_2_COLOR_ATTACHMENT_OUTPUT_BIT_KHR,
      0 },
    { VK_STRUCTURE_TYPE_SEMAPHORE_SUBMIT_INFO_KHR, nullptr,
```

```
            vulkan_compute_semaphore,
            last_compute_semaphore_value,
            VK_PIPELINE_STAGE_2_VERTEX_ATTRIBUTE_INPUT_BIT_KHR,
            0 },
        { VK_STRUCTURE_TYPE_SEMAPHORE_SUBMIT_INFO_KHR, nullptr,
            vulkan_graphics_semaphore,
            absolute_frame - ( k_max_frames - 1 ),
            VK_PIPELINE_STAGE_2_TOP_OF_PIPE_BIT_KHR , 0 },
};
```

The same care must be taken when adding the compute semaphore to the list. We want to wait only if at least one compute submission has been performed. For some frames, we might not have any compute work pending. We don't want to wait for the compute semaphore in this case, either.

In our case, we have set the wait stage to `VK_PIPELINE_STAGE_2_VERTEX_ATTRIBUTE_INPUT_BIT_KHR`, as we are modifying the vertices of our mesh. This will need adjusting if, for instance, you are using the compute queue to update a texture that won't be used until the fragment shader stage. Using the right wait stage is important to obtain the best performance.

In this section, we have demonstrated how to retrieve a separate queue for compute work. We then explained how to use the newly created queue to submit compute work and correctly synchronize data access from different queues to ensure correct results.

In the next section, we are going to show a concrete example by implementing a simple cloth simulation using compute shaders.

Implementing cloth simulation using async compute

In this section, we are going to implement a simple cloth simulation on the GPU as an example use case of a compute workload. We start by explaining why running some tasks on the GPU might be beneficial. Next, we provide an overview of compute shaders. Finally, we show how to port code from the CPU to the GPU and highlight some of the differences between the two platforms.

Benefits of using compute shaders

In the past, physics simulations mainly ran on the CPU. GPUs only had enough compute capacity for graphics work, and most stages in the pipeline were implemented by dedicated hardware blocks that could only perform one task. As GPUs evolved, pipeline stages moved to generic compute blocks that could perform different tasks.

This increase both in flexibility and compute capacity has allowed engine developers to move some workloads on the GPU. Aside from raw performance, running some computations on the GPU avoids expensive copies from CPU memory to GPU memory. Memory speed hasn't evolved as fast as processor speed, and moving data as little as possible between devices is key to application performance.

In our example, the cloth simulation has to update the position of all vertices and copy the updated data to the GPU. Depending on the size of the mesh and the number of meshes to update, this could amount to a significant percentage of frame time.

These workloads can also scale better on the GPU, as we can update a larger number of meshes in parallel.

We are now going to provide an overview of how compute shaders are executed. If you are familiar with compute shaders or have worked with CUDA or OpenCL before, feel free to skim the next section.

Compute shaders overview

The GPU execution model is called **Single Instruction, Multiple Threads (SIMT)**. It is similar to the **Single Instruction, Multiple Data (SIMD)** offered by modern CPUs to operate on multiple data entries with a single instruction.

However, GPUs operate on a larger number of data points within a single instruction. The other main difference is that each thread on the GPU is more flexible compared to a SIMD instruction. GPU architecture is a fascinating topic, but its scope is outside this book. We will provide references for further reading at the end of the chapter.

> **Note**
> A group of threads has different names depending on the GPU vendor. You might see the term warp or wave being mentioned in their documentation. We are going to use thread group to avoid confusion.

Each compute shader invocation can use multiple threads within a compute unit, and it's possible to control how many threads are used. In Vulkan, this is achieved with the following directive inside a compute shader:

```
layout (local_size_x = 8, local_size_y = 8,
local_size_z = 1) in;
```

This defines the local group size; we are going to explain what it does in just a moment. For now, the main point is that we are telling the GPU that we want to execute 64 threads (8x8). Each GPU has an optimal thread group size. You should check the documentation from each vendor and, if possible, adjust the thread group size for optimal performance.

We also have to define a global group size when invoking a compute shader:

```
gpu_commands->dispatch( ceilu32( renderer->
    gpu->swapchain_width * 1.f / 8 ),
```

```
            ceilu32( renderer->gpu->swapchain_height * 1.f / 8 ),
        1 );
```

This code is taken from our lighting pass implementation. In this case, we want to process all the pixels in our render target texture. As you probably noticed, we divide the size by 8. This is needed to ensure we don't process the same pixel multiple times. Let's walk through an example to clarify how the local and global group size works.

Let's say our render target is 1280x720. Multiplying the width by the height will give us the total number of pixels in the image. When we define the local group size, we determine how many pixels are going to be processed by each shader invocation (again, 64 in our case). The number of shader invocations is computed as follows:

```
shader_invocation_count = total_pixels / 64
```

The `dispatch` command requires three values, though, as both the local and global group size are defined as a vector of three values. This is why we divide each dimension by 8:

```
global_group_size_x = width / 8
global_group_size_y = height / 8
```

Since we are operating on a 2D texture, we are not modifying the z value. We can verify that we are processing the right number of pixels with this code:

```
local_thread_group_count = 64
shader_invocation_count = global_group_size_x *
    global_group_size_y
total_pixels =  shader_invocation_count *
    local_thread_group_count
```

We can determine which invocation is being run inside the shader by using this variable provided by GLSL:

```
ivec3 pos = ivec3( gl_GlobalInvocationID.xyz );
```

Each thread will see a unique position value, which we can use to access our texture.

This was only a brief overview of the compute shader execution model. We are going to provide more in-depth resources in the *Further reading* section.

Now that we have a better understanding of how compute shaders are executed, we are going to demonstrate how to convert CPU code to a GPU compute shader.

Writing compute shaders

Writing code for compute shaders is similar to writing vertex or fragment shaders. The main difference is that we have more flexibility in compute shaders to define which data to access. For instance, in vertex shaders, we usually access a single entry in an attribute buffer. The same applies to fragment shaders, where the fragment being shaded by a shader invocation is determined by the GPU.

Because of the added flexibility, we also need to think more carefully about our access patterns and synchronization between threads. If, for instance, more than one thread has to write to the same memory location, we need to add memory barriers to ensure previous writes to that memory have completed and all threads see the correct value. In pseudo-code, this translates to this:

```
// code
MemoryBarrier()
// all threads have run the code before the barrier
```

GLSL also provides atomic operations in case the same memory location has to be accessed across shader invocations.

With that in mind, let's have a look at the pseudo-code for the CPU version of the cloth simulation:

```
for each physics mesh in the scene:
    for each vertex in the mesh:
        compute the force applied to the vertex
    // We need two loops because each vertex references
       other vertices position
    // First we need to compute the force applied to each
       vertex,
    // and only after update each vertex position
        for each vertex in the mesh:
    update the vertex position and store its velocity

    update the mesh normals and tangents
    copy the vertices to the GPU
```

We used a common spring model for the cloth simulation, but its implementation is outside the scope of this chapter. We suggest looking at the code for more detail, and we also reference the paper we used in the *Further reading* section.

As you notice, at the end of the loop, we have to copy the updated vertex, normal, and tangent buffers to the GPU. Depending on the number of meshes and their complexity, this could be a costly operation.

This step could be even more costly if the cloth simulation were to rely on data from other systems that run on the GPU.

If, for instance, the animation system runs on the GPU while the cloth simulation runs on the CPU, we now have two copies to perform, in addition to extra synchronization points in the pipeline. For these reasons, it can be beneficial to move the cloth simulation to the GPU.

Let's start by looking at the vertex buffer setup:

```
BufferCreation creation{ };
sizet buffer_size = positions.size * sizeof( vec3s );
creation.set( flags, ResourceUsageType::Immutable,
    buffer_size ).set_data( positions.data )
        .set_name( nullptr ).set_persistent( true );

BufferResource* cpu_buffer = renderer->
    create_buffer( creation );
cpu_buffers.push( *cpu_buffer );
```

This is the only buffer we needed before. Because we had to update the data on the CPU, we could only use a host coherent buffer so that write on the CPU would be visible on the CPU. Using this type of buffer has performance implications on the GPU, as this type of memory can be slower to access, especially when the buffer size is large.

Since we are now going to perform the update on the GPU, we can use a buffer that is marked as `device_only`. This is how we create the buffer:

```
creation.reset().set( flags, ResourceUsageType::Immutable,
    buffer_size ).set_device_only( true )
        .set_name( "position_attribute_buffer" );

BufferResource* gpu_buffer = renderer->
    create_buffer( creation );
gpu_buffers.push( *gpu_buffer );
```

Finally, we copy the data from the CPU to the GPU only once. After the copy is done, we can free the CPU buffer:

```
async_loader->request_buffer_copy( cpu_buffer->handle,
                                   gpu_buffer->handle );
```

We have shown an example of the position buffer. All the other buffers (normal, tangent, texture coordinates, and indices) are managed in the same way.

Now that we have our buffers, we need to create a descriptor set that will be used by our compute shader:

```
DescriptorSetLayoutHandle physics_layout = renderer->
    gpu->get_descriptor_set_layout
        ( cloth_technique->passes[ 0 ].pipeline,
          k_material_descriptor_set_index );
ds_creation.reset().buffer( physics_cb, 0 )
    .buffer( mesh.physics_mesh->gpu_buffer, 1 )
    .buffer( mesh.position_buffer, 2 )
    .buffer( mesh.normal_buffer, 3 )
    .buffer( mesh.index_buffer, 4 )
    .set_layout( physics_layout );

mesh.physics_mesh->descriptor_set = renderer->
    gpu->create_descriptor_set( ds_creation );
```

We can match the binding of the preceding buffers with the following shader code:

```
layout ( std140, set = MATERIAL_SET, binding = 0 ) uniform
    PhysicsData {
    ...
};

layout ( set = MATERIAL_SET, binding = 1 ) buffer
    PhysicsMesh {
        uint index_count;
        uint vertex_count;

        PhysicsVertex physics_vertices[];
};

layout ( set = MATERIAL_SET, binding = 2 ) buffer
    PositionData {
        float positions[];
```

```
};

layout ( set = MATERIAL_SET, binding = 3 ) buffer
    NormalData {
        float normals[];
};

layout ( set = MATERIAL_SET, binding = 4 ) readonly buffer
    IndexData {
        uint indices[];
};
```

It's important to notice a couple of points. Because we don't know the size of each buffer at runtime, we have to use separate storage blocks. We can only have one runtime array per storage block, and it must be the last member of the block.

We also have to use float arrays instead of `vec3` arrays; otherwise, each entry in the vector would be padded to 16 bytes and the data on the GPU will no longer match the data layout on the CPU. We could use `vec4` as type, but we would be wasting 4 bytes for each vertex. When you have millions, if not billions, of vertices, it adds up!

Finally, we marked the `IndexData` block as `readonly`. This is because we never modify the index buffer in this shader. It's important to mark each block with the right attributes as this will give more opportunities for optimization to the shader compiler.

We could reduce the number of blocks by arranging our data differently, for example:

```
struct MeshVertex {
    vec3 position;
    vec3 normal;
    vec3 tangent;
};

layout ( set = MATERIAL_SET, binding = 2 ) buffer MeshData {
    MeshVertex mesh_vertices[];
};
```

This solution is usually referred to as **Array of Structures** (**AoS**), while the code we presented before used **Structure of Arrays** (**SoA**). While the AoS solution simplifies the bindings, it also makes it impossible to use each array individually. In our depth pass, for instance, we only need the positions. For this reason, we preferred the SoA approach.

We have already shown how to dispatch a compute shader and how to synchronize access between the compute and graphics queue, so we won't repeat that code here. We can now move to the shader implementation. We are only going to show the relevant section; you can refer to the code for the full listing.

We start by computing the force applied to each vertex:

```
vec3 spring_force = vec3( 0, 0, 0 );

for ( uint j = 0; j < physics_vertices[ v ]
    .joint_count; ++j ) {
        pull_direction = ...;
        spring_force += pull_direction;
}

vec3 viscous_damping = physics_vertices[ v ]
    .velocity * -spring_damping;

vec3 viscous_velocity = ...;

vec3 force = g * m;
force -= spring_force;
force += viscous_damping;
force += viscous_velocity;

physics_vertices[ v ].force = force;
```

Notice how we access the `physics_vertices` array each time. In the CPU code, we could simply get a reference to the struct, and each field would be updated correctly. However, GLSL doesn't support references, so we need to be really careful that we are not writing to a local variable.

As in the CPU code, after computing the force vector for each vertex, we need to update its position:

```
vec3 previous_position = physics_vertices[ v ]
    .previous_position;
vec3 current_position = physics_vertices[ v ].position;

vec3 new_position = ...;
```

```
physics_vertices[ v ].position = new_position;
physics_vertices[ v ].previous_position = current_position;

physics_vertices[ v ].velocity = new_position - current_
position;
```

Again, notice that we always read from the buffer each time. Finally, we update the vertex positions of the mesh:

```
for ( uint v = 0; v < vertex_count; ++v ) {
    positions[ v * 3 + 0 ] = physics_vertices[ v ]
        .position.x;
    positions[ v * 3 + 1 ] = physics_vertices[ v ]
        .position.y;
    positions[ v * 3 + 2 ] = physics_vertices[ v ]
        .position.z;
}
```

Because this is all performed on the GPU, the positions could have been updated first by another system, such as animation, but we no longer need costly copy operations to and from the GPU.

Before we conclude, we'd like to point out that we have one shader invocation per mesh and that performance is achieved by updating the cloth simulation for multiple meshes in the same dispatch. Another approach could have been to have one dispatch per mesh where each shader invocation updates an individual vertex.

While technically a valid approach, it requires a lot more synchronization within the thread group and across shader invocations. As we mentioned, we first have to compute the force for each vertex before updating their position. Another solution could be to split the update into two shaders, one that computes the force and a second one that updates the positions.

This still requires pipeline barriers between each shader dispatch. While the GPU must guarantee that each command is executed in the same order it has been recorded; it doesn't guarantee the order of completion. For these reasons, we have decided to use one thread per mesh.

In this section, we have explained the execution model of compute shaders and the benefits of running selected computations on the GPU to improve performance and avoid extra memory copies. We then demonstrated how to port code written for the CPU to the GPU and some of the aspects we need to pay attention to when working with compute shaders.

We suggest looking at the code for more details. Try to make changes to the cloth simulation to implement a different simulation technique or add your own compute shaders to the engine!

Summary

In this chapter, we have built the foundations to support compute shaders in our renderer. We started by introducing timeline semaphores and how they can be used to replace multiple semaphores and fences. We have shown how to wait for a timeline semaphore on the CPU and how a timeline semaphore can be used as part of a queue submission, either for it to be signaled or to be waited on.

Next, we demonstrated how to use the newly introduced timeline semaphore to synchronize execution across the graphics and compute queue.

In the last section, we showed an example of how to approach porting code written for the CPU to the GPU. We first explained some of the benefits of running computations on the GPU. Next, we gave an overview of the execution model for compute shaders and the configuration of local and global workgroup sizes. Finally, we gave a concrete example of a compute shader for cloth simulation and highlighted the main differences with the same code written for the CPU.

In the next chapter, we are going to improve our pipeline by adding mesh shaders, and for the devices that don't support them, we are going to write a compute shader alternative.

Further reading

Synchronization is likely one of the most complex aspects of Vulkan. We have mentioned some of the concepts in this and previous chapters. If you want to improve your understanding, we suggest reading the following resources:

- `https://www.khronos.org/registry/vulkan/specs/1.3-extensions/html/vkspec.html#synchronization`
- `https://www.khronos.org/blog/understanding-vulkan-synchronization`
- `https://github.com/KhronosGroup/Vulkan-Docs/wiki/Synchronization-Examples`

We only touched the surface when it comes to compute shaders. The following resources go more in depth and also provide suggestions to get the most out of individual devices:

- `https://www.khronos.org/opengl/wiki/Compute_Shader`
- `https://docs.nvidia.com/cuda/cuda-c-programming-guide/index.html#programming-model`
- `https://github.com/KhronosGroup/OpenCL-Guide/blob/main/chapters/opencl_programming_model.md`

Further reading

Real-time cloth simulation for computer graphics has been a subject of study for many years. We have based our implementation on this paper: http://graphics.stanford.edu/courses/cs468-02-winter/Papers/Rigidcloth.pdf.

Another popular approach is presented in this paper: http://www.cs.cmu.edu/~baraff/papers/sig98.pdf.

Finally, this GDC talk gave us the idea of using cloth simulation to demonstrate how to use compute shaders:

https://www.gdcvault.com/play/1022350/Ubisoft-Cloth-Simulation-Performance-Postmortem

Part 2: GPU-Driven Rendering

Starting with this part, we are going to focus on modern rendering techniques. We will cover the following chapters in this section:

- *Chapter 6, GPU-Driven Rendering*
- *Chapter 7, Rendering Many Lights with Clustered Deferred Rendering*
- *Chapter 8, Adding Shadows Using Mesh Shaders*
- *Chapter 9, Implementing Variable Rate Shading*
- *Chapter 10, Adding Volumetric Fog*

6
GPU-Driven Rendering

In this chapter, we will upgrade the geometry pipeline to use the latest available technology: **mesh shaders** and **meshlets**. The idea behind this technique is to move the flow of mesh rendering from the CPU to the GPU, moving culling and draw command generation into different shaders.

We will first work on the mesh structure on the CPU, by separating it into different *meshlets* that are groups of up to 64 triangles, each with an individual bounding sphere. We will then use compute shaders to perform culling and write a list of commands to draw the meshlets in the different passes. Finally, we will use the mesh shaders to render the meshlets. There will also be a compute version provided, as mesh shaders are still available only on Nvidia GPUs for now.

Traditionally, geometry culling has been performed on the CPU. Each mesh on the scene is usually represented by an **axis aligned bounding box** (**AABB**). An AABB can easily be culled against the camera frustum, but with the increase in scene complexity, a large portion of frame time could be spent on the culling step.

This is usually the first step in a rendering pipeline, as we need to determine which meshes to submit for drawing. This means it's hard to find other work that could be done in parallel. Another pain point of doing frustum culling on the CPU is that it's hard to determine which objects are occluded and don't need to be drawn.

At every frame, we need to re-sort all elements based on the camera position. When there are hundreds of thousands of elements in the scene, this is usually unfeasible. Finally, some meshes, terrain, for example, are organized in large areas that end up always being drawn, even if only a small part of them is visible.

Thankfully, we can move some of this computation to the GPU and take advantage of its parallel capabilities. The techniques we are going to present in this chapter will allow us to perform frustum and occlusion culling on the GPU. To make the process as efficient as possible, we are going to generate the list of draw commands directly on the GPU.

In this chapter, we're going to cover the following main topics:

- Breaking down large meshes into meshlets
- Processing meshlets using task and mesh shaders to perform back-face and frustum culling
- Performing efficient occlusion culling using compute shaders
- Generating draw commands on the GPU and using indirect drawing functions

Technical requirements

The code for this chapter can be found at the following URL: https://github.com/PacktPublishing/Mastering-Graphics-Programming-with-Vulkan/tree/main/source/chapter6.

Breaking down large meshes into meshlets

In this chapter, we are going to focus primarily on the geometry stage of the pipeline, the one before the shading stage. Adding some complexity to the geometry stage of the pipeline will pay dividends in later stages as we'll reduce the number of pixels that need to be shaded.

> **Note**
> When we refer to the geometry stage of the graphics pipeline, we don't mean geometry shaders. The geometry stage of the pipeline refers to **input assembly** (**IA**), vertex processing, and **primitive assembly** (**PA**). Vertex processing can, in turn, run one or more of the following shaders: vertex, geometry, tessellation, task, and mesh shaders.

Content geometry comes in many shapes, sizes, and complexity. A rendering engine must be able to deal with meshes from small, detailed objects to large terrains. Large meshes (think terrain or buildings) are usually broken down by artists so that the rendering engine can pick out the different levels of details based on the distance from the camera of these objects.

Breaking down meshes into smaller chunks can help cull geometry that is not visible, but some of these meshes are still large enough that we need to process them in full, even if only a small portion is visible.

Meshlets have been developed to address these problems. Each mesh is subdivided into groups of vertices (usually 64) that can be more easily processed on the GPU.

The following image illustrates how meshes can be broken down into meshlets:

Figure 6.1 – A meshlet subdivision example

These vertices can make up an arbitrary number of triangles, but we usually tune this value according to the hardware we are running on. In Vulkan, the recommended value is `126` (as written in `https://developer.nvidia.com/blog/introduction-turing-mesh-shaders/`, the number is needed to reserve some memory for writing the primitive count with each meshlet).

> **Note**
> At the time of writing, mesh and task shaders are only available on Nvidia hardware through its extension. While some of the APIs described in this chapter are specific to this extension, the concepts can be generally applied and implemented using generic compute shaders. A more generic version of this extension is currently being worked on by the Khronos committee so that mesh and task shaders should soon be available from other vendors!

Now that we have a much smaller number of triangles, we can use them to have much finer-grained control by culling meshlets that are not visible or are being occluded by other objects.

Together with the list of vertices and triangles, we also generate some additional data for each meshlet that will be very useful later on to perform back-face, frustum, and occlusion culling.

One additional possibility (that will be added in the future) is to choose the **level of detail** (**LOD**) of a mesh and, thus, a different subset of meshlets based on any wanted heuristic.

The first of this additional data represents the bounding sphere of a meshlet, as shown in the following screenshot:

Figure 6.2 – A meshlet bounding spheres example; some of the larger spheres have been hidden for clarity

Some of you might ask: why not AABBs? AABBs require at least two `vec3` of data: one for the center and one for the half-size vector. Another encoding could be to store the minimum and maximum corners. Instead, spheres can be encoded with a single `vec4`: a `vec3` for the center plus the radius.

Given that we might need to process millions of meshlets, each saved byte counts! Spheres can also be more easily tested for frustum and occlusion culling, as we will describe later in the chapter.

The next additional piece of data that we're going to use is the meshlet cone, as shown in the following screenshot:

Figure 6.3 – A meshlet cone example; not all cones are displayed for clarity

The cone indicates the direction a meshlet is facing and will be used for back-face culling.

Now we have a better understanding of why meshlets are useful and how we can use them to improve the culling of larger meshes, let's see how we generate them in code!

Generating meshlets

We are using an open source library, called **MeshOptimizer** (https://github.com/zeux/meshoptimizer) to generate the meshlets. An alternative library is **meshlete** (https://github.com/JarkkoPFC/meshlete) and we encourage you to try both to find the one that best suits your needs.

After we have loaded the data (vertices and indices) for a given mesh, we are going to generate the list of meshlets. First, we determine the maximum number of meshlets that could be generated for our mesh and allocate memory for the vertices and indices arrays that will describe the meshlets:

```
const sizet max_meshlets = meshopt_buildMeshletsBound(
    indices_accessor.count, max_vertices, max_triangles );

Array<meshopt_Meshlet> local_meshlets;
local_meshlets.init( temp_allocator, max_meshlets,
```

```
        max_meshlets );

Array<u32> meshlet_vertex_indices;
meshlet_vertex_indices.init( temp_allocator, max_meshlets *
    max_vertices, max_meshlets* max_vertices );

Array<u8> meshlet_triangles;
meshlet_triangles.init( temp_allocator, max_meshlets *
    max_triangles * 3, max_meshlets* max_triangles * 3 );
```

Notice the types for the indices and triangle arrays. We are not modifying the original vertex or index buffer, but only generating a list of indices in the original buffers. Another interesting aspect is that we only need 1 byte to store the triangle indices. Again, saving memory is very important to keep meshlet processing efficient!

The next step is to generate our meshlets:

```
const sizet max_vertices = 64;
const sizet max_triangles = 124;
const f32 cone_weight = 0.0f;

sizet meshlet_count = meshopt_buildMeshlets(
    local_meshlets.data,
    meshlet_vertex_indices.data,
    meshlet_triangles.data, indices,
    indices_accessor.count,
    vertices,
    position_buffer_accessor.count,
    sizeof( vec3s ),
    max_vertices,
    max_triangles,
    cone_weight );
```

As mentioned in the preceding step, we need to tell the library the maximum number of vertices and triangles that a meshlet can contain. In our case, we are using the recommended values for the Vulkan API. The other parameters include the original vertex and index buffer, and the arrays we have just created that will contain the data for the meshlets.

Let's have a better look at the data structure of each meshlet:

```
struct meshopt_Meshlet
{
unsigned int vertex_offset;
unsigned int triangle_offset;

unsigned int vertex_count;
unsigned int triangle_count;
};
```

Each meshlet is described by two offsets and two counts, one for the vertex indices and one for the indices of the triangles. Note that these offsets refer to `meshlet_vertex_indices` and `meshlet_triangles` that are populated by the library, not the original vertex and index buffers of the mesh.

Now that we have the meshlet data, we need to upload it to the GPU. To keep the data size to a minimum, we store the positions at full resolution while we compress the normals to 1 byte for each dimension and UV coordinates to half-float for each dimension. In pseudocode, this is as follows:

```
meshlet_vertex_data.normal = ( normal + 1.0 ) * 127.0;
meshlet_vertex_data.uv_coords = quantize_half( uv_coords );
```

The next step is to extract the additional data (bounding sphere and cone) for each meshlet:

```
for ( u32 m = 0; m < meshlet_count; ++m ) {
    meshopt_Meshlet& local_meshlet = local_meshlets[ m ];

    meshopt_Bounds meshlet_bounds =
    meshopt_computeMeshletBounds(
    meshlet_vertex_indices.data +
    local_meshlet.vertex_offset,
    meshlet_triangles.data +
    local_meshlet.triangle_offset,
    local_meshlet.triangle_count,
    vertices,
    position_buffer_accessor
    .count,
    sizeof( vec3s ) );

    ...
}
```

We loop over all the meshlets and we call the MeshOptimizer API that computes the bounds for each meshlet. Let's see in more detail the structure of the data that is returned:

```
struct meshopt_Bounds
{
    float center[3];
    float radius;

    float cone_apex[3];
    float cone_axis[3];
    float cone_cutoff;

    signed char cone_axis_s8[3];
    signed char cone_cutoff_s8;
};
```

The first four floats represent the bounding sphere. Next, we have the cone definition, which is comprised of the cone direction (`cone_axis`) and the cone angle (`cone_cutoff`). We are not using the `cone_apex` value as it makes the back-face culling computation more expensive. However, it can lead to better results.

Once again, notice that quantized values (`cone_axis_s8` and `cone_cutoff_s8`) help us reduce the size of the data required for each meshlet.

Finally, meshlet data is copied into GPU buffers and it will be used during the execution of task and mesh shaders.

For each processed mesh, we will also save an offset and count of meshlets to add a coarse culling based on the parent mesh: if the mesh is visible, then its meshlets will be added.

In this section, we have described what meshlets are and why they are useful to improve the culling of geometry on the GPU. Next, we showed the data structures that are used in our implementation. Now that our data is ready, it's time for it to be consumed by task and mesh shaders. That's the topic of the next section!

Understanding task and mesh shaders

Before we begin, we should mention that mesh shaders can be used without task shaders. If, for instance, you wanted to perform culling or some other pre-processing step on the meshlets on the CPU, you are free to do so.

Also, note that task and mesh shaders replace vertex shaders in the graphics pipeline. The output of mesh shaders is going to be consumed by the fragment shader directly.

The following diagram illustrates the differences between the traditional geometry pipeline and the mesh shader pipeline:

MESHLETS

TRADITIONAL PIPELINE

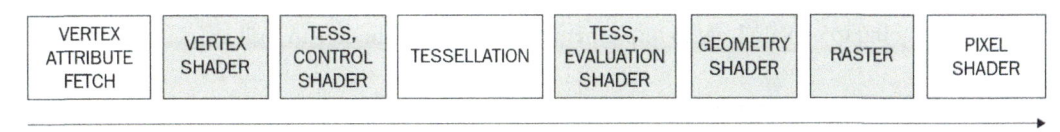

| VERTEX ATTRIBUTE FETCH | VERTEX SHADER | TESS, CONTROL SHADER | TESSELLATION | TESS, EVALUATION SHADER | GEOMETRY SHADER | RASTER | PIXEL SHADER |

keeping interstage data on chip

TASK / MESH PIPELINE

| TASK SHADER | MESH GENERATION | MESH SHADER | RASTER | PIXEL SHADER |

Figure 6.4 – The difference between traditional and mesh pipeline

In this section, we are going to provide an overview of how task and mesh shaders work and then use this information to implement back-face and frustum culling using task shaders.

Both task and mesh shaders use the same execution model of compute shaders, with some minor changes. The output of task shaders is consumed directly by a mesh shader, and for both types, we can specify the thread group size.

Task shaders (sometimes also referred to as amplification shaders) can be thought of as filters. We submit all meshlets for processing when invoking a task shader, and the task shader will output the meshlets that have passed the filter.

The following diagram provides an example of meshlets that are processed by the task shader. The meshlets that are rejected won't be processed further.

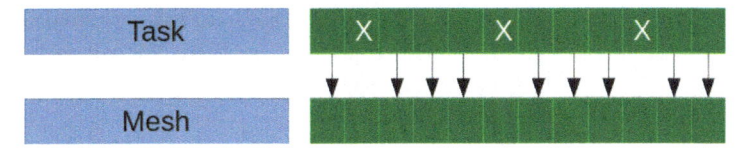

Figure 6.5 – The task shader determines which meshlets to cull. The culled meshlets won't be processed by the mesh shader

The mesh shader then takes the active meshlets and performs the final processing as you normally would in a vertex shader.

While this is only a high-level overview of task and mesh shaders, there isn't much more to it. We will provide more resources in the *Further reading* section if you'd like to know more about the inner workings of this feature.

Next, we are going to explain how to implement task and mesh shaders in Vulkan!

Implementing task shaders

As we mentioned previously, task and mesh shaders are available through an extension of the Vulkan API. We have shown how to check for extensions before, so we are not duplicating the code in this chapter. Please refer to the code for more details.

The extension also introduces two new pipeline stages, VK_PIPELINE_STAGE_TASK_SHADER_BIT_NV and VK_PIPELINE_STAGE_MESH_SHADER_BIT_NV, that can be used to place pipeline barriers to ensure data used by these stages is synchronized correctly.

Task shaders can be treated like any compute shader: we create a pipeline that includes an (optional) task shader module, a mesh shader, and a fragment shader. Invoking a task shader is done with the following API:

```
vkCmdDrawMeshTasksNV( vk_command_buffer, task_count,
    first_task );
```

Think of task_count as the workgroup size of a compute shader. There is also an indirect variant that can read the invocation details for multiple draws from a buffer:

```
vkCmdDrawMeshTasksIndirectCountNV( vk_command_buffer,
    mesh_draw_buffer, 0, draw_count, stride );
```

We use this variant in our code as it allows us to have only one draw call per scene and give the GPU full control over which meshlets will be drawn.

With indirect rendering, we write the commands in a GPU program as we would do on the CPU, and we additionally read a buffer to know how many commands are there. We will see command writing in the *GPU culling using compute* section of this chapter.

We now turn our attention to the shader implementation. Task and mesh shaders require that their GLSL extension be enabled, otherwise, the compiler might treat the code as a regular compute shader:

```
#extension GL_NV_mesh_shader: require
```

Since we are using an indirect command to invoke our shader, we need to enable another extension that will let us access the `draw` ID for the current shader invocation:

```
#extension GL_ARB_shader_draw_parameters : enable
```

Note that this extension is enabled in the `platform.h` header and not directly in the shader code. As we mentioned, task shaders are akin to compute shaders. In fact, the first directive in our shader is to determine the thread group size:

```
layout (local_size_x = 32) in;
```

Here, `local_size_y` and `local_size_z` will be ignored even if specified. We can now move to the main body of the shader. We start by determining which mesh and meshlet we need to process:

```
uint thread_index = gl_LocalInvocationID.x;
uint group_index = gl_WorkGroupID.x;
uint meshlet_index = group_index * 32 + thread_index;

uint mesh_instance_index = draw_commands[ gl_DrawIDARB ]
    .drawId;
```

The `gl_DrawIDARB` draw index comes from the invocation of each `vkCmdDrawMeshTasksNV` through the commands written in the indirect buffer.

Next, we load the data for the current meshlet. First, we determine the world position and the size of the meshlet bounding sphere:

```
vec4 center = model * vec4(meshlets[mi].center, 1);
float scale = length( model[0] );
float radius = meshlets[mi].radius * scale;
```

Next, we restore the `cone_axis` value (remember, they are stored as a single byte) and `cone_cutoff`:

```
vec3 cone_axis = mat3( model ) *
    vec3(int(meshlets[mi].cone_axis[0]) / 127.0,
    int(meshlets[mi].cone_axis[1]) / 127.0,
    int(meshlets[mi].cone_axis[2]) / 127.0);
float cone_cutoff = int(meshlets[mi].cone_cutoff) / 127.0;
```

We now have all of the data we need to perform back-face and frustum culling:

```
accept = !coneCull(center.xyz, radius, cone_axis,
    cone_cutoff, eye.xyz);
```

Next, `coneCull` is implemented as follows:

```
bool coneCull(vec3 center, float radius, vec3 cone_axis,
float cone_cutoff, vec3 camera_position)
{
    return dot(center - camera_position, cone_axis) >=
        cone_cutoff * length(center - camera_position) +
        radius;
}
```

This code first computes the cosine of the angle between the cone axis and the vector toward the camera from the center of the bounding sphere. Then it scales the cone cutoff (which is the cosine of the cut-off half angle) by the distance between the camera and the center of the bounding sphere and adds the radius of the bounding sphere.

This determines whether the cone is pointing away from the camera, and should be culled or, if it's pointing toward the camera, it should be kept.

The next step is to perform frustum culling. First, we transform the center of the bounding sphere into camera space:

```
center = world_to_camera * center;
```

Next, we check against the six frustum planes to determine whether the bounding sphere is inside the frustum:

```
for ( uint i = 0; i < 6; ++i ) {
    frustum_visible = frustum_visible &&
        (dot( frustum_planes[i], center) > -radius);
}
```

We accept the meshlet if it's both visible and not considered back facing:

```
accept = accept && frustum_visible;
```

The final step is to write out the indices of the visible meshlets and their number. The output data structure is defined as follows:

```
out taskNV block
{
    uint meshletIndices[32];
};
```

We use the subgroup instructions of GLSL for this step, and it's worth going through line by line if it's the first time you have seen this syntax. To access these instructions, the following extension must be enabled:

```
#extension GL_KHR_shader_subgroup_ballot : require
```

First, we set a bit for the active shader invocation depending on whether the meshlet is considered visible or not:

```
uvec4 ballot = subgroupBallot(accept);
```

Next, we determine which bit was set by the previous call and use it to store the active meshlet index:

```
uint index = subgroupBallotExclusiveBitCount(ballot);

if (accept)
    meshletIndices[index] = meshlet_index;
```

Finally, we count all the bits set across this thread group and store them in the `gl_TaskCountNV` variable:

```
uint count = subgroupBallotBitCount(ballot);

if (ti == 0)
    gl_TaskCountNV = count;
```

The `gl_TaskCountNV` variable is used by the GPU to determine how many mesh shader invocations are needed to process the meshlets that have not been occluded. The `if` is needed so that we write `TaskCount` only once per meshlet.

This concludes our implementation of task shaders. Next, we are going to look at our mesh shader implementation.

Implementing mesh shaders

After performing meshlet culling in the task shader, we need to process the active meshlets. This is similar to a regular vertex shader, however, there are some important differences that we'd like to point out.

Like task shaders, mesh shaders can be considered compute shaders, and the first directive is to determine the thread group size:

```
layout(local_size_x = 32) in;
```

We then have to read the data that has been written by the task shader:

```
in taskNV block
{
    uint meshletIndices[32];
};
```

Next, we define the data we are going to output. We first determine the maximum number of vertices and primitives (triangles in our case) that we could write:

```
layout(triangles, max_vertices = 64, max_primitives = 124) out;
```

We follow with the same data we might usually output from a vertex shader:

```
layout (location = 0) out vec2 vTexcoord0[];
layout (location = 1) out vec4 vNormal_BiTanX[];
layout (location = 2) out vec4 vTangent_BiTanY[];
layout (location = 3) out vec4 vPosition_BiTanZ[];
layout (location = 4) out flat uint mesh_draw_index[];
```

Notice, though, that we are using an array of values, as we can output up to 64 vertices per invocation.

Now that we have our input and output values, we can move to the shader implementation. Like before, we first determine our mesh and meshlet index:

```
uint ti = gl_LocalInvocationID.x;
uint mi = meshletIndices[gl_WorkGroupID.x];

MeshDraw mesh_draw = mesh_draws[ meshlets[mi].mesh_index ];

uint mesh_instance_index = draw_commands[gl_DrawIDARB + total_count].drawId;
```

Next, we determine the vertex and index offset and count for the active meshlet:

```
uint vertexCount = uint(meshlets[mi].vertexCount);
uint triangleCount = uint(meshlets[mi].triangleCount);
uint indexCount = triangleCount * 3;

uint vertexOffset = meshlets[mi].dataOffset;
uint indexOffset = vertexOffset + vertexCount;
```

We then process the vertices for the active meshlet:

```
for (uint i = ti; i < vertexCount; i += 32)
{
    uint vi = meshletData[vertexOffset + i];

vec3 position = vec3(vertex_positions[vi].v.x,
    vertex_positions[vi].v.y,
    vertex_positions[vi].v.z);

    // normals, tangents, etc.

    gl_MeshVerticesNV[ i ].gl_Position = view_projection *
        (model * vec4(position, 1));

    mesh_draw_index[ i ] = meshlets[mi].mesh_index;
}
```

Notice we are writing to the `gl_MeshVerticesNV` variable. This variable is used by the GPU to keep track of the vertices we output and their index. This data will then be used by the rasterizer to draw the resulting triangles on the screen.

Next, we write out the indices:

```
uint indexGroupCount = (indexCount + 3) / 4;

for (uint i = ti; i < indexGroupCount; i += 32)
{
    writePackedPrimitiveIndices4x8NV(i * 4,
        meshletData[indexOffset + i]);
}
```

The `writePackedPrimitiveIndices4x8NV` instruction has been introduced specifically for mesh shaders and it allows them to write four indices at once. As we mentioned previously, indices require only 1 byte to be stored, as we can't have values greater than 64. They are packed into `meshletData`, which is an unsigned `int` array.

If indices were stored in a different format, we would need to write them out individually to the `gl_PrimitiveIndicesNV` variable.

Finally, we write the primitive count in the appropriate variable:

```
if (ti == 0)
    gl_PrimitiveCountNV = uint(meshlets[mi].triangleCount);
```

This concludes our mesh shader implementation.

In this section, we have given an overview of how task and mesh shaders work and how they relate to compute shaders. Next, we provided a walk-through of our task and mesh shader implementation and highlighted the main differences from regular vertex shaders.

In the next section, we are going to extend our implementation by adding occlusion culling.

GPU culling using compute

In the previous section, we demonstrated how to perform back-face and frustum culling on meshlets. In this section, we are going to implement frustum and occlusion culling using compute shaders.

Depending on the rendering pipeline, occlusion culling is usually done through a depth pre-pass, where we write only the depth buffer. The depth buffer can then be used during the G-Buffer pass to avoid shading fragments that we already know are occluded.

The downside of this approach is that we have to draw the scene twice and, unless there is other work that can overlap with the depth pre-pass, have to wait for the depth pre-pass to complete before proceeding to the next step.

The algorithm described in this section was first presented at `https://advances.realtimerendering.com/s2015/aaltonenhaar_siggraph2015_combined_final_footer_220dpi.pdf`.

Here's how it works:

1. Using the depth buffer from the previous frame, we render the visible objects in the scene and perform mesh and meshlet frustum and occlusion culling. This could lead to false negatives, for example, meshes or meshlets that are visible in this frame but were not visible before. We store the list of these objects so that any false positives can be resolved in the next phase.

2. The previous step generates a list of draw commands directly in a compute shader. This list will be used to draw the visible objects using an indirect draw command.

3. We now have an updated depth buffer, and we update the depth pyramid as well.

4. We can now re-test the objects that have been culled in the first phase and generate a new draw list to remove any false positives.

5. We draw the remaining objects and generate our final depth buffer. This will then be used as the starting point for the next frame, and the process will repeat.

Now that we have a better understanding of the steps of the occlusion algorithm, let's see in detail how it is implemented.

Depth pyramid generation

When describing the occlusion algorithm, we mentioned the use of the depth buffer. However, we are not using the depth buffer directly. What we use instead is called a **depth pyramid**. You can think of it as the mipmap of the depth buffer.

The main difference from traditional mipmaps is that we can't use bi-linear interpolation to compute the lower level. If we were to use regular interpolation, we would compute depth values that don't exist in the scene.

> **Note**
> As we'll see later in the book, this applies in general to sampling depth textures. You should either use nearest neighbor sampling or specific samplers with min/max compare operations. Check out https://www.khronos.org/registry/vulkan/specs/1.3-extensions/man/html/VkSamplerReductionMode.html for more info.

Instead, we read the four fragments we want to reduce and pick the maximum value. We pick the maximum because our depth value goes from 0 to 1 and we need to make sure we cover the full range of values. If you are using inverted-z, the depth values go from 1 to 0 and the minimum value has to be used instead.

We perform this step using a compute shader. We start by transitioning the depth texture to a read state:

```
util_add_image_barrier( gpu, gpu_commands->
    vk_command_buffer, depth_texture,
        RESOURCE_STATE_SHADER_RESOURCE, 0, 1, true );
```

Then, we loop over the levels of the depth pyramid:

```
u32 width = depth_pyramid_texture->width;
u32 height = depth_pyramid_texture->
    height for ( u32 mip_index = 0; mip_index <
    depth_pyramid_texture->mipmaps; ++mip_index ) {
    util_add_image_barrier( gpu, gpu_commands->
    vk_command_buffer, depth_pyramid_texture->
    vk_image, RESOURCE_STATE_UNDEFINED,
    RESOURCE_STATE_UNORDERED_ACCESS,
    mip_index, 1, false );
```

The barrier in the preceding example is needed to ensure the image we are writing to is correctly set up. Next, we compute the group size for this level and invoke the compute shader:

```
u32 group_x = ( width + 7 ) / 8;
u32 group_y = ( height + 7 ) / 8;

gpu_commands->dispatch( group_x, group_y, 1 );
```

As we'll see in a moment, the thread group size of the compute shader is set to 8x8. We have to take this into account to compute the right group size.

Finally, we transition the image of the current level so that we can safely read from it at the next iteration:

```
    util_add_image_barrier( gpu, gpu_commands->
        vk_command_buffer, depth_pyramid_texture->
        vk_image, RESOURCE_STATE_UNORDERED_ACCESS,
        RESOURCE_STATE_SHADER_RESOURCE, mip_index,
        1, false );

    width /= 2;
    height /= 2;
}
```

We also update the width and height to match the size of the next level. The compute shader implementation is relatively simple:

```
ivec2 texel_position00 = ivec2( gl_GlobalInvocationID.xy )
    * 2;
ivec2 texel_position01 = texel_position00 + ivec2(0, 1);
ivec2 texel_position10 = texel_position00 + ivec2(1, 0);
ivec2 texel_position11 = texel_position00 + ivec2(1, 1);
```

We first compute the positions for the texels we want to reduce. Next, we read the depth value for these texels:

```
float color00 = texelFetch( src, texel_position00, 0 ).r;
float color01 = texelFetch( src, texel_position01, 0 ).r;
float color10 = texelFetch( src, texel_position10, 0 ).r;
float color11 = texelFetch( src, texel_position11, 0 ).r;
```

Finally, we compute the maximum value and store it in the right position of the next level in the pyramid:

```
float result = max( max( max( color00, color01 ),
    color10 ), color11 );
imageStore( dst, ivec2( gl_GlobalInvocationID.xy ),
    vec4( result, 0, 0, 0 ) );
```

The max operation is needed because the depth goes from 0 (close to the camera) to 1 (far from the camera). When using inverse-depth, it should be set to min. When down-sampling, we want the farthest of the four samples to avoid over-occluding.

Now that we have computed the depth pyramid, let's see how it's going to be used for occlusion culling.

Occlusion culling

The implementation of this step is done entirely in a compute shader. We are going to highlight the main sections of the code. We start by loading the current mesh:

```
uint mesh_draw_index =
    mesh_instance_draws[mesh_instance_index]
    .mesh_draw_index;

MeshDraw mesh_draw = mesh_draws[mesh_draw_index];

mat4 model =
    mesh_instance_draws[mesh_instance_index].model;
```

Next, we compute the bounding sphere position and radius in view space:

```
vec4 bounding_sphere = mesh_bounds[mesh_draw_index];

vec4 world_bounding_center = model *
    vec4(bounding_sphere.xyz, 1);
vec4 view_bounding_center = world_to_camera *
    world_bounding_center;

float scale = length( model[0] );
float radius = bounding_sphere.w * scale;
```

Note that this is the bounding sphere for the full mesh, not the meshlet. We are going to process the meshlets in the same way.

The next step is to perform frustum culling on the bounding sphere. This is the same code we presented in the *Implementing task shaders* section, and we are not going to replicate it here.

If the mesh passes the frustum culling, we check for occlusion culling next. First, we compute the bounding square of the perspective projected sphere. This step is necessary as the projected sphere shape could be an ellipsoid. Our implementation is based on this paper: https://jcgt.org/published/0002/02/05/ and the Niagara project (https://github.com/zeux/niagara/).

We are going to highlight only the final implementation; we suggest reading the full paper for more details about the theory and derivation.

We start by checking whether the sphere is fully behind the near plane. If that's the case, no further processing is required:

```
bool project_sphere(vec3 C, float r, float znear,
    float P00, float P11, out vec4 aabb) {
        if (-C.z - r < znear)
        return false;
```

Why -C.z? Because in our implementation, we look at a negative direction vector, thus the visible pixel's z is always negative.

Next, we compute the minimum and maximum points on the *x* axis. We do so by considering only the xz plane, finding the projection of the sphere onto this plane, and computing the minimum and maximum x coordinates of this projection:

```
vec2 cx = vec2(C.x, -C.z);
vec2 vx = vec2(sqrt(dot(cx, cx) - r * r), r);
vec2 minx = mat2(vx.x, vx.y, -vx.y, vx.x) * cx;
vec2 maxx = mat2(vx.x, -vx.y, vx.y, vx.x) * cx;
```

We repeat the same procedure for the y coordinate (omitted here). The computed points are in world space, but we need their value in perspective-projected space. This is accomplished with the following code:

```
aabb = vec4(minx.x / minx.y * P00, miny.x / miny.y * P11,
    maxx.x / maxx.y * P00, maxy.x / maxy.y * P11);
```

P00 and P11 are the first two diagonal values of the view-projection matrix. The final step is to transform these values from screen space to UV space. Operating in UV space will be useful for the next part of the algorithm.

The transformation is performed by the following code:

```
aabb = aabb.xwzy * vec4(0.5f, -0.5f, 0.5f, -0.5f) +
vec4(0.5f);
```

Coordinates in screen space are in the [-1, 1] range, while UV coordinates are in the [0, 1] range. This transformation performs the mapping from one range to the other. We use a negative offset for y as screen space has a bottom-left origin, while UV space has a top-left origin.

Now that we have the 2D bounding box for the mesh sphere, we can check whether it's occluded. First, we determine which level of the depth pyramid we should use:

```
ivec2 depth_pyramid_size =
    textureSize(global_textures[nonuniformEXT
    (depth_pyramid_texture_index)], 0);
float width = (aabb.z - aabb.x) * depth_pyramid_size.x ;
float height = (aabb.w - aabb.y) * depth_pyramid_size.y ;

float level = floor(log2(max(width, height)));
```

We simply scale the size of the bounding box in UV coordinates, computed in the previous step, by the size of the top level of the depth pyramid texture. We then take the logarithm of the largest between the width and height to determine which level of the pyramid we should use for the depth value lookup.

With this step, we reduce the bounding box to an individual pixel lookup. Remember, when computing the levels of the pyramid, the reduction step stores the farthest depth value. Thanks to this, we can safely look up an individual fragment to determine whether the bounding box is occluded or not.

This is accomplished with the following code:

```
float depth =
    textureLod(global_textures[nonuniformEXT
    (depth_pyramid_texture_index)], (aabb.xy + aabb.zw)
    0.5, level).r;
```

First, we look up the depth value in the pyramid for the sphere bounding box. Next, we compute the closest depth of the bounding sphere.

We also compute the closest depth for the bounding sphere:

```
float depth_sphere = z_near / (view_bounding_center.z -
                    radius);
```

Finally, we determine whether the sphere is occluded by checking its depth against the depth we read from the pyramid:

```
occlusion_visible = (depth_sphere <= depth);
```

If the mesh passes both the frustum and occlusion culling, we add the command to draw it in the command list:

```
draw_commands[draw_index].drawId = mesh_instance_index;
draw_commands[draw_index].taskCount =
    (mesh_draw.meshlet_count + 31) / 32;
draw_commands[draw_index].firstTask =
    mesh_draw.meshlet_offset / 32;
```

We will then use this list of commands to draw the meshlets for the visible meshes (as shown in the *Understanding task and mesh shaders* section) and update the depth pyramid.

The last step will be to rerun the culling for the meshes that were discarded in this first pass. Using the updated depth pyramid, we can generate a new command list to draw any meshes that had been incorrectly culled.

This concludes our implementation of occlusion culling. In this section, we have explained an algorithm for efficient occlusion culling on the GPU. We started by detailing the steps performed by this technique.

We then highlighted the main sections of the code that perform the creation of the depth pyramid, which is used for occlusion culling based on the bounding sphere of each mesh.

Performing culling on the GPU is a powerful technique that has helped developers overcome some of the limitations of the traditional geometry pipeline and allows us to render more complex and detailed scenes.

Summary

In this chapter, we have introduced the concept of meshlets, a construct that helps us break down large meshes into more manageable chunks and that can be used to perform occlusion computations on the GPU. We have demonstrated how to use the library of our choice (MeshOptimizer) to generate meshlets, and we also illustrated the extra data structures (cones and bounding spheres) that are useful for occlusion operations.

We introduced mesh and task shaders. Conceptually similar to compute shaders, they allow us to quickly process meshlets on the GPU. We demonstrated how to use task shaders to perform backface and frustum culling, and how mesh shaders replace vertex shaders by processing and generating multiple primitives in parallel.

Finally, we went through the implementation of occlusion culling. We first listed the steps that compose this technique. Next, we demonstrated how to compute a depth pyramid from our existing depth buffer. Lastly, we analyzed the occlusion culling implementation and highlighted the most relevant part of the compute shader. This step also generates a list of commands that can be used with an indirect draw call.

So far, our scene only uses one light. In the next chapter, we are going to implement clustered-deferred lighting, which will allow us to render hundreds of lights in our scene.

Further reading

As we mentioned in a previous section, task and mesh shaders are only available on Nvidia GPUs. This blog post has more details about their inner workings: `https://developer.nvidia.com/blog/introduction-turing-mesh-shaders/`.

Our implementation has been heavily inspired by the algorithms and techniques described in these resources:

- `https://www.gdcvault.com/play/1023463/contactUs`
- `http://advances.realtimerendering.com/s2015/aaltonenhaar_siggraph2015_combined_final_footer_220dpi.pdf`

Our go-to reference implementation for a task and mesh shader has been this project: `https://github.com/zeux/niagara`, which is also accompanied by a series of videos showing its development: `https://www.youtube.com/playlist?list=PL0JVLUVCkk-l7CWCn3-cdftR0oajugYvd`.

These libraries can be used to generate meshlets:

- `https://github.com/zeux/meshoptimizer` (the one we use)
- `https://github.com/JarkkoPFC/meshlete`

A more recent development in occlusion culling is the concept of a visibility buffer. The technique is described in detail in these resources:

- `http://www.conffx.com/Visibility_Buffer_GDCE.pdf`
- `http://filmicworlds.com/blog/visibility-buffer-rendering-with-material-graphs/`
- `https://www.youtube.com/watch?v=eviSykqSUUw`

7
Rendering Many Lights with Clustered Deferred Rendering

Until now, our scene has been lit by a single point light. While this has worked fine so far as we focused our attention more on laying the foundations of our rendering engine, it's not a very compelling and realistic use case. Modern games can have hundreds of lights in a given scene, and it's important that the lighting stage is performed efficiently and within the budget of a frame.

In this chapter, we will first describe the most common techniques that are used both in deferred and forward shading. We will highlight the pros and cons of each technique so that you can determine which one best fits your needs.

Next, we are going to provide an overview of our G-buffer setup. While the G-buffer has been in place from the very beginning, we haven't covered its implementation in detail. This is a good time to go into more detail, as the choice of a deferred renderer will inform our strategy for clustered lighting.

Finally, we are going to describe our clustering algorithm in detail and highlight the relevant sections of the code. While the algorithm itself is not too complex, there are a lot of details that are important to get a stable solution.

In this chapter, we're going to cover the following main topics:

- A brief history of clustered lighting
- Our G-buffer setup and implementation
- Implementing clustered lighting using screen tiles and Z-binning

Technical requirements

By the end of the chapter you will have a solid understanding of our G-buffer implementation. You will also learn how to implement a state of the art light clustering solution that can handle hundreds of lights.

The code for this chapter can be found at the following URL: `https://github.com/PacktPublishing/Mastering-Graphics-Programming-with-Vulkan/tree/main/source/chapter7`.

A brief history of clustered lighting

In this section, we are going to explore the background of how clustered lighting came to be and how it has evolved over the years.

In real-time applications, until the early 2000s, the most common way to handle lighting was by using the so-called **forward rendering**, a technique that renders each object on the screen with all the information needed, including light information. The problem with this approach is that it would limit the number of lights that could be processed to a low number, such as 4 or 8, a number that in the early 2000s would be enough.

The concept of Deferred Rendering, and more specifically, shading the same pixel only once, was already pioneered by Michael Deering and colleagues in a seminal paper called *The triangle processor and normal vector shader: a VLSI system for high performance graphics* in 1988, even though the term *deferred* was still not used.

Another key concept, the **G-buffer**, or **geometric buffer**, was pioneered by Takafumi Saito and Tokiichiro Takahashi in another pioneering paper, *Comprehensible Rendering of 3D Shapes*. In this paper, the authors cache depth and normals for each pixel to post-process the image – in this case, to add visual aids and comprehensibility to the image.

Although the first commercial game with a deferred renderer was *Shrek* in 2001 on the original Xbox, it became increasingly popular with the game *Stalker* and its accompanying paper, *Deferred Shading in Stalker* (`https://developer.nvidia.com/gpugems/gpugems2/part-ii-shading-lighting-and-shadows/chapter-9-deferred-shading-stalker`), and exploded in popularity with the CryEngine presentation at Siggraph 2010 called *Reaching the Speed of Light* (`http://advances.realtimerendering.com/s2010/Kaplanyan-CryEngine3%28SIGGRAPH%202010%20Advanced%20RealTime%20Rendering%20Course%29.pdf`).

In the late 2000s/early 2010s, Deferred Rendering was all the rage, and basically, all engines were implementing some variations of it.

Forward rendering made a comeback in 2012 when AMD launched a demo called *Leo* in which, thanks to the new *Compute Shaders* technology, they introduced the light list for each screen space tile and created *Forward+*.

The AMD Leo paper can be found here: `https://takahiroharada.files.wordpress.com/2015/04/forward_plus.pdf`.

A few weeks after that paper, the first commercial game to use Forward+ was *Dirt Showdown*, but only the PC version, as consoles still did not have support for APIs that would help in that area: `https://web.archive.org/web/20210621112015/https://www.rage3d.com/articles/gaming/codemaster_dirt_showdown_tech_review/`.

With this, the Forward+ technology came back into usage, as the light limitations were gone, and it added a lot of algorithmic exploration in different areas (such as post-process anti-aliasing for a deferred depth prepass).

In the following years, more refined subdivision algorithms were developed, with tiles becoming clusters and moving from simple 2D screen space tiles to fully frustum-shaped 3D clusters.

This became famous with the *Just Cause 3* paper by Emil Persson, `https://www.humus.name/Articles/PracticalClusteredShading.pdf`, and the concept was further enhanced by others for both deferred and forward rendering (`https://www.cse.chalmers.se/~uffe/clustered_shading_preprint.pdf`).

Clustering has been a great idea, but the memory consumption of having a 3D grid can be big, especially with the increasing rendering resolutions.

The current state of the art of clustering comes from Activision, which is our chosen solution, and we will see it in detail in the *Implementing light clusters* section of this chapter.

Now that we have provided a brief historical overview of real-time light rendering techniques, we are going to go into more depth about the differences between forward and Deferred Rendering in the next section.

Differences between forward and deferred techniques

After talking about the history of forward and Deferred Rendering techniques, we want to highlight the key differences and talk about their common problem: **light assignment**.

The main advantages of forward rendering are as follows:

- Total freedom when rendering materials
- Same rendering path for opaque and transparent objects
- Support for **Multi Sampled Anti-Aliasing (MSAA)**
- Lower memory bandwidth within the GPU

The main disadvantages of forward rendering are as follows:

- A depth prepass could be necessary to reduce the number of fragments shaded. Without this preprocessing step, scenes that contain a large number of objects could waste a lot of processing time by shading fragments for objects that are not visible. For this reason, a pass that only writes to the depth buffer is executed at the beginning of a frame.

  The `depth-test` function is then set to equal so that only the fragments for the visible objects will be shaded. Depending on the complexity of your scene, this pre-pass could be expensive, and in some cases, simplified geometry is used to reduce the cost of this pass at the expense of slightly less accurate results. You must also be careful and ensure that the Early-Z test is not disabled in the graphics pipeline.

This happens when writing to the depth buffer from a fragment shader or when a fragment shader contains a discard instruction.

- The complexity of shading a scene is the number of objects (N) multiplied by the number of lights (L). All the lights must be processed for each object as we don't know in advance which lights affect a given fragment.

- Shaders become increasingly more complex, having to do a lot of operations and thus having a very high GPU register pressure (number of registers used), impacting performance.

Deferred Rendering (sometimes referred to as **deferred shading**) was introduced primarily to decouple the rendering of the geometry and the light computations. In Deferred Rendering, we create multiple render targets. Usually, we have a render target for albedo, normals, PBR parameters (roughness, metalness, and occlusion – see *Chapter 2, Improving Resources Management,* for more details), and depth.

Once these render targets have been created, for each fragment we process the lights in the scene. We still have the same problem as before, since we still don't know which lights affect a given shader; however, our scene complexity has gone from $N \times L$ to $N + L$.

The main advantages of deferred shading are as follows:

- Decreased shading complexity
- No need for a depth pre-pass
- Less complex shaders, as writing information on the G-buffer and processing lights are separate operations

However, there are some disadvantages to this approach, as follows:

- **High memory usage**: We listed three render targets that have to be stored in memory. With increasing resolutions of modern games, these start to add up, especially when more render targets are needed for other techniques – for example, motion vectors for **Temporal Anti-Aliasing (TAA)**, which will be discussed in a later chapter. For this reason, developers tend to compress some of this data, which helps to reduce the amount of memory required by the G-buffer.

- **Loss of normals precision**: Normals are usually encoded as full floats (or possibly as 16-bit floats) as part of the geometry. To save memory when writing the normals render target, these values get compressed to 8 bits, significantly reducing the accuracy of these values.

  To further reduce memory usage, developers take advantage of the fact that normals are normalized. This allows us to store only two values and reconstruct the third. There are other techniques that can be used to compress normals, which will be referenced in the *Further reading* section. We will explain in detail the one we use in the next section.

- Transparent objects need a separate pass and need to be shaded using a forward technique.

- Special materials need to have all their parameters packed into the G-buffer.

As you probably noticed, one problem is common to both techniques: we have to go through all the lights when processing an individual object or fragment. We are now going to describe the two most common techniques that are used to solve this issue: tiles and clusters.

Light tiles

One approach to reducing the number of lights processed for a given fragment is to create a grid in screen space and determine which lights affect a given tile. When rendering the scene, we determine which tile the fragment we are shading belongs to and we iterate only over the lights that cover that tile.

The following figure shows the debug visualization for a light in the scene (the green sphere) and the screen area that it covers (in yellow). We will use this data to determine which tiles are affected by a given light.

Figure 7.1 – The area covered by a point light in screen space

Building the tiles can be done on the CPU or with a compute shader on the GPU. Tile data can be stored in a flat array; we will explain this data structure in more detail later in the chapter.

Traditional light tiles require a depth pre-pass to determine the minimum and maximum Z values. This approach can suffer from depth discontinuities; however, the final data structure is usually densely packed, meaning we are not wasting memory.

Light clusters

Light clusters subdivide the frustum in a 3D grid. As for tiles, lights are assigned to each cell, and at render time, we only iterate over the lights that a given fragment belongs to.

The following figure illustrates the shape of the clusters for one of the camera axes. Each cluster is composed of a smaller frustum:

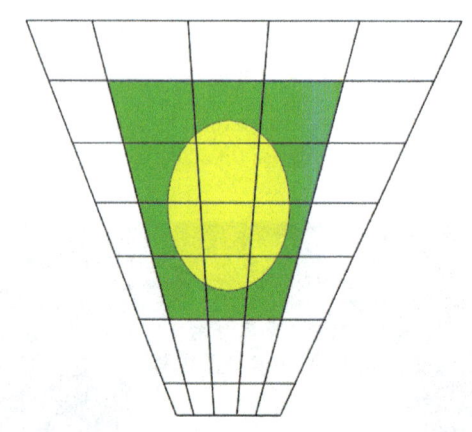

Figure 7.2 – The frustum clusters covered by a point light

Lights can be stored in a 3D grid (a 3D texture, for instance) or more complex data structures – for example, a **Bounded Volume Hierarchy** (**BVH**) or octree.

To build light clusters, we don't need a depth pre-pass. Most implementations build **Axis Aligned Bounding Boxes** (**AABBs**) for each light and project them into clip space. This approach allows easy 3D lookups and, depending on the amount of memory that can be allocated for the data structure, it's possible to achieve quite accurate results.

In this section, we have highlighted the advantages and disadvantages of both forward and Deferred Rendering. We have introduced tiling and clustering techniques that can help reduce the number of lights that need to be processed for each fragment.

In the next section, we are going to provide an overview of our G-buffer implementation.

Implementing a G-buffer

From the beginning of this project, we decided we would implement a deferred renderer. It's one of the more common approaches, and some of the render targets will be needed in later chapters for other techniques:

1. The first step in setting up multiple render targets in Vulkan is to create the framebuffers – the textures that will store the G-buffer data – and the render pass.

This step is automated, thanks to the frame graph (see *Chapter 4, Implementing a Frame Graph*, for details); however, we want to highlight our use of a new Vulkan extension that simplifies render pass and framebuffer creation. The extension is `VK_KHR_dynamic_rendering`.

> **Note**
>
> This extension has become part of the core specification in Vulkan 1.3, so it's possible to omit the KHR suffix on the data structures and API calls.

2. With this extension, we don't have to worry about creating the render pass and framebuffers ahead of time. We'll start by analyzing the changes required when creating a pipeline:

   ```
   VkPipelineRenderingCreateInfoKHR pipeline_rendering_
   create_info{
     VK_STRUCTURE_TYPE_PIPELINE_RENDERING_CREATE_INFO_KHR };
   pipeline_rendering_create_info.viewMask = 0;
   pipeline_rendering_create_info.colorAttachmentCount =
       creation.render_pass.num_color_formats;
   pipeline_rendering_create_info.pColorAttachmentFormats
       = creation.render_pass.num_color_formats > 0 ?
           creation.render_pass.color_formats : nullptr;
   pipeline_rendering_create_info.depthAttachmentFormat =
       creation.render_pass.depth_stencil_format;
   pipeline_rendering_create_info.stencilAttachmentFormat
       = VK_FORMAT_UNDEFINED;

   pipeline_info.pNext = &pipeline_rendering_create_info;
   ```

   We have to populate a `VkPipelineRenderingCreateInfoKHR` structure with the number of attachments we are going to use and their format. We also need to specify the depth and stencil formats, if used.

   Once this structure has been filled, we chain it to the `VkGraphicsPipelineCreateInfo` structure. When using this extension we don't populate the `VkGraphicsPipelineCreateInfo::renderPass` member.

3. At render time, instead of calling `vkCmdBeginRenderPass`, we call a new API, `vkCmdBeginRenderingKHR`. We start by creating an array to hold our attachments details:

   ```
   Array<VkRenderingAttachmentInfoKHR> color_attachments_
   info;
   color_attachments_info.init( device->allocator,
   ```

```
                framebuffer->num_color_attachments,
                    framebuffer->num_color_attachments );
```

4. Next, we populate each entry with the details of each attachment:

```
        for ( u32 a = 0; a < framebuffer->
            num_color_attachments; ++a ) {
                Texture* texture = device->
                    access_texture( framebuffer->
                        color_attachments[a] );

            VkAttachmentLoadOp color_op = ...;

        VkRenderingAttachmentInfoKHR&
        color_attachment_info = color_attachments_info[ a ];
        color_attachment_info.sType =
            VK_STRUCTURE_TYPE_RENDERING_ATTACHMENT_INFO_KHR;
        color_attachment_info.imageView = texture->
            vk_image_view;
        color_attachment_info.imageLayout =
            VK_IMAGE_LAYOUT_COLOR_ATTACHMENT_OPTIMAL;
        color_attachment_info.resolveMode =
            VK_RESOLVE_MODE_NONE;
        color_attachment_info.loadOp = color_op;
        color_attachment_info.storeOp =
            VK_ATTACHMENT_STORE_OP_STORE;
        color_attachment_info.clearValue = render_pass->
            output.color_operations[ a ] ==
                RenderPassOperation::Enum::Clear ? clears[ 0 ]
                    : VkClearValue{ };
        }
```

5. We have to fill a similar data structure for the depth attachment:

```
        VkRenderingAttachmentInfoKHR depth_attachment_info{
            VK_STRUCTURE_TYPE_RENDERING_ATTACHMENT_INFO_KHR };

        bool has_depth_attachment = framebuffer->
```

```
            depth_stencil_attachment.index != k_invalid_index;

    if ( has_depth_attachment ) {
        Texture* texture = device->access_texture(
            framebuffer->depth_stencil_attachment );

        VkAttachmentLoadOp depth_op = ...;
        depth_attachment_info.imageView = texture->
            vk_image_view;
        depth_attachment_info.imageLayout =
            VK_IMAGE_LAYOUT_DEPTH_STENCIL_ATTACHMENT_OPTIMAL;
        depth_attachment_info.resolveMode =
            VK_RESOLVE_MODE_NONE;
        depth_attachment_info.loadOp = depth_op;
        depth_attachment_info.storeOp =
            VK_ATTACHMENT_STORE_OP_STORE;
        depth_attachment_info.clearValue = render_pass->
            output.depth_operation ==
                RenderPassOperation::Enum::Clear ? clears[ 1 ]
                    : VkClearValue{ };
    }
```

6. Finally, we fill the VkRenderingInfoKHR structure that will be passed to vkCmdBeginRenderingKHR:

```
    VkRenderingInfoKHR rendering_info{
        VK_STRUCTURE_TYPE_RENDERING_INFO_KHR };
    rendering_info.flags = use_secondary ?
        VK_RENDERING_CONTENTS_SECONDARY_COMMAND
            _BUFFERS_BIT_KHR : 0;
    rendering_info.renderArea = { 0, 0, framebuffer->
        width, framebuffer->height };
    rendering_info.layerCount = 1;
    rendering_info.viewMask = 0;
    rendering_info.colorAttachmentCount = framebuffer->
        num_color_attachments;
    rendering_info.pColorAttachments = framebuffer->
```

```
            num_color_attachments > 0 ?
                color_attachments_info.data : nullptr;
        rendering_info.pDepthAttachment =
            has_depth_attachment ? &depth_attachment_info :
                nullptr;
        rendering_info.pStencilAttachment = nullptr;
```

Once we are done rendering, we are going to call `vkCmdEndRenderingKHR` instead of `vkCmdEndRenderPass`.

Now that we have set up our render targets, we are going to describe how they are used in our G-buffer shader. Our G-buffer has four render targets plus the depth buffer. As we mentioned in the previous section, there is no need for a depth pre-pass, although you might notice this was enabled in some of the earlier chapters for testing purposes.

The first step is to declare multiple outputs in the fragment shader:

```
layout (location = 0) out vec4 color_out;
layout (location = 1) out vec2 normal_out;
layout (location = 2) out vec4
    occlusion_roughness_metalness_out;
layout (location = 3) out vec4 emissive_out;
```

The location index must correspond to the order in which the attachments have been specified when calling `vkCmdBeginRenderingKHR` (or when creating the render pass and framebuffer objects). Writing to a given render target is done simply by writing to one of the variables we just declared:

```
colour_out = texture(global_textures[nonuniformEXT
    (albedo_texture)], uv);
```

As we mentioned in the previous section, we must be conscious of memory usage. As you might have noticed, we only store two channels for normals. We use an octahedral encoding that allows storing only two values. We can reconstruct the full normal in the lighting pass.

Here's the encoding function:

```
vec2 octahedral_encode(vec3 n) {
    // Project the sphere onto the octahedron, and then
        onto the xy plane
    vec2 p = n.xy * (1.0f / (abs(n.x) + abs(n.y) +
        abs(n.z)));
    // Reflect the folds of the lower hemisphere over the
        diagonals
    return (n.z < 0.0f) ? ((1.0 - abs(p.yx)) *
        sign_not_zero(p)) : p;
}
```

And here is the decoding function:

```
vec3 octahedral_decode(vec2 f) {
    vec3 n = vec3(f.x, f.y, 1.0 - abs(f.x) - abs(f.y));
    float t = max(-n.z, 0.0);
    n.x += n.x >= 0.0 ? -t : t;
    n.y += n.y >= 0.0 ? -t : t;

    return normalize(n);
}
```

The following table illustrates the data arrangement of our G-buffer pass:

Albedo	R8	G8	B8	
Normals	R16		G16	
PBR	R8	G8	B8	

Table 7.1 – G-buffer memory layout

Here are the screenshots for our render targets:

Figure 7.3 – From top to bottom: albedo, normals, and combined occlusion (red), roughness (green), and metalness (blue)

We could probably reduce the number of render targets further: we know that in the G-buffer pass, we are only shading opaque objects, so we don't need the alpha channel. Also, nothing prevents us from mixing data for different render targets – for instance, we could have something like the following:

- **RGBA8**: `r`, `g`, `b`, and `normal_1`
- **RGBA8**: `normal_2`, `roughness`, `metalness`, and `occlusion`
- **RGBA8**: `emissive`

We can also try to use different texture formats (**R11G11B10**, for example) to increase the accuracy of our data. We encourage you to experiment with different solutions and find the one that works best for your use case!

In this section, we have introduced a new Vulkan extension that simplifies the creation and use of the render pass and framebuffer. We also provided details on the implementation of our G-buffer and highlighted potential optimizations. In the next section, we are going to look at the light clustering solution that we have implemented.

Implementing light clusters

In this section, we are going to describe our implementation of the light clustering algorithm. It's based on this presentation: `https://www.activision.com/cdn/research/2017_Sig_Improved_Culling_final.pdf`. The main (and very smart) idea is to separate the *XY* plane from the *Z* range, combining the advantages of both tiling and clustering approaches. The algorithms are organized as follows:

1. We sort the lights by their depth value in camera space.
2. We then divide the depth range into bins of equal size, although a logarithmic subdivision might work better depending on your depth range.
3. Next, we assign the lights to each bin if their bounding box falls within the bin range. We only store the minimum and maximum light index for a given bin, so we only need 16 bits for each bin, unless you need more than 65,535 lights!
4. We then divide the screen into tiles (8x8 pixels, in our case) and determine which lights cover a given tile. Each tile will store a bitfield representation for the active lights.
5. Given a fragment that we want to shade, we determine the depth of the fragment and read the bin index.
6. Finally, we iterate from the minimum to the maximum light index in that bin and read the corresponding tile to see whether the light is visible, this time using *x* and *y* coordinates to retrieve the tile.

This solution provides a very efficient way to loop through the active lights for a given fragment.

CPU lights assignment

We'll now look at the implementation. During each frame, we perform the following steps:

1. We start by sorting the lights by their depth value:

   ```
   float z_far = 100.0f;
   for ( u32 i = 0; i < k_num_lights; ++i ) {
       Light& light = lights[ i ];



       vec4s p{ light.world_position.x,
           light.world_position.y,
               light.world_position.z, 1.0f };
       vec3s p_min = glms_vec3_add( light.world_position,
           glms_vec3_scale(
               light_camera_dir,
                   -light.radius ) );
       vec3s p_max = glms_vec3_add( light.world_position,
           glms_vec3_scale(
               light_camera_dir,
                   light.radius ) );


       vec4s projected_p = glms_mat4_mulv(
           world_to_camera, p );
       vec4s projected_p_min = glms_mat4_mulv(
           world_to_camera, p_min4 );
       vec4s projected_p_max = glms_mat4_mulv(
           world_to_camera, p_max4 );

       SortedLight& sorted_light = sorted_lights[ i ];
       sorted_light.light_index = i;
       sorted_light.projected_z = ( -projected_p.z -
           scene_data.z_near ) / ( z_far -
               scene_data.z_near );
       sorted_light.projected_z_min = ( -
           projected_p_min.z - scene_data.z_near ) / (
   ```

```
                  z_far - scene_data.z_near );
    sorted_light.projected_z_max = ( -
        projected_p_max.z - scene_data.z_near ) / (
                  z_far - scene_data.z_near );
}
```

We compute the minimum and maximum point of the light sphere from the camera's point of view. Notice that we use a closer `far` depth plane to gain precision in the depth range.

2. To avoid having to sort the light list, we only sort the light indices:

```
qsort( sorted_lights.data, k_num_lights, sizeof(
    SortedLight ), sorting_light_fn );
u32* gpu_light_indices = ( u32* )gpu.map_buffer(
    cb_map );
if ( gpu_light_indices ) {
    for ( u32 i = 0; i < k_num_lights; ++i ) {
        gpu_light_indices[ i ] = sorted_lights[ i ]
            .light_index;
    }

    gpu.unmap_buffer( cb_map );
}
```

This optimization allows us to upload the light array only once, while we only need to update the light indices.

3. Next, we proceed with the tile assignment. We start by defining our bitfield array and some helper variables that will be used to compute the index within the array:

```
Array<u32> light_tiles_bits;
light_tiles_bits.init( context.scratch_allocator,
    tiles_entry_count, tiles_entry_count );

float near_z = scene_data.z_near;
float tile_size_inv = 1.0f / k_tile_size;

u32 tile_stride = tile_x_count * k_num_words;
```

4. We then transform the light position in camera space:

```
for ( u32 i = 0; i < k_num_lights; ++i ) {
    const u32 light_index = sorted_lights[ i ]
        .light_index;
    Light& light = lights[ light_index ];

    vec4s pos{ light.world_position.x,
        light.world_position.y,
            light.world_position.z, 1.0f };
    float radius = light.radius;

    vec4s view_space_pos = glms_mat4_mulv(
        game_camera.camera.view, pos );
    bool camera_visible = view_space_pos.z - radius <
        game_camera.camera.near_plane;

    if ( !camera_visible &&
        context.skip_invisible_lights ) {
        continue;
    }
}
```

If the light is behind the camera, we don't do any further processing.

5. Next, we compute the corners of the AABB projected to clip space:

```
for ( u32 c = 0; c < 8; ++c ) {
    vec3s corner{ ( c % 2 ) ? 1.f : -1.f, ( c & 2 ) ?
        1.f : -1.f, ( c & 4 ) ? 1.f : -1.f };
    corner = glms_vec3_scale( corner, radius );
    corner = glms_vec3_add( corner, glms_vec3( pos ) );

    vec4s corner_vs = glms_mat4_mulv(
        game_camera.camera.view,
            glms_vec4( corner, 1.f ) );
    corner_vs.z = -glm_max(
        game_camera.camera.near_plane, -corner_vs.z );

    vec4s corner_ndc = glms_mat4_mulv(
```

```
            game_camera.camera.projection, corner_vs );
        corner_ndc = glms_vec4_divs( corner_ndc,
            corner_ndc.w );

        aabb_min.x = glm_min( aabb_min.x, corner_ndc.x );
        aabb_min.y = glm_min( aabb_min.y, corner_ndc.y );

        aabb_max.x = glm_max( aabb_max.x, corner_ndc.x );
        aabb_max.y = glm_max( aabb_max.y, corner_ndc.y );
    }

    aabb.x = aabb_min.x;
    aabb.z = aabb_max.x;
    aabb.w = -1 * aabb_min.y;
    aabb.y = -1 * aabb_max.y;
```

6. We then proceed to determine the size of the quad in screen space:

```
    vec4s aabb_screen{ ( aabb.x * 0.5f + 0.5f ) * (
        gpu.swapchain_width - 1 ),
        ( aabb.y * 0.5f + 0.5f ) * (
        gpu.swapchain_height - 1 ),
        ( aabb.z * 0.5f + 0.5f ) * (
        gpu.swapchain_width - 1 ),
        ( aabb.w * 0.5f + 0.5f ) *
        ( gpu.swapchain_height - 1 ) };

    f32 width = aabb_screen.z - aabb_screen.x;
    f32 height = aabb_screen.w - aabb_screen.y;

    if ( width < 0.0001f || height < 0.0001f ) {
        continue;
    }

    float min_x = aabb_screen.x;
    float min_y = aabb_screen.y;
```

```
float max_x = min_x + width;
float max_y = min_y + height;

if ( min_x > gpu.swapchain_width || min_y >
    gpu.swapchain_height ) {
    continue;
}

if ( max_x < 0.0f || max_y < 0.0f ) {
    continue;
}
```

If the light is not visible on the screen, we move to the next light.

7. The final step is to set the bit for the light we are processing on all the tiles it covers:

```
min_x = max( min_x, 0.0f );
min_y = max( min_y, 0.0f );

max_x = min( max_x, ( float )gpu.swapchain_width );
max_y = min( max_y, ( float )gpu.swapchain_height );

u32 first_tile_x = ( u32 )( min_x * tile_size_inv );
u32 last_tile_x = min( tile_x_count - 1, ( u32 )(
    max_x * tile_size_inv ) );

u32 first_tile_y = ( u32 )( min_y * tile_size_inv );
u32 last_tile_y = min( tile_y_count - 1, ( u32 )(
    max_y * tile_size_inv ) );

for ( u32 y = first_tile_y; y <= last_tile_y; ++y ) {
    for ( u32 x = first_tile_x; x <= last_tile_x; ++x
         ) {
            u32 array_index = y * tile_stride + x;
            u32 word_index = i / 32;
            u32 bit_index = i % 32;

        light_tiles_bits[ array_index + word_index ] |= (
```

```
                  1 << bit_index );
        }
}
```

We then upload all the light tiles and bin data to the GPU.

At the end of this computation, we will have a bin table containing the minimum and maximum light ID for each depth slice. The following table illustrates an example of the values for the first few slices:

Slice Index	MIN	MAX
0	MAX_LIGHT_ID	0 (empty)
1	2	8
2	7	7
3	4	9

Table 7.2 – Example of the data contained in the depth bins

The other data structure we computed is a 2D array, where each entry contains a bitfield tracking the active lights for the corresponding screen tile. The following table presents an example of the content of this array:

Tile Index	0	1	2	3
0	0010	0110	0110	0000
1	1000	1011	0011	1101
2	0110	1001	0001	0010
3	1111	0101	1100	1010

Table 7.3 – Example of the bitfield values tracking the active lights per tile

In the preceding example, we have divided the screen into a 4x4 grid, and each tile entry has a bit set for every light that covers that tile. Note that each tile entry can be composed of multiple 32-bit values depending on the number of lights in the scene.

In this section, we provided an overview of the algorithm we have implemented to assign lights to a given cluster. We then detailed the steps to implement the algorithm. In the next section, we are going to use the data we have just obtained to process lights on the GPU.

GPU light processing

Now that we have all the data we need on the GPU, we can use it in our lighting computation:

1. We start by determining which depth bin our fragment belongs to:

   ```
   vec4 pos_camera_space = world_to_camera * vec4(
       world_position, 1.0 );
   
   float z_light_far = 100.0f;
   float linear_d = ( -pos_camera_space.z - z_near ) / (
       z_light_far - z_near );
   int bin_index = int( linear_d / BIN_WIDTH );
   uint bin_value = bins[ bin_index ];
   
   uint min_light_id = bin_value & 0xFFFF;
   uint max_light_id = ( bin_value >> 16 ) & 0xFFFF;
   ```

2. We extract the minimum and maximum light index, as they are going to be used in the light computation loop:

   ```
   uvec2 position = gl_GlobalInvocationID.xy;
   
   uvec2 tile = position / uint( TILE_SIZE );
   
   uint stride = uint( NUM_WORDS ) *
       ( uint( resolution.x ) / uint( TILE_SIZE ) );
   uint address = tile.y * stride + tile.x;
   ```

3. We first determine the address in the tile bitfield array. Next, we check whether there are any lights in this depth bin:

   ```
   if ( max_light_id != 0 ) {
       min_light_id -= 1;
       max_light_id -= 1;
   ```

4. If `max_light_id` is 0, it means we didn't store any lights in this bin, so no lights will affect this fragment. Next, we loop over the lights for this depth bin:

    ```
    for ( uint light_id = min_light_id; light_id <=
        max_light_id; ++light_id ) {
            uint word_id = light_id / 32;
            uint bit_id = light_id % 32;
    ```

5. After we compute the word and bit index, we determine which lights from the depth bin also cover the screen tile:

    ```
    if ( ( tiles[ address + word_id ] &
        ( 1 << bit_id ) ) != 0 ) {
            uint global_light_index =
                light_indices[ light_id ];
            Light point_light = lights[
                global_light_index ];

            final_color.rgb +=
                calculate_point_light_contribution
                    ( albedo, orm, normal, emissive,
                        world_position, V, F0, NoV,
                            point_light );
        }
      }
    }
    ```

This concludes our light clustering algorithm. The shader code also contains an optimized version that makes use of the subgroup instructions to improve register utilization. There are plenty of comments to explain how it works.

We covered a fair amount of code in this section, so don't worry if some things were not clear on the first read. We started by describing the steps of the algorithm. We then explained how the lights are sorted in depth bins and how we determine the lights that cover a given tile on the screen. Finally, we showed how these data structures are used in the lighting shader to determine which lights affect a given fragment.

Note that this technique can be used both in forward and Deferred Rendering. Now that we have a performant lighting solution, one element is sorely missing from our scene: shadows! This will be the topic for the next chapter.

Summary

In this chapter, we have implemented a light clustering solution. We started by explaining forward and Deferred Rendering techniques and their main advantages and shortcomings. Next, we described two approaches to group lights to reduce the computation needed to shade a single fragment.

We then outlined our G-buffer implementation by listing the render targets that we use. We detailed our use of the `VK_KHR_dynamic_rendering` extension, which allows us to simplify the render pass and framebuffer use. We also highlighted the relevant code in the G-buffer shader to write to multiple render targets, and we provided the implementation for our normal encoding and decoding. In closing, we suggested some optimizations to further reduce the memory used by our G-buffer implementation.

In the last section, we described the algorithm we selected to implement light clustering. We started by sorting the lights by their depth value into depth bins. We then proceeded to store the lights that affect a given screen tile using a bitfield array. Finally, we made use of these two data structures in our lighting shader to reduce the number of lights that need to be evaluated for each fragment.

Optimizing the lighting stage of any game or application is paramount to maintaining interactive frame rates. We described one possible solution, but other options are available, and we suggest you experiment with them to find the one that best suits your use case!

Now that we have added many lights, the scene still looks flat as there's one important element missing: shadows. That's the topic for the next chapter!

Further reading

- Some history about the first Deferred Rendering in the *Shrek* game, 2001: `https://sites.google.com/site/richgel99/the-early-history-of-deferred-shading-and-lighting`
- Stalker Deferred Rendering paper: `https://developer.nvidia.com/gpugems/gpugems2/part-ii-shading-lighting-and-shadows/chapter-9-deferred-shading-stalker`
- This is one of the first papers that introduced the concept of clustered shading: `http://www.cse.chalmers.se/~uffe/clustered_shading_preprint.pdf`
- These two presentations are often cited as the inspiration for many implementations:
  - `https://www.activision.com/cdn/research/2017_Sig_Improved_Culling_final.pdf`
  - `http://www.humus.name/Articles/PracticalClusteredShading.pdf`

- In this chapter, we only covered point lights, but in practice, many other types of lights are used (spotlights, area lights, polygonal lights, and a few others). This article describes a way to determine the visibility of a spotlight approximated by a cone:

    - `https://bartwronski.com/2017/04/13/cull-that-cone/`

- These presentations describe variants of the clustering techniques we described in this chapter:

    - `https://www.intel.com/content/dam/develop/external/us/en/documents/lauritzen-deferred-shading-siggraph-2010-181241.pdf`
    - `https://advances.realtimerendering.com/s2016/Siggraph2016_idTech6.pdf`
    - `https://www.ea.com/frostbite/news/parallel-graphics-in-frostbite-current-future`

8
Adding Shadows Using Mesh Shaders

In the previous chapter, we added support for multiple lights using clustered deferred techniques with the latest innovations.

We added a hard limit of 256 maximum lights, with the possibility for each one to be dynamic and unique in its properties.

In this chapter, we will add the possibility for each of these lights to cast shadows to further enhance the visuals of any asset displayed in Raptor Engine, and we will exploit the possibilities given by mesh shaders of having many of these lights cast shadows and still be in a reasonable frame time.

We will also have a look at using sparse resources to improve shadow map memory usage, moving the possibility of having many shadow-casting lights from something almost impossible to something possible and performant with current hardware.

In this chapter, we're going to cover the following main topics:

- A brief history of shadow techniques
- Implementing shadow mapping using mesh shaders
- Improving shadow memory with Vulkan's sparse resources

Technical requirements

The code for this chapter can be found at the following URL: `https://github.com/PacktPublishing/Mastering-Graphics-Programming-with-Vulkan/tree/main/source/chapter8`

A brief history of shadow techniques

Shadows are one of the biggest additions to any rendering framework as they really enhance the perception of depth and volume across a scene. Being a phenomenon linked to lights, they have been studied in graphics literature for decades, but the problem is still far from being solved.

The most used shadow technique right now is shadow mapping, but recently, thanks to hardware-enabled ray tracing, ray traced shadows are becoming popular as a more realistic solution.

There were some games—especially *Doom 3*—that also used shadow volumes as a solution to make lights cast shadows, but they are not used anymore.

Shadow volumes

Shadow volumes are an old concept, already proposed by Frank Crow in 1977. They are defined as the projection of each vertex of a triangle along the light direction and toward infinity, thus creating a volume.

The shadows are sharp, and they require each triangle and each light to process accordingly. The most recent implementation uses the stencil buffer, and this change enabled it to be used in real time.

The problem with shadow volumes is that they require a lot of geometry work and become fill-rate intensive, and in this case, shadow maps are a clear winner.

Shadow mapping

The most used technique of all, first appearing around 1978, shadow mapping is the industry standard in both real-time and offline rendering. The idea behind shadow mapping is to render the scene from the perspective of the light and save the depth of each pixel.

After that, when rendering the scene from the camera point of view, the pixel position can be converted to the shadow coordinate system and tested against the corresponding pixel in the shadow map to see whether the current pixel is in shadow or not.

The resolution of a shadow map is very important, as well as what type of information is saved inside it. With time, filters started to appear, using mathematical tools to add the possibility to soften the shadows, or adding calculations to harden the shadows the closer they are to the blocker geometry.

Shadow mapping suffers from a lot of issues as well, but being the de facto standard, many techniques are used to alleviate them. Some problems that can be encountered are aliasing, shadow acne, and Peter Panning.

Finding a robust shadow solution is one of the most intricate steps of a rendering engine and normally requires a lot of trial and error and custom solutions tailored to different scenes and situations.

Raytraced shadows

In the last few years, raytracing—a technique that uses rays to trace any kind of rendering information—got hardware support on customer GPUs, enabling rendering programmers to use a different scene representation to trace rays and enhance the look of different rendering phenomena.

We will look at raytracing toward the end of the book, but for now, it is sufficient to say that using this special representation of the scene (different from mesh and meshlets we already use), it is possible to trace, for each pixel on the screen, one ray toward each light affecting the pixel and calculate the final shadow contribution to that pixel.

It is the most advanced and realistic form of a shadow, but still, performance-wise—despite the hardware support—it can be slow, and the diffusion of GPUs supporting it is not as elevated as needed to make it the new standard.

That is why shadow mapping is still the standard—any hardware, including mobile phones, can render shadow maps, and they can still achieve a convincing look. Based on this consideration, we chose to implement shadow mapping as the main shadow technique for Raptor Engine.

Implementing shadow mapping using mesh shaders

Now that we have looked at the different ways to render a shadow, we will describe the algorithm and the implementation's detail used to render many shadow maps at once leveraging the mesh shader power.

Overview

In this section, we will give an overview of the algorithm. What we are trying to achieve is to render shadows using meshlets and mesh shaders, but this will require some compute work to generate commands to actually draw the meshlets.

We will draw shadows coming from point lights, and we will use cubemaps as textures to store the necessary information. We will talk about cubemaps in the following section.

Back to the algorithm, the first step will be to cull mesh instances against lights. This is done in a compute shader and will save a per-light list of visible mesh instances. Mesh instances are used to retrieve associated meshes later on, and per-meshlet culling will be performed using task shaders later on.

The second step is to write indirect draw meshlet arguments to perform the actual rendering of meshlets into shadow maps, again in a compute shader. There is a caveat here that will be explained in the *A note about multiview rendering* section.

The third step is to draw meshlets using indirect mesh shaders, drawing into the actual shadow maps.

We will use a layered cubemap shadow texture as we are drawing, with each layer corresponding to each light.

The fourth and final step is to sample the shadow texture when lighting the scene.

We will render shadows with almost no filtering, as the focus of this chapter is on mesh shader-driven shadows, but we will give links to filtering options at the end of the chapter.

Here is a visual overview of the algorithm:

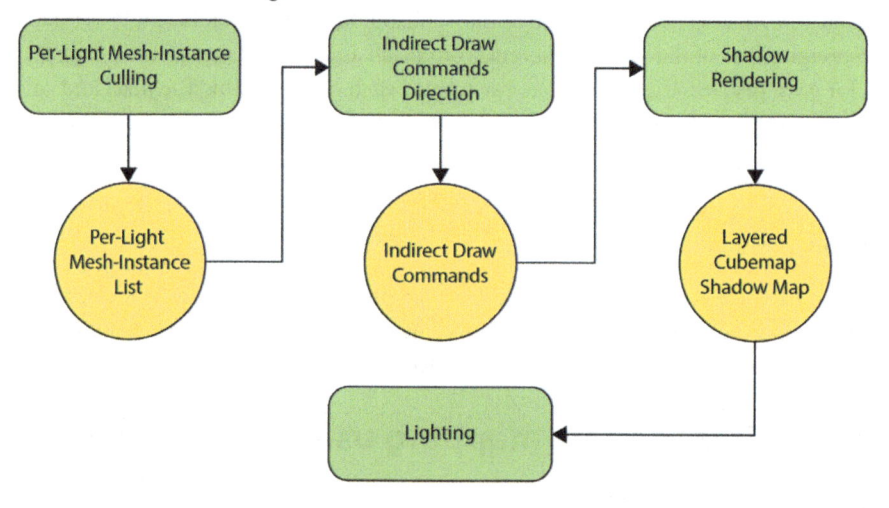

Figure 8.1 – Algorithm overview

In the next section, we will talk about cubemap shadows, used to store shadows from point lights.

Cubemap shadows

Cubemaps are a general way of mapping a 3D direction (x, y, z) with six faces containing image information.

They are used not only for shadow rendering but in general to draw environments as well (such as sky boxes, or far distant landscapes), and they are so standardized that even hardware contains support for cubemap sampling and filtering.

Each direction of the cubemap has normally a name and an orientation and a single texture associated with it:

- Positive x
- Negative x
- Positive y
- Negative y
- Positive z
- Negative z

Implementing shadow mapping using mesh shaders   183

When rendering to a face, we need to provide matrices that will look in the correct direction.

When reading, a single vector will be translated (behind the scenes) to the corresponding image. For shadows, the process will be manual, as we will provide for each face a view projection matrix that will be read by the meshlets to direct the rendering to the correct face.

A caveat for that also is that we will need to duplicate the drawing commands for each face, as one vertex can be rendered only to one image view associated with each face.

There are some extensions that can associate a vertex with more than one image, as we will see in the next section, but their support in mesh shaders at the time of writing is still limited.

Another important aspect of the proposed shadow rendering is that we will use an array of cubemaps so that we can both read and write every shadow using layered rendering.

Here is the unrolled cubemap shadow rendering for one point light, with a texture for each cubemap face:

Figure 8.2 – The six cubemap faces rendered from the light point of view

As we can see, only the positive Z is rendering something. We will provide some culling mechanisms to avoid rendering meshlets in empty cubemap faces.

A note about multiview rendering

As written in the previous section, there is an extension that helps with rendering a vertex on more than a cubemap face: Multiview Rendering. This extension is widely used in virtual reality applications to render a vertex in both the views of a stereographic projection and can be used as well with cubemaps.

At the time of writing, mesh shaders don't have a proper extension supported, so we are using the NVIDIA Vulkan extension, and this is not supporting Multiview Rendering properly, thus we are manually generating commands for each face and drawing using those commands.

We are aware that a multi-vendor extension is on the way, so we will update the code accordingly, but the core algorithm does not change, as multiview rendering is more of an optimization.

We are now ready to see the algorithm steps.

Per-light mesh instance culling

The first step in preparing for shadow rendering is a coarse grain culling done in a compute shader. In Raptor, we have both mesh and meshlet representations, thus we can use meshes and their bounding volumes as a *higher hierarchy* linked to meshlets.

We will perform a very simple light sphere to mesh sphere intersection, and if intersecting, we will add the corresponding meshlets. The first thing to know is that we will dispatch this compute shader using mesh instances and light together, so we will calculate for each light and for each mesh instance if the light influences the mesh instance.

We will then output a list of per-light meshlet instances, defined as both a mesh instance and global meshlet index combined. We will also write the per-light meshlet instances count, to skip empty lights and to correctly read the indices.

The first step is thus to reset the per-light counts:

```
layout (local_size_x = 32, local_size_y = 1, local_size_z =
        1) in;
void main() {
    if (gl_GlobalInvocationID.x == 0 ) {
        for ( uint i = 0; i < NUM_LIGHTS; ++i ) {
            per_light_meshlet_instances[i * 2] = 0;
            per_light_meshlet_instances[i * 2 + 1] = 0;
        }
    }
    global_shader_barrier();
```

Implementing shadow mapping using mesh shaders 185

We will then skip threads that will work on out-of-bounds lights. When we dispatch, we round up the numbers after dividing by 32, so some threads can be working on empty lights.

The dispatch of this compute will be done by linking each mesh instance with each light, like so:

Mesh Instance 0	Mesh Instance 0	Mesh Instance 1	Mesh Instance 1	Mesh Instance 2	Mesh Instance 2
Light 0	Light 1	Light 0	Light 1	Light 0	Light 1
Dispatch 0	Dispatch 1	Dispatch 2	Dispatch 3	Dispatch 4	Dispatch 5

Figure 8.3 – Organization of the command buffer to render the cubemaps for multiple lights using a single draw call

Here is the early out and light index calculation:

```
uint light_index = gl_GlobalInvocationID.x %
                   active_lights;
if (light_index >= active_lights) {
    return;
}
const Light = lights[light_index];
```

In a similar way, we calculate the mesh instance index, and *early out* again if the dispatch rounding up is too much:

```
uint mesh_instance_index = gl_GlobalInvocationID.x /
                           active_lights;
if (mesh_instance_index >= num_mesh_instances) {
    return;
}
uint mesh_draw_index = mesh_instance_draws
                       [mesh_instance_index].
                       mesh_draw_index;
// Skip transparent meshes
MeshDraw mesh_draw = mesh_draws[mesh_draw_index];
if ( ((mesh_draw.flags & (DrawFlags_AlphaMask |
    DrawFlags_Transparent)) != 0 ) ){
```

Adding Shadows Using Mesh Shaders

```
        return;
    }
```

We can finally gather the bounding sphere of the mesh instance and the model and simply calculate the world space bounding sphere:

```
vec4 bounding_sphere = mesh_bounds[mesh_draw_index];
mat4 model = mesh_instance_draws
             [mesh_instance_index].model;

// Calculate mesh instance bounding sphere
vec4 mesh_world_bounding_center = model * vec4
    (bounding_sphere.xyz, 1);

float scale = length( model[0] );
float mesh_radius = bounding_sphere.w * scale * 1.1;
// Artificially inflate bounding sphere

// Check if mesh is inside light
const bool mesh_intersects_sphere =
sphere_intersect(mesh_world_bounding_center.xyz,
    mesh_radius, light.world_position, light.radius )
        || disable_shadow_meshes_sphere_cull();
if (!mesh_intersects_sphere) {
    return;
}
```

At this point, we know that the mesh instance is influenced by the light, so increase the per-light meshlet count and add all the indices necessary to draw the meshlets:

```
uint per_light_offset =
    atomicAdd(per_light_meshlet_instances[light_index],
        mesh_draw.meshlet_count);

// Mesh inside light, add meshlets
for ( uint m = 0; m < mesh_draw.meshlet_count; ++m ) {
    uint meshlet_index = mesh_draw.meshlet_offset + m;
    meshlet_instances[light_index *
```

```
                    per_light_max_instances + per_light_offset
                        + m] = uvec2( mesh_instance_index,
                    meshlet_index );
        }
}
```

We will end up writing both the mesh instance index—to retrieve the world matrix—and the global meshlet index—to retrieve meshlet data in the following task shader. But before that, we need to generate an indirect draw commands list, and we will see that in the next section.

Also, based on the scene, we have a maximum number of meshlet instances, and we allocate them upfront for each light.

Indirect draw commands generation

This compute shader will generate a list of indirect commands for each light. We will use the last element of the per-light meshlet instances' **Shader Storage Buffer Object** (**SSBO**) to atomically count the number of indirect commands.

As before, reset `atomic int` used for the indirect commands count:

```
layout (local_size_x = 32, local_size_y = 1, local_size_z =
        1) in;
void main() {
    if (gl_GlobalInvocationID.x == 0 ) {
        // Use this as atomic int
        per_light_meshlet_instances[NUM_LIGHTS] = 0;
    }
    global_shader_barrier();
```

We will early out execution for rounded-up light indices:

```
    // Each thread writes the command of a light.
    uint light_index = gl_GlobalInvocationID.x;
    if ( light_index >= active_lights ) {
        return;
    }
```

We can finally write the indirect data and the packed light index, only if the light contains visible meshes.

Note that we write six commands, one for each cubemap face:

```
// Write per light shadow data
const uint visible_meshlets =
    per_light_meshlet_instances[light_index];
if (visible_meshlets > 0) {
    const uint command_offset =
        atomicAdd(per_light_meshlet_instances[
            NUM_LIGHTS], 6);
    uint packed_light_index = (light_index & 0xffff)
                                    << 16;
    meshlet_draw_commands[command_offset] =
        uvec4( ((visible_meshlets + 31) / 32), 1, 1,
            packed_light_index | 0 );
    meshlet_draw_commands[command_offset + 1] =
        uvec4( ((visible_meshlets + 31) / 32), 1, 1,
            packed_light_index | 1 );
... same for faces 2 to 5.
}
}
```

We now have a list of indirect drawing commands, six for each light. We will perform further culling in the task shader, shown in the next section.

Shadow cubemap face culling

In the indirect drawing task shader, we will add a mechanism to cull a meshlet against a cubemap to optimize the rendering. To do that, we have a utility method that will calculate, given a cubemap and an axis-aligned bounding box, which face will be visible in the cubemap. It is using cubemap face normals to calculate whether the center and extents are enclosed in the four planes used to define one of the six cubemap faces:

```
uint get_cube_face_mask( vec3 cube_map_pos, vec3 aabb_min,
                        vec3 aabb_max ) {
    vec3 plane_normals[] = {
        vec3(-1, 1, 0), vec3(1, 1, 0), vec3(1, 0, 1),
            vec3(1, 0, -1), vec3(0, 1, 1), vec3(0, -1, 1)
    };
    vec3 abs_plane_normals[] = {
```

```
                vec3(1, 1, 0), vec3(1, 1, 0), vec3(1, 0, 1),
                    vec3(1, 0, 1), vec3(0, 1, 1), vec3(0, 1, 1) };

        vec3 aabb_center = (aabb_min + aabb_max) * 0.5f;
        vec3 center = aabb_center - cube_map_pos;
        vec3 extents = (aabb_max - aabb_min) * 0.5f;

        bool rp[ 6 ];
        bool rn[ 6 ];

        for ( uint i = 0; i < 6; ++i ) {
            float dist = dot( center, plane_normals[ i ] );
            float radius = dot( extents, abs_plane_normals[ i ]
            );
            rp[ i ] = dist > -radius;
            rn[ i ] = dist < radius;
        }

        uint fpx = (rn[ 0 ] && rp[ 1 ] && rp[ 2 ] && rp[ 3 ] &&
                    aabb_max.x > cube_map_pos.x) ? 1 : 0;
        uint fnx = (rp[ 0 ] && rn[ 1 ] && rn[ 2 ] && rn[ 3 ] &&
                    aabb_min.x < cube_map_pos.x) ? 1 : 0;
        uint fpy = (rp[ 0 ] && rp[ 1 ] && rp[ 4 ] && rn[ 5 ] &&
                    aabb_max.y > cube_map_pos.y) ? 1 : 0;
        uint fny = (rn[ 0 ] && rn[ 1 ] && rn[ 4 ] && rp[ 5 ] &&
                    aabb_min.y < cube_map_pos.y) ? 1 : 0;
        uint fpz = (rp[ 2 ] && rn[ 3 ] && rp[ 4 ] && rp[ 5 ] &&
                    aabb_max.z > cube_map_pos.z) ? 1 : 0;
        uint fnz = (rn[ 2 ] && rp[ 3 ] && rn[ 4 ] && rn[ 5 ] &&
                    aabb_min.z < cube_map_pos.z) ? 1 : 0;

        return fpx | ( fnx << 1 ) | ( fpy << 2 ) | ( fny << 3 )
        | ( fpz << 4 ) | ( fnz << 5 );
}
```

These methods return a bitmask with each of the six bits set as 1 when the current axis-aligned bounding box is visible in that face.

Adding Shadows Using Mesh Shaders

Meshlet shadow rendering – task shader

Now that we have this utility method in place, we can look at the task shader. We changed some things with the other task shaders to accommodate the indirect drawing and to use layered rendering to write on different cubemaps.

We will pass uint to the mesh shader that packs a light and a face index to retrieve the corresponding cubemap view projection matrix and write to the correct layer:

```
out taskNV block {
    uint meshlet_indices[32];
     uint light_index_face_index;
};

void main() {
    uint task_index = gl_LocalInvocationID.x;
     uint meshlet_group_index = gl_WorkGroupID.x;
```

The meshlet calculation is tricky, as indices need to be calculated globally. We first calculate the meshlet index global to the indirect draw:

```
    // Calculate meshlet and light indices
    const uint meshlet_index = meshlet_group_index * 32 +
                               task_index;
```

We then extrapolate the light index and the read offset in the meshlet instances written in the culling compute shader:

```
    uint packed_light_index_face_index =
        meshlet_draw_commands[gl_DrawIDARB].w;
    const uint light_index =
        packed_light_index_face_index >> 16;
    const uint meshlet_index_read_offset =
        light_index * per_light_max_instances;
```

We can finally read the correct meshlet and mesh instance indices:

```
    uint global_meshlet_index =
      meshlet_instances[meshlet_index_read_offset +
      meshlet_index].y;
    uint mesh_instance_index =
```

```
            meshlet_instances[meshlet_index_read_offset +
                meshlet_index].x;
```

Now, we calculate the face index, and we can start the culling phase:

```
        const uint face_index = (packed_light_index_face_index
                                        & 0xf);
        mat4 model = mesh_instance_draws[mesh_instance_index]
                        .model;
```

Culling is performed similarly to previous task shaders, but we added also per-face culling:

```
        vec4 world_center = model * vec4(meshlets
                            [global_meshlet_index].center, 1);
        float scale = length( model[0] );
        float radius = meshlets[global_meshlet_index].radius *
                        scale * 1.1;    // Artificially inflate
                                            bounding sphere
 vec3 cone_axis =
    mat3( model ) * vec3(int(meshlets
    [global_meshlet_index].cone_axis[0]) / 127.0,
    int(meshlets[global_meshlet_index].
    cone_axis[1]) / 127.0,
    int(meshlets[global_meshlet_index].
    cone_axis[2]) / 127.0);
    float cone_cutoff = int(meshlets[global_meshlet_index].
                            cone_cutoff) / 127.0;

    bool accept = false;
    const vec4 camera_sphere = camera_spheres[light_index];

    // Cone cull
    accept = !coneCull(world_center.xyz, radius, cone_axis,
            cone_cutoff, camera_sphere.xyz) ||
            disable_shadow_meshlets_cone_cull();

    // Sphere culling
```

```glsl
    if ( accept ) {
        accept = sphere_intersect( world_center.xyz,
                radius, camera_sphere.xyz,
                camera_sphere.w) ||
                disable_shadow_meshlets_sphere_cull();
    }

    // Cubemap face culling
    if ( accept ) {

        uint visible_faces =
        get_cube_face_mask( camera_sphere.xyz,
            world_center.xyz - vec3(radius),
                world_center.xyz + vec3(radius));

        switch (face_index) {
            case 0:
                accept = (visible_faces & 1) != 0;
                break;
            case 1:
                accept = (visible_faces & 2) != 0;
                break;
...same for faces 2 to 5.
        }

        accept = accept || disable_shadow_meshlets_cubemap
                _face_cull();
    }
```

At this point of the shader we write each visible meshlet:

```glsl
        uvec4 ballot = subgroupBallot(accept);
    uint index = subgroupBallotExclusiveBitCount(ballot);

    if (accept)
        meshlet_indices[index] = global_meshlet_index;
    uint count = subgroupBallotBitCount(ballot);
```

```
        if (task_index == 0)
            gl_TaskCountNV = count;
```

And finally, we write the packed light and face index:

```
            light_index_face_index =
                packed_light_index_face_index;
    }
```

Next, we will see the mesh shader.

Meshlet shadow rendering – mesh shader

In this mesh shader, we will need to retrieve the layer index in the cubemap array to write to, and the light index to read the correct view-projection transform.

It's important to note that each face has its own transform, as we effectively render to each face separately.

Note that each face of the cubemap is considered a layer, thus the first cubemap will be rendered in layers 0-5, the second in layers 6-11, and so on.

Here is the code:

```
void main() {
    ...
    const uint light_index = light_index_face_index >> 16;
    const uint face_index = (light_index_face_index & 0xf);
    const int layer_index = int(CUBE_MAP_COUNT *
                                light_index + face_index);

    for (uint i = task_index; i < vertex_count; i +=
        32)    {
        uint vi = meshletData[vertexOffset + i];
        vec3 position = vec3(vertex_positions[vi].v.x,
                        vertex_positions[vi].v.y,
                        vertex_positions[vi].v.z);
        gl_MeshVerticesNV[ i ].gl_Position =
        view_projections[layer_index] *
            (model * vec4(position, 1));
    }
```

```
            uint indexGroupCount = (indexCount + 3) / 4;

            for (uint i = task_index; i < indexGroupCount; i += 32) {
                writePackedPrimitiveIndices4x8NV(i * 4,
                    meshletData[indexOffset + i]);
            }
```

Here, we write the layer index for each primitive. The usage of these offsets is to avoid bank conflict when writing, as seen on previous shaders:

```
            gl_MeshPrimitivesNV[task_index].gl_Layer =
                layer_index;
            gl_MeshPrimitivesNV[task_index + 32].gl_Layer =
                layer_index;
            gl_MeshPrimitivesNV[task_index + 64].gl_Layer =
                layer_index;
            gl_MeshPrimitivesNV[task_index + 96].gl_Layer =
                layer_index;

            if (task_index == 0) {
                gl_PrimitiveCountNV =
                    uint(meshlets[global_meshlet_index]
                        .triangle_count);
            }
        }
```

After this mesh shader rendering of shadows is complete, as there is no fragment shader associated. We can now read the generated shadow texture in the lighting shader, as explained in the next section.

Shadow map sampling

Given that we are just using hard shadow maps without filtering, the code to sample it is standard cubemap code. We calculate the world-to-light vector and use it to sample the cubemap.

Being a layered cubemap, we need both the 3D direction vector and the layer index, which we saved in the light itself:

```
    vec3 shadow_position_to_light = world_position -
                                    light.world_position;
const float closest_depth =
    texture(global_textures_cubemaps_array
    [nonuniformEXT(cubemap_shadows_index)],
    vec4(shadow_position_to_light,
    shadow_light_index)).r;
```

We then convert the depth to raw depth values with the `vector_to_depth_value` utility method, which takes the major axis from the light vector and converts it to raw depth so that we can compare the value read from the cubemap:

```
    const float current_depth = vector_to_depth_value
                                (shadow_position_to_light,
                                light.radius);
    float shadow = current_depth - bias < closest_depth ?
                   1 : 0;
```

The `vector_to_depth_value` method is shown here:

```
float vector_to_depth_value( inout vec3 Vec, float radius) {
    vec3 AbsVec = abs(Vec);
    float LocalZcomp = max(AbsVec.x, max(AbsVec.y,
                           AbsVec.z));
    const float f = radius;
    const float n = 0.01f;
    float NormZComp = -(f / (n - f) - (n * f) / (n - f) /
                       LocalZcomp);
    return NormZComp;
}
```

It takes the major axis from the direction vector and converts it to the raw depth using the formula coming from the projection matrix. This value is now usable with any depth value stored in a shadow map.

Here is an example of shadow coming from a point light:

Figure 8.4 – Shadows produced by a single point light in the scene

As we can see, shadows are a great improvement in rendering, giving the viewer a fundamental visual cue of an object's relationship with its environment.

Until here, we saw how to implement mesh shader-based shadows, but there is still room for improvement, especially in memory usage. Right now, this solution allocates upfront a single cubemap for each light, and the memory can become big quickly if we consider that we have six textures for each light.

We will look at a solution to lower the shadow map memory using sparse resources in the next section.

Improving shadow memory with Vulkan's sparse resources

As we mentioned at the end of the last section, we currently allocate the full memory for each cubemap for all the lights. Depending on the screen size of the light, we might be wasting memory as distant and small lights won't be able to take advantage of the high resolution of the shadow map.

For this reason, we have implemented a technique that allows us to dynamically determine the resolution of each cubemap based on the camera position. With this information, we can then manage a sparse texture and re-assign its memory at runtime depending on the requirements for a given frame.

Sparse textures (sometimes also referred to as **virtual textures**) can be implemented manually, but luckily, they are supported natively in Vulkan. We are now going to describe how to use the Vulkan API to implement them.

Creating and allocating sparse textures

Regular resources in Vulkan must be bound to a single memory allocation, and it's not possible to bind a given resource to a different allocation. This works well for resources that are known at runtime and that we don't expect to change.

However, when using cubemaps with a dynamic resolution, we need to be able to bind different portions of memory to a given resource. Vulkan exposes two methods to achieve this:

- Sparse resources allow us to bind a resource to non-contiguous memory allocations, but the full resource needs to be bound.
- Sparse residency allows us to partially bind a resource to different memory allocations. This is what we need for our implementation, as we are likely to use only a subsection of each layer of a cubemap.

Both methods allow users to re-bind a resource to different allocations at runtime. The first step needed to start using sparse resources is to pass the right flag when creating resources:

```
VkImageCreateInfo image_info = {
    VK_STRUCTURE_TYPE_IMAGE_CREATE_INFO };
image_info.flags = VK_IMAGE_CREATE_SPARSE_RESIDENCY_BIT |
                   VK_IMAGE_CREATE_SPARSE_BINDING_BIT;
```

Here, we are requesting a resource that supports sparse residency. Once an image is created, we don't need to immediately allocate memory for it. Instead, we are going to allocate a region of memory from which we will sub-allocate individual pages.

It's important to note that Vulkan has strict requirements for the size of individual pages. These are the required sizes taken from the Vulkan specification:

TEXEL SIZE (bits)	Block Shape (2D)	Block Shape (3D)
8-bit	256 × 256 × 1	64 × 32 × 32
16-bit	256 × 128 × 1	32 × 32 × 32
32-bit	128 × 128 × 1	32 × 32 × 16
64-bit	128 × 64 × 1	32 × 16 × 16
128-bit	64 × 64 × 1	16 × 16 × 16

Table 8.1 – Sparse block sizes for images

We will need this information to determine how many pages to allocate for a cubemap of a given size. We can retrieve the details for a given image with the following code:

```
VkPhysicalDeviceSparseImageFormatInfo2 format_info{
    VK_STRUCTURE_TYPE_PHYSICAL_DEVICE_SPARSE_IMAGE_FORMAT
        _INFO_2 };
format_info.format = texture->vk_format;
format_info.type = to_vk_image_type( texture->type );
format_info.samples = VK_SAMPLE_COUNT_1_BIT;
format_info.usage = texture->vk_usage;
format_info.tiling = VK_IMAGE_TILING_OPTIMAL;
```

The information for this structure is already available in our texture data structure. Next, we retrieve the block size for the given image:

```
Array<VkSparseImageFormatProperties2> properties;
vkGetPhysicalDeviceSparseImageFormatProperties2(
    vulkan_physical_device, &format_info, &property_count,
        properties.data );

u32 block_width = properties[ 0 ].properties.
                imageGranularity.width;
u32 block_height = properties[ 0 ].properties.
                imageGranularity.height;
```

With this information, we can now allocate a pool of pages. First, we retrieve the memory requirements for the image:

```
VkMemoryRequirements memory_requirements{ };
vkGetImageMemoryRequirements( vulkan_device, texture->
                              vk_image,
                              &memory_requirements );
```

This is the same code we would use for a regular texture; however, `memory_requirements.alignment` will contain the block size for the given image format.

Next, we compute the number of blocks we need to allocate for the given pool size:

```
u32 block_count = pool_size / ( block_width * block_height );
```

The final step is to allocate the pages that we will use later to write into our cubemaps:

```
VmaAllocationCreateInfo allocation_create_info{ };
allocation_create_info.usage = VMA_MEMORY_USAGE_GPU_ONLY;

VkMemoryRequirements page_memory_requirements;
page_memory_requirements.memoryTypeBits =
    memory_requirements.memoryTypeBits;
page_memory_requirements.alignment =
    memory_requirements.alignment;
page_memory_requirements.size =
    memory_requirements.alignment;

vmaAllocateMemoryPages( vma_allocator,
                        &page_memory_requirements,
                        &allocation_create_info,
                        block_count, page_pool->
                        vma_allocations.data, nullptr );
```

The **Vulkan Memory Allocator** (**VMA**) library provides a convenient API, `vmaAllocateMemoryPages`, to allocate multiple pages at once.

Now that we have allocated the memory for our shadow maps, we need to determine the resolution for each cubemap.

Choosing per-light shadow memory usage

To determine the resolution of the cubemap for a given light, we need to find how much influence it has on the scene. Intuitively, a more distant light will have less influence, depending on its radius (at least for point lights), but we need to quantify its amount of influence. We have implemented a solution similar to the one proposed in the *More Efficient Virtual Shadow Maps for Many Lights* paper.

We are going to reuse the concept introduced in the previous chapter: clusters. We subdivide the screen into tiles and *slice* the frustum on the *z* axis. This will give us smaller frustums (approximated by axis-aligned bounding boxes) that we will use to determine which regions are covered by a given light.

Let's look at the code to achieve this:

1. We start by computing the bounding box for each light in camera space:

    ```
    for ( u32 l = 0; l < light_count; ++l ) {
        Light& light = scene->lights[ l ];

        vec4s aabb_min_view = glms_mat4_mulv(
                                   last_camera.view,
                                   light.aabb_min );
        vec4s aabb_max_view = glms_mat4_mulv(
                                   last_camera.view,
                                   light.aabb_max );

        lights_aabb_view[ l * 2 ] = vec3s{
            aabb_min_view.x, aabb_min_view.y,
            aabb_min_view.z };
        lights_aabb_view[ l * 2 + 1 ] = vec3s{
            aabb_max_view.x, aabb_max_view.y,
            aabb_max_view.z };
    }
    ```

2. Next, we iterate over the tiles and each depth slice to compute each cluster position and size. We start by computing the camera space position of each tile:

    ```
    vec4s max_point_screen = vec4s{ f32( ( x + 1 ) *
                                tile_size ), f32( ( y + 1 ) *
                                tile_size ), 0.0f, 1.0f };
                                // Top Right
    ```

```
vec4s min_point_screen = vec4s{ f32( x * tile_size ),
                                f32( y * tile_size ),
                                0.0f, 1.0f }; // Top Right

vec3s max_point_view = screen_to_view(
                                max_point_screen );
vec3s min_point_view = screen_to_view(
                                min_point_screen );
```

3. We then need to determine the minimum and maximum depth for each slice:

```
f32 tile_near = z_near * pow( z_ratio, f32( z ) *
                                z_bin_range );
f32 tile_far  = z_near * pow( z_ratio, f32( z + 1 ) *
                                z_bin_range );
```

4. Finally, we combine both values to retrieve the position and size of the cluster:

```
vec3s min_point_near = line_intersection_to_z_plane(
                                eye_pos, min_point_view,
                                tile_near );
vec3s min_point_far  = line_intersection_to_z_plane(
                                eye_pos, min_point_view,
                                tile_far );
vec3s max_point_near = line_intersection_to_z_plane(
                                eye_pos, max_point_view,
                                tile_near );
vec3s max_point_far  = line_intersection_to_z_plane(
                                eye_pos, max_point_view,
                                tile_far );

vec3s min_point_aabb_view = glms_vec3_minv( glms_vec3_
minv( min_point_near, min_point_far ), glms_vec3_minv(
max_point_near, max_point_far ) );
vec3s max_point_aabb_view = glms_vec3_maxv( glms_vec3_
maxv( min_point_near, min_point_far ), glms_vec3_maxv(
max_point_near, max_point_far ) );
```

Now that we have obtained the cluster, we iterate over each light to determine whether it covers the cluster and the projection of the cluster onto the light; we'll clarify what this means in a moment.

5. The next step is a box intersection test between the light and the cluster:

```
f32 minx = min( min( light_aabb_min.x,
                light_aabb_max.x ), min(
                min_point_aabb_view.x,
                max_point_aabb_view.x ) );
f32 miny = min( min( light_aabb_min.y,
                light_aabb_max.y ), min(
                min_point_aabb_view.y,
                max_point_aabb_view.y ) );
f32 minz = min( min( light_aabb_min.z,
                light_aabb_max.z ), min(
                min_point_aabb_view.z,
                max_point_aabb_view.z ) );

f32 maxx = max( max( light_aabb_min.x,
                light_aabb_max.x ), max(
                min_point_aabb_view.x,
                max_point_aabb_view.x ) );
f32 maxy = max( max( light_aabb_min.y,
                light_aabb_max.y ), max(
                min_point_aabb_view.y,
                max_point_aabb_view.y ) );
f32 maxz = max( max( light_aabb_min.z,
                light_aabb_max.z ), max(
                min_point_aabb_view.z,
                max_point_aabb_view.z ) );

f32 dx = abs( maxx - minx );
f32 dy = abs( maxy - miny );
f32 dz = abs( maxz - minz );

f32 allx = abs( light_aabb_max.x - light_aabb_min.x )
         + abs( max_point_aabb_view.x -
           min_point_aabb_view.x );
f32 ally = abs( light_aabb_max.y - light_aabb_min.y )
         + abs( max_point_aabb_view.y -
```

```
                    min_point_aabb_view.y );
   f32 allz = abs( light_aabb_max.z - light_aabb_min.z )
            + abs( max_point_aabb_view.z -
                    min_point_aabb_view.z );
     bool intersects = ( dx <= allx ) && ( dy < ally ) &&
                       ( dz <= allz );
```

If they do intersect, we compute an approximation of the projected area of the light onto the cluster:

```
   f32 d = glms_vec2_distance( sphere_screen, tile_center );

   f32 diff = d * d - tile_radius_sq;

   if ( diff < 1.0e-4 ) {
       continue;
   }

   f32 solid_angle = ( 2.0f * rpi ) * ( 1.0f - ( sqrtf(
                       diff ) / d ) );

   f32 resolution = sqrtf( ( 4.0f * rpi * tile_pixels ) /
                       ( 6 * solid_angle ) );
```

The idea is to take the distance between the light and cluster center in screen space, compute the solid angle subtended by the cluster onto the light position, and compute the resolution of the cubemap using the size in pixels of the cluster. We refer you to the paper for more details.

We keep the maximum resolution, and we will use the computed value to bind the memory for each cubemap.

Rendering into a sparse shadow map

Now that we have determined the resolution of the cubemaps for a given frame, we need to assign the pre-allocated pages to our textures:

1. The first step is to record which pages are assigned to each image:

    ```
    VkImageAspectFlags aspect = TextureFormat::has_depth(
    texture->vk_format ) ? VK_IMAGE_ASPECT_DEPTH_BIT : VK_
    IMAGE_ASPECT_COLOR_BIT;
    for ( u32 block_y = 0; block_y < num_blocks_y;
    ```

```cpp
                    ++block_y ) {
            for ( u32 block_x = 0; block_x < num_blocks_x;
                ++block_x ) {
                    VkSparseImageMemoryBind sparse_bind{ };

                    VmaAllocation allocation =
                        page_pool-> vma_allocations
                            [ page_pool->used_pages++ ];
                    VmaAllocationInfo allocation_info{ };
                    vmaGetAllocationInfo( vma_allocator,
                                        allocation,
                                        &allocation_info );
```

We start by getting the details for the allocation that we are going to use for a given block, as we need to access the `VkDeviceMemory` handle and the offset into the pool it was allocated from.

2. Next, we compute the texture offset for each block:

```cpp
            i32 dest_x = ( i32 )( block_x * block_width +
                                    x );
            i32 dest_y = ( i32 )( block_y * block_height +
                                    y );
```

3. Then, we record this information into a `VkSparseImageMemoryBind` data structure that will be used later to update the memory bound to the cubemap texture:

```cpp
                sparse_bind.subresource.aspectMask = aspect;
                sparse_bind.subresource.arrayLayer = layer;
                sparse_bind.offset = { dest_x, dest_y, 0 };
                sparse_bind.extent = { block_width,
                                    block_height, 1 };
                sparse_bind.memory =
                    allocation_info.deviceMemory;
                sparse_bind.memoryOffset =
                    allocation_info.offset;

                pending_sparse_queue_binds.push( sparse_bind
                                                );
            }
        }
```

It's important to note that, as we mentioned previously, we only use one image with many layers. The layer variable determines which layer each allocation will belong to. Please refer to the full code for more details.

4. Finally, we record which image these pages will be bound to:

```
SparseMemoryBindInfo bind_info{ };
bind_info.image = texture->vk_image;
bind_info.binding_array_offset = array_offset;
bind_info.count = num_blocks;

pending_sparse_memory_info.push( bind_info );
```

`array_offset` is an offset into the `pending_sparse_queue_binds` array so that we can store all pending allocations in a single array.

Now that we have recorded the list of allocation updates, we need to submit them to a queue for them to be executed by the GPU.

5. First, we populate a `VkSparseImageMemoryBindInfo` structure for each layer:

```
for ( u32 b = 0; b < pending_sparse_memory_info.size;
    ++b ) {
    SparseMemoryBindInfo& internal_info =
        pending_sparse_memory_info[ b ];

    VkSparseImageMemoryBindInfo& info =
        sparse_binding_infos[ b ];
    info.image = internal_info.image;
    info.bindCount = internal_info.count;
    info.pBinds = pending_sparse_queue_binds.data +
                  internal_info.binding_array_offset;
}
```

6. Next, we submit all pending binding operations to the main queue:

```
VkBindSparseInfo sparse_info{
    VK_STRUCTURE_TYPE_BIND_SPARSE_INFO };
sparse_info.imageBindCount =
    sparse_binding_infos.size;
sparse_info.pImageBinds = sparse_binding_infos.data;
sparse_info.signalSemaphoreCount = 1;
```

```
          sparse_info.pSignalSemaphores =
            &vulkan_bind_semaphore;

          vkQueueBindSparse( vulkan_main_queue, 1, &sparse_info,
                             VK_NULL_HANDLE );
```

It's important to note that it's the responsibility of the user to make sure this operation is completed before accessing the resources whose allocations we just updated. We achieve this by signaling a semaphore, `vulkan_bind_semaphore`, which will then be waited on by the main rendering work submission.

It's important to note that the queue we call `vkQueueBindSparse` on must have the `VK_QUEUE_SPARSE_BINDING_BIT` flag.

In this section, we have covered the steps necessary to allocate and use sparse textures. We first explained how sparse textures work and why they are useful for our cubemap use case.

Next, we illustrated the algorithm we used to dynamically determine the resolution of each cubemap based on each light contribution to the scene. Finally, we demonstrated how to use the Vulkan API to bind memory to sparse resources.

Summary

In this chapter, we extended our lighting system to support many point lights with an efficient implementation. We started with a brief history of shadow algorithms, and their benefits and shortcomings, up until some of the most recent techniques that take advantage of raytracing hardware.

Next, we covered our implementation of shadows for many point lights. We explained how cubemaps are generated for each light and the optimizations we implemented to make the algorithm scale to many lights. In particular, we highlighted the culling method we reused from the main geometry pass and the use of a single indirect draw call for each light.

In the last section, we introduced sparse textures, a technique that allows us to dynamically bind memory to a given resource. We highlighted the algorithm we used to determine the contribution of each point light to the scene and how we use that information to determine the resolution of each cubemap. Finally, we demonstrated how to use sparse resources with the Vulkan API.

While we only covered point lights in this chapter, some of the techniques can be reused with other types of lights. Some steps could also be optimized further: for instance, it's possible to further reduce the cubemap resolution to account only for the area where geometry is visible.

The cluster computation is currently done on the CPU for clarity and to avoid having to read back the cluster data from the GPU, which could be a slow operation, but it might be worth moving the implementation to the GPU. We encourage you to experiment with the code and add more features!

Further reading

The book *Real-Time Shadows* provides a good overview of many techniques to implement shadows, many of which are still in use today.

GPU Pro 360 Guide to Shadows collects articles from the *GPU Pro* series that are focused on shadows.

An interesting technique described in the book is called tetrahedron shadow mapping: the idea is to project the shadow map to a tetrahedron and then unwrap it to a single texture.

The original concept was introduced in the *Shadow Mapping for Omnidirectional Light Using Tetrahedron Mapping* chapter (originally published in *GPU Pro*) and later expanded in *Tile-based Omnidirectional Shadows* (originally published in *GPU Pro 6*).

For more details, we refer you to the code provided by the author: http://www.hd-prg.com/tileBasedShadows.html.

Our sparse texture implementation is based on this SIGGRAPH presentation: https://efficientshading.com/wp-content/uploads/s2015_shadows.pdf.

This expands on their original paper, found here: http://newq.net/dl/pub/MoreEfficientClusteredShadowsPreprint.pdf.

While we haven't implemented it in this chapter, shadow map caching is an important technique to reduce the cost of computing shadow maps and amortize the shadow map updates over several frames.

A good starting point is this presentation: https://www.activision.com/cdn/research/2017_DD_Rendering_of_COD_IW.pdf.

Our cluster computation closely follows the one presented in this article: http://www.aortiz.me/2018/12/21/CG.html#part-2.

The Vulkan specification provides many more details on how to use the API for sparse resources: https://registry.khronos.org/vulkan/specs/1.2-extensions/html/vkspec.html#sparsememory.

9
Implementing Variable Rate Shading

In this chapter, we are going to implement a technique that has become quite popular recently: variable rate shading. This technique allows developers to specify at which rate to shade individual pixels while maintaining the same perceived visual quality. This approach allows us to reduce the time taken for some rendering passes, and the time savings can be used to implement more features or render at higher resolutions.

Vulkan provides multiple options to integrate this technique into an application, and we are going to provide an overview of all of them. This feature is provided through an extension that is supported only on recent hardware, but it's possible to implement it manually using compute shaders. We won't cover this option here, but we are going to point you to the relevant resources in the *Further reading* section.

In this chapter, we'll cover the following main topics:

- Introducing variable rate shading
- Implementing variable rate shading using the Vulkan API
- Using specialization constants to configure compute shaders

Technical requirements

The code for this chapter can be found at the following URL: https://github.com/PacktPublishing/Mastering-Graphics-Programming-with-Vulkan/tree/main/source/chapter9.

Introducing variable rate shading

Variable rate shading (**VRS**) is a technique that allows developers to control the rate at which fragments are shaded. When this feature is disabled, all fragments are shaded using a 1x1 rate, meaning that the fragment shader will run for all fragments in the image.

With the introduction of **virtual reality** (**VR**) headsets, developers have started to investigate ways to reduce the amount of time it takes to render a frame. This is crucial, not only because VR requires rendering two frames (one for the right eye and one for the left) but also because VR is quite sensitive to frame latency, and higher frame rates are required to avoid users experiencing motion sickness.

One technique that was developed is called **foveated rendering**: the idea is to render the center of the image at full rate while lowering the quality outside the center. Developers have noticed that users are focused primarily on the central region of the image and don't notice the lower quality in the surrounding area.

It turns out that this approach can be generalized outside of VR. For this reason, APIs such as DirectX® and Vulkan have added support for this feature natively.

With this more general approach, it's possible to specify multiple shading rates for individual fragments. The rates that are usually recommended are 1x1, 1x2, 2x1, and 2x2. While it might be possible to adopt higher shading rates, it usually leads to a visible artifact in the final frame.

As we mentioned, a 1x1 rate implies that the fragment shader will run for all fragments within an image, and there are no time savings. This is the default behavior when VRS is not enabled.

A rate of 1x2 or 2x1 means that two fragments will be shaded by a single fragment shader invocation, and the computed value is applied to both fragments. Likewise, with a 2x2 shading rate, a single fragment invocation will compute and apply a single value to four fragments.

Determining the shading rate

There are multiple options to choose the shading rate for individual fragments, and the one we have implemented is to run an edge detection filter based on luminance after the lighting pass.

The idea is to reduce the shading rate in the areas of the image where luminance is uniform and use a full rate in transition areas. This approach works because the human eye is more susceptible to noticing changes in those areas compared to ones that have more uniform values.

The filter we have used is the traditional Sobel filter in a 3x3 configuration. For each fragment, we compute two values:

$$G_x = \begin{bmatrix} +1 & 0 & -1 \\ +2 & 0 & -2 \\ +1 & 0 & -1 \end{bmatrix} * A \text{ and } G_y = \begin{bmatrix} +1 & +2 & +1 \\ 0 & 0 & 0 \\ -1 & -2 & -1 \end{bmatrix} * A$$

Figure 9.1 – The filters used to approximate the x and y derivative for a given fragment (source: Wikipedia –https://en.wikipedia.org/wiki/Sobel_operator)

Introducing variable rate shading | 211

We then compute the final derivative value with the following formula:

$$G = \sqrt{G_x{}^2 + G_y{}^2}$$

Figure 9.2 – The formula to approximate the derivative value (source: Wikipedia –https://en.wikipedia.org/wiki/Sobel_operator)

Let's apply the Sobel filter to the following image:

Figure 9.3 – The rendered frame after the lighting pass

It gives us the following shading rate mask:

Figure 9.4 – The computed shading rate mask

In our implementation, we are going to use a full 1x1 rate for fragments that have a G value (as computed by the formula in *Figure 9.2*) greater than 0.1. These are the black pixels in *Figure 9.4*.

For fragments whose G value is below 0.1, we are going to use a 2x2 rate, and these fragments are the red pixels in the screenshot in *Figure 9.4*. We will explain how the values in the mask are computed in the next section.

In this section, we have introduced the concepts behind variable rate shading and provided the details for our implementation. In the next section, we will demonstrate how to implement this feature using the Vulkan API.

Integrating variable rate shading using Vulkan

As we mentioned in the previous section, the fragment shading rate functionality is provided through the VK_KHR_fragment_shading_rate extension. As with other option extensions, make sure the device you are using supports it before calling the related APIs.

Vulkan provides three methods to control the shading rate:

- Per draw
- Per primitive
- Using an image attachment for a render pass

To use a custom shading rate per draw, there are two options. We can pass a `VkPipelineFragmentShadingRateStateCreateInfoKHR` structure when creating a pipeline, or we can call `vkCmdSetFragmentShadingRateKHR` at runtime.

This approach is useful when we know in advance that some draws can be performed at a lower rate without affecting quality. This could include the sky or objects we know are far away from the camera.

It's also possible to provide a shading rate per primitive. This is accomplished by populating the `PrimitiveShadingRateKHR` built-in shader variable from a vertex or mesh shader.

This can be useful if, for instance, we have determined we can use a lower level of details in the mesh shader and a lower rate to render that particular primitive.

For our implementation, we decided to use the third approach as it is more flexible for our use case. As we mentioned in the previous section, we first need to compute the variable rate shading mask. This is done using a compute shader that populates the shading rate image.

We start by populating a table that is shared within a shader invocation:

```
shared float local_image_data[ LOCAL_DATA_SIZE ][
    LOCAL_DATA_SIZE ];

local_image_data[ local_index.y ][ local_index.x ] =
    luminance( texelFetch( global_textures[
    color_image_index ], global_index, 0 ).rgb );

barrier();
```

Each entry in the table contains the luminance value for the fragment for this shader invocation.

We used this approach to reduce the number of texture reads we needed to perform. If each shader thread had to read the values it needs individually, we would need eight texture reads. With this solution, only one read per thread is needed.

There is a caveat for the threads of the fragments on the border of the region we are processing. With each shader invocation, we process 16x16 fragments, but because of how the Sobel filter works, we need to fill an 18x18 table. For the threads on the border, we need to do some extra processing to make sure the table is fully filled. We have omitted the code here for brevity.

Notice that we have to use the `barrier()` method to guarantee that all threads within this workgroup have completed their write. Without this call, threads will compute the wrong value, as the table will not be filled correctly.

Implementing Variable Rate Shading

Next, we compute the value of the derivative for a given fragment:

```
float dx = local_image_data[ local_index.y - 1 ][
    local_index.x - 1 ] - local_image_data[
    local_index.y - 1 ][ local_index.x + 1 ] +
    2 * local_image_data[ local_index.y ][
    local_index.x - 1 ] -
    2 * local_image_data[ local_index.y ][
    local_index.x + 1 ] +
    local_image_data[ local_index.y + 1][
    local_index.x - 1 ] -
    local_image_data[ local_index.y + 1 ][
    local_index.x + 1 ];

float dy = local_image_data[ local_index.y - 1 ][
    local_index.x - 1 ] +
    2 * local_image_data[ local_index.y - 1 ][
    local_index.x ] +
    local_image_data[ local_index.y - 1 ][
    local_index.x + 1 ] -
    local_image_data[ local_index.y + 1 ][
    local_index.x - 1 ] -
    2 * local_image_data[ local_index.y + 1 ][
    local_index.x ] -
    local_image_data[ local_index.y + 1 ][
    local_index.x + 1 ];

float d = pow( dx, 2 ) + pow( dy, 2 );
```

This is simply applying the formula we introduced in the previous section. Now that we have computed the derivative, we need to store the shading rate for this fragment:

```
uint rate = 1 << 2 | 1;

if ( d > 0.1 ) {
    rate = 0;
}
```

```
imageStore( global_uimages_2d[ fsr_image_index ], ivec2(
    gl_GlobalInvocationID.xy ), uvec4( rate, 0, 0, 0 ) );
```

The rate is computed following the formula from the Vulkan specification:

```
size_w = 2^( ( texel / 4 ) & 3 )
size_h = 2^( texel & 3 )
```

In our case, we are computing the `texel` value in the previous formula. We are setting the exponent (`0` or `1`) for the `x` and `y` shading rates and storing the value in the shading rate image.

Once the shading rate image has been filled, we can use it to provide the shading rate for the render pass for the next frame. Before using this image, we need to transition it to the correct layout:

```
VK_IMAGE_LAYOUT_FRAGMENT_SHADING_RATE_ATTACHMENT_OPTIMAL_
    KHR
```

We also need to use a new pipeline stage:

```
VK_PIPELINE_STAGE_FRAGMENT_SHADING_RATE_ATTACHMENT_BIT_KHR
```

There are a few options to use the newly created shading rate image as part of a render pass. The `VkSubpassDescription2` structure can be extended by a `VkFragmentShadingRateAttachmentInfoKHR` structure, which specifies which attachment to use as the fragment shading rate. Since we aren't using the `RenderPass2` extension just yet, we opted to extend our existing dynamic rendering implementation.

We have to extend the `VkRenderingInfoKHR` structure using the following code:

```
VkRenderingFragmentShadingRateAttachmentInfoKHR
shading_rate_info {
    VK_STRUCTURE_TYPE_RENDERING_FRAGMENT_SHADING
        _RATE_ATTACHMENT_INFO_KHR };
shading_rate_info.imageView = texture->vk_image_view;
shading_rate_info.imageLayout =
    VK_IMAGE_LAYOUT_FRAGMENT_SHADING_RATE
        _ATTACHMENT_OPTIMAL_KHR;
shading_rate_info.shadingRateAttachmentTexelSize = { 1, 1 };

rendering_info.pNext = ( void* )&shading_rate_info;
```

And that's it! The shader used for rendering doesn't require any modifications.

216   Implementing Variable Rate Shading

In this section, we have detailed the changes required to our rendering code to make use of a shading rate image. We have also provided the implementation of the compute shader that implements an edge detection algorithm based on the Sobel filter.

The result of this algorithm is then used to determine the shading rate for each fragment.

In the next section, we are going to introduce specialization constants, a Vulkan feature that allows us to control the workgroup size of compute shaders for optimal performance.

Taking advantage of specialization constants

Specialization constants are a Vulkan feature that allows developers to define constant values when creating a pipeline. This is particularly useful when the same shader is needed for multiple use cases that differ only for some constant values, for example, materials. This is a more elegant solution compared to pre-processor definitions as they can be dynamically controlled at runtime without having to recompile the shaders.

In our case, we want to be able to control the workgroup size of compute shaders based on the hardware we are running to obtain the best performance:

1. The first step in the implementation is to determine whether a shader uses specialization constants. We now identify any variables that have been decorated with the following type when parsing the shader SPIR-V:

   ```
   case ( SpvDecorationSpecId ):
   {
       id.binding = data[ word_index + 3 ];
       break;
   }
   ```

2. When parsing all the variables, we now save the specialization constants' details so that they can be used when compiling a pipeline that uses this shader:

   ```
   switch ( id.op ) {
       case ( SpvOpSpecConstantTrue ):
       case ( SpvOpSpecConstantFalse ):
       case ( SpvOpSpecConstant ):
       case ( SpvOpSpecConstantOp ):
       case ( SpvOpSpecConstantComposite ):
       {
           Id& id_spec_binding = ids[ id.type_index ];
   ```

```
      SpecializationConstant&
         specialization_constant = parse_result->
         specialization_constants[
         parse_result->
         specialization_constants_count
         ];
            specialization_constant.binding =
               id_spec_binding.binding;
            specialization_constant.byte_stride =
               id.width / 8;
            specialization_constant.default_value =
               id.value;

            SpecializationName& specialization_name =
             parse_result->specialization_names[
                parse_result->
                specialization_constants_count ];
            raptor::StringView::copy_to(
               id_spec_binding.name,
                  specialization_name.name, 32 );

            ++parse_result->
               specialization_constants_count;

            break;
      }
   }
```

3. Now that we have the specialization constants' information, we can change their values when creating a pipeline. We start by filling a `VkSpecializationInfo` structure:

```
VkSpecializationInfo specialization_info;
VkSpecializationMapEntry specialization_entries[
    spirv::k_max_specialization_constants ];
u32 specialization_data[
    spirv::k_max_specialization_constants ];
```

218 Implementing Variable Rate Shading

```
       specialization_info.mapEntryCount = shader_state->
           parse_result->specialization_constants_count;
       specialization_info.dataSize = shader_state->
           parse_result->specialization_constants_count *
               sizeof( u32 );
       specialization_info.pMapEntries =
           specialization_entries
           ;
       specialization_info.pData = specialization_data;
```

4. We then set the value for each specialization constant entry:

```
       for ( u32 i = 0; i < shader_state->parse_result->
           specialization_constants_count; ++i ) {

           const spirv::SpecializationConstant&
               specialization_constant = shader_state->
                   parse_result->
                       specialization_constants[ i ];
           cstring specialization_name = shader_state->
               parse_result->specialization_names[ i ].name;
           VkSpecializationMapEntry& specialization_entry =
               specialization_entries[ i ];

           if ( strcmp(specialization_name, "SUBGROUP_SIZE")
               == 0 ) {
                           specialization_entry.constantID =
                               specialization_constant.binding;
               specialization_entry.size = sizeof( u32 );
               specialization_entry.offset = i * sizeof( u32 );

               specialization_data[ i ] = subgroup_size;
           }
       }
```

In our case, we are looking for a variable named `SUBGROUP_SIZE`. The final step is to store the specialization constant details in the shader stage structure that will be used when creating the pipeline:

```
shader_stage_info.pSpecializationInfo =
    &specialization_info;
```

During compilations, the driver and compiler will override the existing value in the shader with the one we specified.

In this section, we have illustrated how to take advantage of specialization constants to modify shader behavior at runtime. We detailed the changes we made to identify specialization constants when parsing the SPIR-V binary. We then highlighted the new code required to override a specialization constant value when creating a pipeline.

Summary

In this chapter, we introduced the variable rate shading technique. We gave a brief overview of this approach and how it can be used to improve the performance of some rendering passes without a loss in perceived quality. We also explained the edge detection algorithm used to determine the shading rate for each fragment.

In the next section, we illustrated the changes necessary to enable and use this feature with the Vulkan API. We detailed the options available to change the shading rate at the draw, primitive, and render pass level. We then explained the implementation of the edge detection algorithm using a compute shader and how the result is used to generate the shading rate image.

In the last section, we introduced specialization constants, a mechanism provided by the Vulkan API to modify shader constant values at compile time. We illustrated how this feature can be used to control the group size of compute shaders for optimal performance based on the device our code is running on.

In the next chapter, we will introduce volumetric effects into our scene. This technique allows us to set the mood of the environment and can be used to direct the attention of the player to a particular area.

Further reading

We only gave a brief overview of the Vulkan APIs for variable rate shading. We recommend reading the specification for further details: https://registry.khronos.org/vulkan/specs/1.3-extensions/html/vkspec.html#primsrast-fragment-shading-rate.

Most of the resources available online seem to be focused on the DirectX API, but the same approach can be translated to Vulkan. This blog post provides some details on the benefits of VRS: https://devblogs.microsoft.com/directx/variable-rate-shading-a-scalpel-in-a-world-of-sledgehammers/.

These two videos provide in-depth details on integrating VRS into existing game engines. The section on how to implement VRS using compute shader is particularly interesting:

- `https://www.youtube.com/watch?v=pPyN9r5QNbs`
- `https://www.youtube.com/watch?v=Sswuj7BFjGo`

This article illustrates how VRS can also have other use cases, for instance, to accelerate raytracing: `https://interplayoflight.wordpress.com/2022/05/29/accelerating-raytracing-using-software-vrs/`.

10
Adding Volumetric Fog

After adding variable rate shading in the previous chapter, we will implement another modern technique that will enhance the visuals of the Raptor Engine: **Volumetric Fog**. Volumetric rendering and fog are very old topics in rendering literature, but until a few years ago, they were considered impossible for real-time usage.

The possibility of making this technique feasible in real-time stems from the observation that fog is a low-frequency effect; thus the rendering can be at a much lower resolution than the screen, increasing the performance in real-time usage.

Also, the introduction of compute shaders, and thus generic GPU programming, paired with clever observations about approximations and optimizations of the volumetric aspect of the technique, paved the way to unlocking real-time Volumetric Fog.

The main idea comes from the seminal paper by Bart Wronski (https://bartwronski.files.wordpress.com/2014/08/bwronski_volumetric_fog_siggraph2014.pdf) at Siggraph 2014, where he described what is still the core idea behind this technique even after almost 10 years.

Implementing this technique will also be important for learning more about the synergies between different rendering parts of a frame: developing a single technique can be challenging, but the interaction with the rest of the technology is a very important part as well and can add to the challenge of the technique

In this chapter, we'll cover the following main topics:

- Introducing Volumetric Fog rendering
- Implementing the Volumetric Fog base technique
- Adding spatial and temporal filtering to improve visuals

By the end of this chapter, we will have Volumetric Fog integrated into the Raptor Engine, interacting with the scenery and all the dynamic lights, as shown in the following figure:

Figure 10.1 – Volumetric Fog with a density volume and three shadow casting lights

Technical requirements

The code for this chapter can be found at the following URL: `https://github.com/PacktPublishing/Mastering-Graphics-Programming-with-Vulkan/tree/main/source/chapter10`.

Introducing Volumetric Fog Rendering

What exactly is **Volumetric Fog Rendering**? As the name suggests, it is the combination of Volumetric Rendering and the fog phenomena. We will now give some background on those components and see how they are combined in the final technique.

Let's begin with Volumetric Rendering.

Volumetric Rendering

This rendering technique describes the visuals associated with what happens to light when it travels through a participating medium. A participating medium is a volume that contains local changes to density or albedo.

The following diagram summarizes what happens to photons in a participating medium:

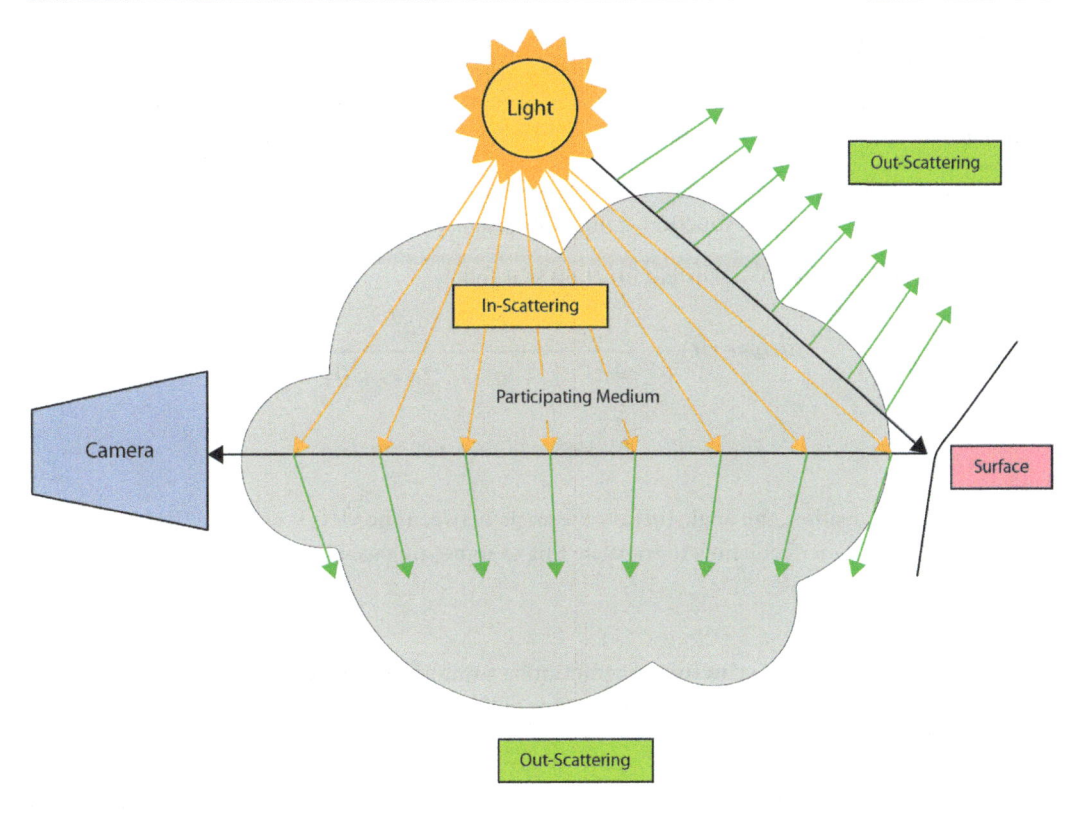

Figure 10.2 – Light behavior in a participating medium

What we are trying to describe is how light changes when going through a participating medium, namely a fog volume (or clouds or atmospheric scattering).

There are three main phenomena that happen, as follows:

- **Absorption**: This happens when light is simply trapped inside the medium and does not go outside. It is a net loss of energy.
- **Out-scattering**: This is depicted using green arrows in *Figure 10.2* and is again a loss of energy coming out (and thus visible) from the medium.
- **In-scattering**: This is the energy coming from the lights that are interacting with the medium.

While these three phenomena are enough to describe what happens to light, there are three other components that need to be understood before having a complete picture of volumetric rendering.

Phase function

The first component is the **phase function**. This function describes the scattering of light in different directions. It is dependent on the angle between the light vector and the outgoing directions.

This function can be complex and tries to describe scattering in a realistic way, but the most commonly used is the Henyey-Greenstein function, a function that also takes into consideration anisotropy.

The formula for the Henyey-Greenstein function is as follows:

$$phase(\theta) = \frac{1}{4\pi} \frac{1-g^2}{(1+g^2-2g\cos\theta)^{3/2}}$$

Figure 10.3 – The Henyey-Greenstein function

In the preceding equation, the angle theta is the angle between the view vector and the light vector. We will see in the shader code how to translate this to something usable.

Extinction

The second component is **extinction**. Extinction is a quantity that describes how much light is scattered. We will use this in the intermediate steps of the algorithm, but to apply the calculated fog, we will need transmittance.

Transmittance

The third and final component is **transmittance**. Transmittance is the extinction of light through a segment of the medium, and it is calculated using the Beer-Lambert law:

$$T(A \to B) = e^{-\int_A^B \beta e(x)dx}$$

Figure 10.4 – The Beer-Lambert law

In the final integration step, we will calculate the transmittance and use it to choose how to apply fog to the scene. The important thing here is to get a basic grasp of the concepts; there will be links provided to deepen your understanding of the mathematical background at the end of the chapter.

We now have all the concepts needed to see the implementation details of Volumetric Fog.

Volumetric Fog

Now that we have an idea of the different components that contribute to Volumetric Rendering, we can take a bird's-eye view of the algorithm. One of the first and most clever ideas that Bart Wronski had while developing this technique is the usage of a Frustum Aligned Volume Texture, like so:

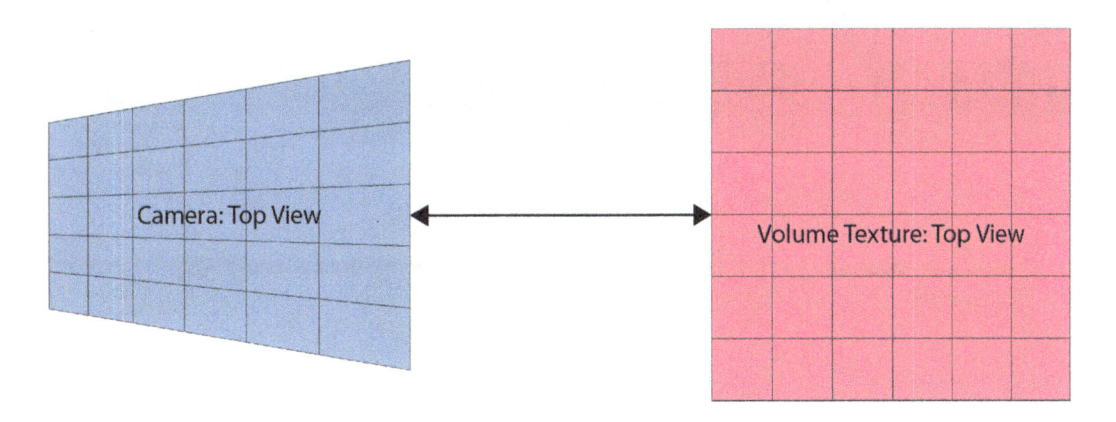

Figure 10.5 – Frustum Aligned Volume Texture

Using a volume texture and math associated with standard rasterization rendering, we can create a mapping between the camera frustum and the texture. This mapping is already happening in the different stages of rendering, for example, when multiplying a vertex position for the view-projection matrix, so it is not something new.

What is new is storing information in a volume texture to calculate the volumetric rendering. Each element of this texture is commonly called the **froxel**, that stands for **frustum voxel**.

We chose to have a texture with a width, height, and depth of 128 units, but other solutions use a width and height dependent on the screen resolution, similar to clustered shading.

We will use different textures with this resolution as an intermediate step, and for additional filtering, we will discuss this later. One additional decision is to increase the resolution of the camera by using a non-linear depth distribution to map a linear range to an exponential one.

We will use a distribution function, such as the one used by Id in their iD Tech engine, like so:

$$Zslice = Near_z * (Far_z/Near_z)^{slice/numSlices}$$

Figure 10.6 – Volume texture depth slice on the Z coordinate function

Now that we have decided on the mapping between the volumetric texture and world units, we can describe the steps needed to have a fully working Volumetric Fog solution.

The algorithm is outlined in the following diagram, where rectangles represent shader executions while ellipses represent textures:

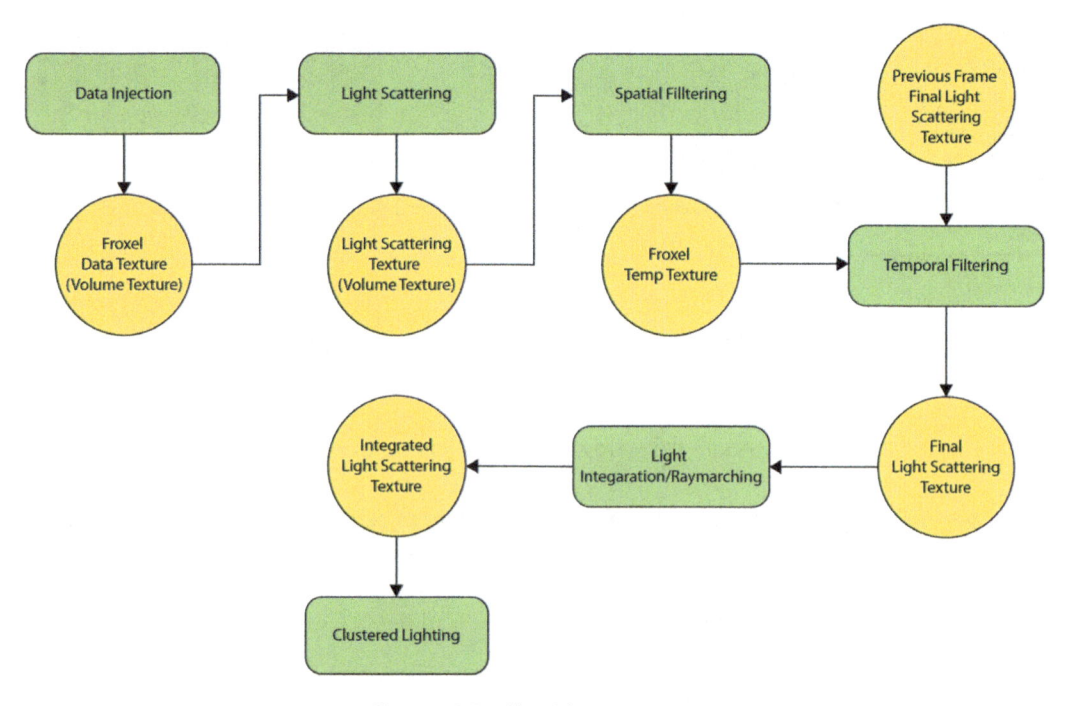

Figure 10.7 – Algorithm overview

We will now see each step of the algorithm to create a mind model of what is happening, and we will review the shader later in the chapter.

Data injection

The first step is the data injection. This shader will add some colored fog in the form of color and density into the first Frustum Aligned Texture containing only data. We decided to add a constant fog, a height-based fog, and a fog volume to mimic a more realistic game development setup.

Light scattering

When performing the light scattering, we calculate the in-scattering coming from the lights in the scene.

Having a working Clustered Lighting algorithm, we will reuse the same data structures to calculate the light contribution for each froxel, paying attention to treating the light in a different way than the standard Clustered Lighting – we don't have diffuse or specular here, but just a global term given by attenuation, shadow, and phase.

We also sample shadow maps associated with the lights for even more realistic behavior.

Spatial filtering

To remove some of the noise, we apply a Gaussian filter only on the X and Y axis of the Frustum Aligned Texture, and then we pass to the most important filter, the temporal one.

Temporal filtering

This filter is what really improves the visuals by giving the possibility of adding some noise at different steps of the algorithm to remove some banding. It will read the previous frame's final texture (the one before the integration) and blend the current light scattering result with the previous one based on some constant factor.

This is a very difficult topic, as temporal filtering and reprojection can cause a few issues. We will have a much bigger discussion in the next chapter when talking about **Temporal Anti-Aliasing (TAA)**

With the scattering and extinction finalized, we can perform the light integration and thus prepare the texture that will be sampled by the scene.

Light integration

This step prepares another Frustum Aligned Volumetric Texture to contain an integration of the fog. Basically, this shader simulates a low-resolution ray marching so that this result can be sampled by the scene.

Ray marching normally starts from the camera toward the far plane of the scene. The combination of the Frustum Aligned Texture and this integration gives, for each froxel, a cached ray marching of the light scattering to be easily sampled by the scene. In this step, from all the extinction saved in previous textures, we finally calculate the transmittance with the Beer-Lambert law and use that to merge the fog into the scene.

This and temporal filtering are some of the big innovations that unlocked the real-time possibility of this algorithm. In more advanced solutions, such as in the game Red Dead Redemption 2, an additional ray marching can be added to simulate fog at much further distances.

It also allows for blending fog and Volumetric Clouds, which use a pure ray marching approach, to have an almost seamless transition. This is explained in detail in the Siggraph presentation about Red Dead Redemption 2 rendering.

Scene application in Clustered Lighting

The final step is to read the Volumetric Texture in the lighting shader using the world position. We can read the depth buffer, calculate the world position, calculate the froxel coordinates and sample the texture.

An additional step to further smooth the volumetric look is to render to a half-resolution texture the scene application and then apply it to the scene with a geometry-aware upsampling, but this will be left as an exercise for you to complete.

Implementing Volumetric Fog Rendering

We now have all the knowledge necessary to read the code needed to get this algorithm fully working. From a CPU perspective, it is just a series of compute shaders dispatches, so it is straightforward.

The core of this technique is implemented throughout various shaders, and thus on the GPU, working for almost all steps on the frustum aligned Volumetric Texture we talked about in the previous section.

Figure 10.7 shows the different algorithm steps, and we will see each one individually in the following sections.

Data injection

In the first shader, we will write scattering and extinction, starting from the color and density of different fog phenomena.

We decided to add three different fog effects, as follows:

- A constant fog
- Height fog
- Fog in a volume

For each fog, we need to calculate scattering and extinction and accumulate them.

The following code converts color and density to scattering and extinction:

```
vec4 scattering_extinction_from_color_density( vec3 color,
    float density ) {
    const float extinction = scattering_factor * density;
    return vec4( color * extinction, extinction );
}
```

We can now have a look at the main shader. This shader, as most of the others in this chapter, will be scheduled to have one thread for one froxel cell.

In the first section, we will see the dispatch and code to calculate world position:

```
layout (local_size_x = 8, local_size_y = 8, local_size_z =
        1) in;
void main() {
    ivec3 froxel_coord = ivec3(gl_GlobalInvocationID.xyz);
    vec3 world_position = world_from_froxel(froxel_coord);

    vec4 scattering_extinction = vec4(0);
```

We add an optional noise to animate the fog and break the constant density:

```
vec3 sampling_coord = world_position *
   volumetric_noise_position_multiplier +
   vec3(1,0.1,2) * current_frame *
   volumetric_noise_speed_multiplier;

vec4 sampled_noise = texture(
   global_textures_3d[volumetric_noise_texture_index],
   sampling_coord);
float fog_noise = sampled_noise.x;
```

Here, we add and accumulate constant fog:

```
// Add constant fog
float fog_density = density_modifier * fog_noise;
scattering_extinction +=
   scattering_extinction_from_color_density(
   vec3(0.5), fog_density );
```

Then, add and accumulate height fog:

```
// Add height fog
float height_fog = height_fog_density *
   exp(-height_fog_falloff * max(world_position.y, 0)) *
   fog_noise;
scattering_extinction +=
   scattering_extinction_from_color_density(
   vec3(0.5), height_fog );
```

And finally, add density from a box:

```
// Add density from box
vec3 box = abs(world_position - box_position);
if (all(lessThanEqual(box, box_size))) {
   vec4 box_fog_color = unpack_color_rgba( box_color
                                            );
   scattering_extinction +=
       scattering_extinction_from_color_density(
```

```
                    box_fog_color.rgb, box_fog_density *
                        fog_noise);
    }
```

We finally store the scattering and extinction, ready to be lit in the next shader:

```
    imageStore(global_images_3d[froxel_data_texture_index],
            froxel_coord.xyz, scattering_extinction );
}
```

Calculating the lighting contribution

Lighting will be performed using the Clustered Lighting data structures already used in general lighting functions. In this shader, we calculate the in-scattering of light.

Shader dispatching is the same as for the previous shader, one thread for one froxel:

```
layout (local_size_x = 8, local_size_y = 8, local_size_z =
        1) in;
void main() {
    ivec3 froxel_coord = ivec3(gl_GlobalInvocationID.xyz);
    vec3 world_position = world_from_froxel(froxel_coord);
    vec3 rcp_froxel_dim = 1.0f / froxel_dimensions.xyz;
```

We read scattering and extinction from the result of the injection shader:

```
vec4 scattering_extinction = texture(global_textures_3d
    [nonuniformEXT(froxel_data_texture_index)],
    froxel_coord * rcp_froxel_dim);
    float extinction = scattering_extinction.a;
```

We then start accumulating light and using clustered bins.

Notice the cooperation between different rendering algorithms: having the clustered bin already developed, we can use that to query lights in a defined volume starting from the world space position:

```
vec3 lighting = vec3(0);
vec3 V = normalize(camera_position.xyz - world_position);
// Read clustered lighting data
// Calculate linear depth
float linear_d = froxel_coord.z * 1.0f /
    froxel_dimension_z;
```

```
linear_d = raw_depth_to_linear_depth(linear_d,
    froxel_near, froxel_far) / froxel_far;
// Select bin
int bin_index = int( linear_d / BIN_WIDTH );
uint bin_value = bins[ bin_index ];

// As in calculate_lighting method, cycle through
// lights to calculate contribution
for ( uint light_id = min_light_id;
    light_id <= max_light_id;
    ++light_id ) {

    // Same as calculate_lighting method

    // Calculate point light contribution
    // Read shadow map for current light
    float shadow = current_depth -
        bias < closest_depth ? 1 : 0;
    const vec3 L = normalize(light_position -
        world_position);
    float attenuation = attenuation_square_falloff(
        L, 1.0f / light_radius) * shadow;
```

Up until now, the code is almost identical to the one used in lighting, but we add `phase_function` to finalize the lighting factor:

```
    lighting += point_light.color *
        point_light.intensity *
        phase_function(V, -L,
          phase_anisotropy_01) *
        attenuation;
                }
```

Final scattering is calculated and stored, as follows:

```
vec3 scattering = scattering_extinction.rgb * lighting;
imageStore( global_images_3d
            [light_scattering_texture_index],
```

```
            ivec3(froxel_coord.xyz), vec4(scattering,
                extinction) );
}
```

We will now have a look at the integration/ray marching shader to conclude the main shaders needed to have the algorithm work for the volumetric part.

Integrating scattering and extinction

This shader is responsible for performing the ray marching in the froxel texture and performing the intermediate calculations in each cell. It will still write in a frustum-aligned texture, but each cell will contain the accumulated scattering and transmittance starting from that cell.

Notice that we now use transmittance instead of extinction, transmittance being a quantity that integrates extinction to a certain space. The dispatch is just on the *X* and *Y* axis of the frustum texture, reading the light scattering texture, as we will perform the integration steps and write to each froxel in the main loop.

The final stored result is scattering and transmittance, so it can be easier to apply it to the scene:

```
// Dispatch with Z = 1 as we perform the integration.
layout (local_size_x = 8, local_size_y = 8, local_size_z =
        1) in;
void main() {
    ivec3 froxel_coord = ivec3(gl_GlobalInvocationID.xyz);
    vec3 integrated_scattering = vec3(0,0,0);
    float integrated_transmittance = 1.0f;
    float current_z = 0;
    vec3 rcp_froxel_dim = 1.0f / froxel_dimensions.xyz;
```

We integrate on the *Z* axis as this texture is frustum aligned.

First, we calculate the depth difference to have the thickness needed for the extinction integral:

```
    for ( int z = 0; z < froxel_dimension_z; ++z ) {
        froxel_coord.z = z;
        float next_z = slice_to_exponential_depth(
                    froxel_near, froxel_far, z + 1,
                    int(froxel_dimension_z) );
```

```
            const float z_step = abs(next_z - current_z);
            current_z = next_z;
```

We will calculate scattering and transmittance and accumulate them for the following cell on the Z axis:

```
            // Following equations from Physically Based Sky,
               Atmosphere and Cloud Rendering by Hillaire
            const vec4 sampled_scattering_extinction =
            texture(global_textures_3d[
            nonuniformEXT(light_scattering_texture_index)],
            froxel_coord * rcp_froxel_dim);
            const vec3 sampled_scattering =
                sampled_scattering_extinction.xyz;
            const float sampled_extinction =
                sampled_scattering_extinction.w;
            const float clamped_extinction =
                max(sampled_extinction, 0.00001f);
            const float transmittance = exp(-sampled_extinction
                                            * z_step);
            const vec3 scattering = (sampled_scattering -
                                    (sampled_scattering *
                                    transmittance)) /
                                    clamped_extinction;

            integrated_scattering += scattering *
                                     integrated_transmittance;
            integrated_transmittance *= transmittance;

            imageStore( global_images_3d[
               integrated_light_scattering_texture_index],
               froxel_coord.xyz,
               vec4(integrated_scattering,
                  integrated_transmittance) );
     }
}
```

We now have a volume texture containing ray marched scattering and transmittance values that can be queried from anywhere in the frame to know how much fog there is and what color it is at that point.

This concludes the main volumetric rendering aspect of the algorithm. We will now have a look at how easy it is to apply the fog to a scene.

Applying Volumetric Fog to the scene

We can finally apply the Volumetric Fog. To do that, we use the screen space coordinates to calculate the sampling coordinates for the texture. This function will be used at the end of the lighting calculations for both deferred and forward rendering paths.

We first calculate the sampling coordinates:

```
vec3 apply_volumetric_fog( vec2 screen_uv, float raw_depth,
                           vec3 color ) {
    const float near = volumetric_fog_near;
    const float far = volumetric_fog_far;
    // Fog linear depth distribution
    float linear_depth = raw_depth_to_linear_depth(
                         raw_depth, near, far );
    // Exponential
    float depth_uv = linear_depth_to_uv( near, far,
        linear_depth, volumetric_fog_num_slices );
vec4 scattering_transmittance =
    texture(global_textures_3d
    [nonuniformEXT(volumetric_fog_texture_index)],
    froxel_uvw);
```

After we read the scattering and transmittance at the specified position, we use the transmittance to modulate the current scene color and add the fog scattered color, like so:

```
    color.rgb = color.rgb * scattering_transmittance.a +
                scattering_transmittance.rgb;

    return color;
}
```

And this concludes the necessary steps to fully implement Volumetric Fog rendering. But still, there is a big problem: **banding**.

This is a large topic covered in several papers, but for the sake of simplicity, we can say that having a low-resolution volume texture adds banding problems, but it is necessary for achieving real-time performance.

Adding filters

To further improve the visuals, we add two different filters: a temporal and a spatial one.

The temporal filter is what really makes the difference because it gives us the possibility of adding noise in different parts of the algorithm and thus removing banding. The spatial filter smooths out the fog even further.

Spatial filtering

This shader will smooth out the volumetric texture in the *X* and *Y* axis by applying a Gaussian filter. It will read the result of the light scattering and write into the froxel data texture, unused at this point of the frame, removing the need to create a temporary texture.

We first define the Gaussian function and its representing code:

```
#define SIGMA_FILTER 4.0
#define RADIUS 2

float gaussian(float radius, float sigma) {
    const float v = radius / sigma;
    return exp(-(v*v));
}
```

We then read the light scattering texture and accumulate values and weight only if the calculated coordinates are valid:

```
    vec4 scattering_extinction =
        texture( global_textures_3d[
        nonuniformEXT(light_scattering_texture_index)],
        froxel_coord * rcp_froxel_dim );
    if ( use_spatial_filtering == 1 ) {

        float accumulated_weight = 0;
        vec4 accumulated_scattering_extinction = vec4(0);

        for (int i = -RADIUS; i <= RADIUS; ++i ) {
```

```
            for (int j = -RADIUS; j <= RADIUS; ++j ) {
                ivec3 coord = froxel_coord + ivec3(i, j,
                                                        0);
                // if inside
                if (all(greaterThanEqual(coord, ivec3(0)))
                    && all(lessThanEqual(coord,
                    ivec3(froxel_dimension_x,
                    froxel_dimension_y,
                    froxel_dimension_z)))) {
                    const float weight =
                        gaussian(length(ivec2(i, j)),
                            SIGMA_FILTER);
                    const vec4 sampled_value =
                        texture(global_textures_3d[
                            nonuniformEXT(
                                light_scattering_texture_index)],
                                coord * rcp_froxel_dim);
                    accumulated_scattering_extinction.rgba +=
                        sampled_value.rgba * weight;
                    accumulated_weight += weight;
                }
            }
        }

        scattering_extinction =
            accumulated_scattering_extinction /
            accumulated_weight;
    }
```

We store the result in the froxel data texture:

```
    imageStore(global_images_3d[froxel_data_texture_index],
            froxel_coord.xyz, scattering_extinction );
}
```

The next step is temporal filtering.

Temporal filtering

This shader will take the currently calculated 3D light scattering texture and apply a temporal filter. In order to do that it will need two textures, one for the current and one for the previous frame, and thanks to bindless, we just need to change the indices to use them.

Dispatch is like most of the shaders in this chapter, with one thread for each froxel element of the volume texture. Let's begin with reading the current light scattering texture.

This currently resides in froxel_data_texture, coming from the spatial filtering:

```
vec4 scattering_extinction =
    texture( global_textures_3d[
    nonuniformEXT(froxel_data_texture_index)],
    froxel_coord * rcp_froxel_dim );
```

We need to calculate the previous screen space position to read the previous frame texture.

We will calculate the world position and then use the previous view projection to get the UVW coordinates to read the texture:

```
// Temporal reprojection
if (use_temporal_reprojection == 1) {
    vec3 world_position_no_jitter =
        world_from_froxel_no_jitter(froxel_coord);
    vec4 sceen_space_center_last =
        previous_view_projection *
            vec4(world_position_no_jitter, 1.0);
    vec3 ndc = sceen_space_center_last.xyz /
            sceen_space_center_last.w;

    float linear_depth = raw_depth_to_linear_depth(
                    ndc.z, froxel_near, froxel_far
                    );
    float depth_uv = linear_depth_to_uv( froxel_near,
                    froxel_far, linear_depth,
                    int(froxel_dimension_z) );
    vec3 history_uv = vec3( ndc.x * .5 + .5, ndc.y * -
                    .5 + .5, depth_uv );
```

We then check whether the calculated UVWs are valid and if so, we will read the previous texture:

```
// If history UV is outside the frustum, skip
if (all(greaterThanEqual(history_uv, vec3(0.0f)))
    && all(lessThanEqual(history_uv, vec3(1.0f)))) {
    // Fetch history sample
    vec4 history = textureLod(global_textures_3d[
        previous_light_scattering_texture_index],
        history_uv, 0.0f);
```

Once we read the sample, we can merge the current result with the previous one based on a user-defined percentage:

```
    scattering_extinction.rgb = mix(history.rgb,
        scattering_extinction.rgb,
            temporal_reprojection_percentage);
    scattering_extinction.a = mix(history.a,
        scattering_extinction.a,
            temporal_reprojection_percentage);
    }
}
```

We store the result back into the light scattering texture so that the integration can use it for the last step of the volumetric side of the algorithm.

```
    imageStore(global_images_3d[light_scattering_texture_in
        dex],
        froxel_coord.xyz, scattering_extinction );
}
```

At this point, we have seen all of the steps for the complete algorithm for the Volumetric Fog.

The last thing to see is the volumetric noise generation used to animate the fog and briefly talk about noise and jittering used to remove banding.

Volumetric noise generation

To break the fog density up a bit so that it is more interesting, we can sample a volumetric noise texture to modify the density a little. We can add a single execution compute shader that creates and stores Perlin noise in a 3D texture and then reads it when sampling the fog density.

Additionally, we can animate this noise to simulate wind animation. The shader is straightforward and uses Perlin noise functions as follows:

```
layout (local_size_x = 8, local_size_y = 8, local_size_z =
        1) in;
void main() {
    ivec3 pos = ivec3(gl_GlobalInvocationID.xyz);

    vec3 xyz = pos / volumetric_noise_texture_size;

    float perlin_data = get_perlin_7_octaves(xyz, 4.0);

    imageStore( global_images_3d[output_texture_index],
            pos, vec4(perlin_data, 0, 0, 0) );
}
```

The result is a volume texture with a single channel and Perlin noise to be sampled. We also use a special Sampler that has a repeat filter on the U, V, and W axes.

Blue noise

As an additional noise used to offset sampling in different areas of the algorithm, we use blue noise, reading it from a texture and adding a temporal component to it.

There are many interesting properties of blue noise and much literature on why it is a great noise for visual perception, and we will post links at the end of this chapter, but for now, we just read the noise from a texture with two channels and map it to the -1 to 1 range.

The mapping function is as follows:

```
float triangular_mapping( float noise0, float noise1 ) {
    return noise0 + noise1 - 1.0f;
}
```

And the following is performed to read the blue noise:

```
float generate_noise(vec2 pixel, int frame, float scale) {
    vec2 uv = vec2(pixel.xy / blue_noise_dimensions.xy);
    // Read blue noise from texture
    vec2 blue_noise = texture(global_textures[
        nonuniformEXT(blue_noise_128_rg_texture_index)],
                uv ).rg;
```

```
        const float k_golden_ratio_conjugate = 0.61803398875;
        float blue_noise0 = fract(ToLinear1(blue_noise.r) +
            float(frame % 256) * k_golden_ratio_conjugate);
        float blue_noise1 = fract(ToLinear1(blue_noise.g) +
            float(frame % 256) * k_golden_ratio_conjugate);
        return triangular_noise(blue_noise0, blue_noise1) *
            scale;
}
```

The final value will be between -1 and 1 and can be scaled to any need and used everywhere.

There is an animated blue noise paper that promises even better quality, but due to licensing problems, we opted to use this free version.

Summary

In this chapter, we introduced the Volumetric Fog rendering technique. We provided a brief mathematical background and algorithmic overview before showing the code. We also showed the different techniques available to improve banding – a vast topic that requires a careful balance of noise and temporal reprojection.

The algorithm presented is also an almost complete implementation that can be found behind many commercial games. We also talked about filtering, especially the temporal filter, which is linked to the next chapter, where we will talk about an anti-aliasing technique that uses temporal reprojection.

In the next chapter, we will see how the synergy between Temporal Anti-Aliasing and noises used to jitter the sampling in Volumetric Fog will ease out the visual bandings. We will also show a feasible way to generate custom textures with a single-use compute shader used to generate a volumetric noise.

This technique is also used for other volumetric algorithms, such as Volumetric Clouds, to store more custom noises used for generating the cloud shapes.

Further reading

There are many different papers that are referenced in this chapter, but the most important is the *Real-Time Volumetric Rendering* paper for general GPU-based volumetric rendering: https://patapom.com/topics/Revision2013/Revision%202013%20-%20Real-time%20Volumetric%20Rendering%20Course%20Notes.pdf.

The algorithm is still a derivation of the seminal paper from Bart Wronski: https://bartwronski.files.wordpress.com/2014/08/bwronski_volumetric_fog_siggraph2014.pdf.

With some evolutions and mathematical improvements in the following link: https://www.ea.com/frostbite/news/physically-based-unified-volumetric-rendering-in-frostbite.

For the depth distribution, we referenced the formula used in iD Tech 6: https://advances.realtimerendering.com/s2016/Siggraph2016_idTech6.pdf.

For banding and noise, the most comprehensive papers come from Playdead:

- https://loopit.dk/rendering_inside.pdf
- https://loopit.dk/banding_in_games.pdf

For information on animated blue noise: https://blog.demofox.org/2017/10/31/animating-noise-for-integration-over-time/

For information on dithering, blue noise, and the golden ratio sequence: https://bartwronski.com/2016/10/30/dithering-part-two-golden-ratio-sequence-blue-noise-and-highpass-and-remap/

A free blue noise texture can be found here: http://momentsingraphics.de/BlueNoise.html.

Part 3: Advanced Rendering Techniques

In this part, we will continue to add advanced techniques to our renderer and we will also explore how to replace or improve some of the techniques developed in earlier chapters using ray tracing.

We will cover the following chapters in this section:

- *Chapter 11, Temporal Anti-Aliasing*
- *Chapter 12, Getting Started with Ray Tracing*
- *Chapter 13, Revisiting Shadows with Ray Tracing*
- *Chapter 14, Adding Dynamic Diffuse Global Illumination with Ray Tracing*
- *Chapter 15, Adding Reflections with Ray Tracing*

11
Temporal Anti-Aliasing

In this chapter, we will expand on a concept touched on in the previous one when we talked about temporal reprojection. One of the most common ways to improve image quality is to sample more data (super-sampling) and filter it down to the needed sampling frequency.

The primary technique used in rendering is **Multi-Sample Anti-Aliasing**, or **MSAA**. Another technique used for super-sampling is temporal super-sampling or using the samples from two or more frames to reconstruct a higher-quality image.

In the Volumetric Fog technique, a similar approach is used to remove banding given by the low resolution of the Volume Texture in a very effective way. We will see how we can achieve better image quality using **Temporal Anti-Aliasing** (**TAA**).

This technique has become widely used in recent years after more and more games started using Deferred Rendering at their core and because of the difficulty in applying MSAA on it. There were various attempts to make MSAA and Deferred Rendering work together, but performance (both time- and memory-wise) has always been proven to not be feasible at the time and thus alternative solutions started to be developed.

Enter **Post-Process Anti-Aliasing** and its plethora of acronyms. The first one to be widely used was **Morphological Anti-Aliasing**, or **MLAA**, developed by Alexander Reshetov, working at Intel at the time, and presented at High-Performance Graphics in 2009.

The algorithm was developed to work on the CPU using Intel's **Streaming SIMD Extensions** (**SSE**) instructions and introduced some interesting solutions to find and improve geometrical edge rendering, which fueled successive implementations. Later, Sony Santa Monica adopted MLAA for God of War III using the Cell **Synergisic Processing Unit** (**SPUs**) to be performed with real-time performances.

Post-Process Anti-Aliasing finally found a GPU implementation developed by Jorge Jimenez and others in 2011, opening a new rendering research field. Various other game studios started developing custom Post Process Anti-Aliasing techniques and sharing their details.

All those techniques were based on geometrical edge recognition and image enhancement.

Another aspect that started to emerge was the reuse of information from previous frames to further enhance visual quality, such as in **Sharp Morphological Anti-Aliasing**, or **SMAA**, which started adding a temporal component to enhance the final image.

The most adopted anti-aliasing technique is TAA, which comes with its own set of challenges but fits nicely within the rendering pipeline and lets other techniques (such as Volumetric Fog) increase their visual quality by reducing banding with the introduction of animated dithering.

TAA is now the standard in most game engines, both commercial and private. It comes with its own challenges, such as handling transparent objects and image blurriness, but we will see how to tackle those problems as well.

In the rest of the chapter, we will first see an overview of the algorithm and then dive into the implementation. We will also create an initial, incredibly simple implementation just to show the basic building blocks of the algorithm, allowing you to understand how to write a custom TAA implementation from scratch. Finally, we will see the different areas of improvement within the algorithm.

Let's see an example scene and highlight the TAA improvements:

Figure 11.1 – Temporally anti-aliased scene

The following are a couple of screenshots of the final result, with and without TAA enabled.

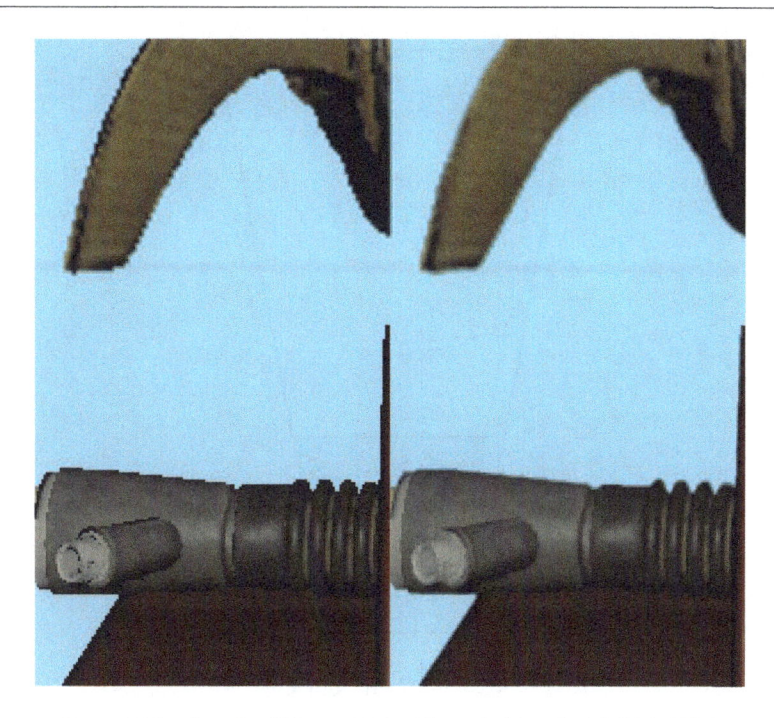

Figure 11.2 – Details of Figure 11.1 without (left) and with (right) TAA

In this chapter, we will have a look at the following topics:

- Creating the simplest TAA implementation
- Step-by-step improvement of the technique
- Overview of image-sharpening techniques outside of TAA
- Improving banding in different image areas with noise and TAA

Technical requirements

The code for this chapter can be found at the following URL: `https://github.com/PacktPublishing/Mastering-Graphics-Programming-with-Vulkan/tree/main/source/chapter11`.

Overview

In this section, we will see the algorithm overview of the TAA rendering technique.

TAA is based on the collection of samples over time by applying small offsets to the camera projection matrix and applying some filters to generate the final image, like so:

248 Temporal Anti-Aliasing

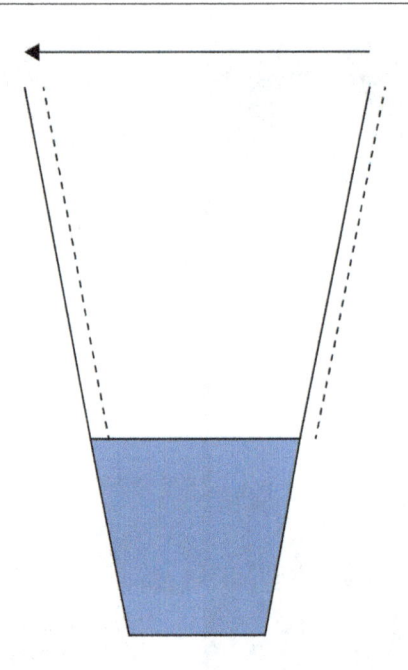

Figure 11.3 – Frustum jitter

There are various numerical sequences that can be used to offset the camera, as we will see in the implementation section. Moving the camera is called **jittering**, and by jittering the camera, we gather additional data that we can use to enhance the image.

The following is an overview of the TAA shader:

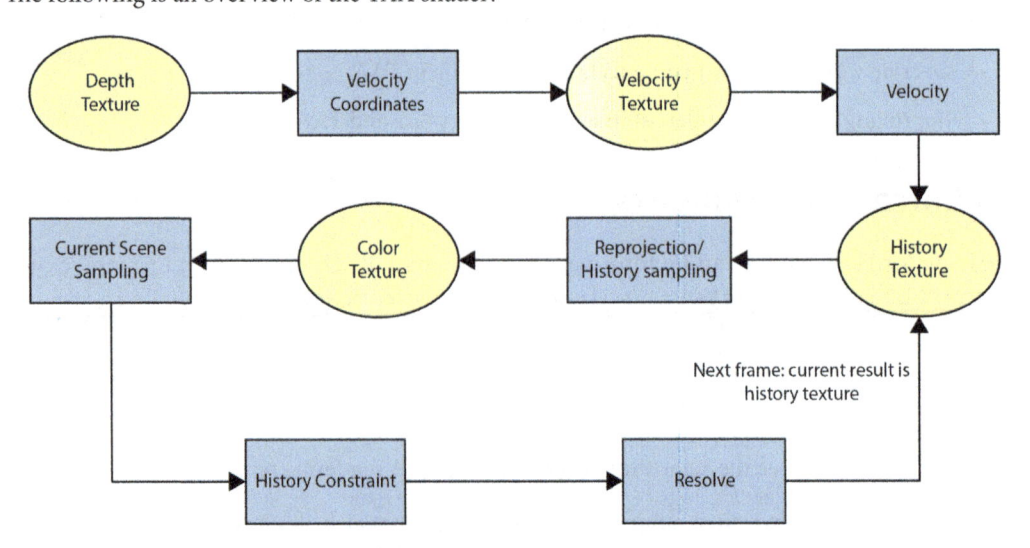

Figure 11.4 – TAA algorithm overview

Based on *Figure 11.4*, we've separated the algorithm into steps (blue rectangles) and texture reads (yellow ellipses:.

1. We calculate the coordinates to read the velocity from, represented by the **Velocity Coordinates** block.

   This is normally done by reading a neighborhood of 3x3 pixels around the current pixel position and finding the closest pixel, using the current frame's **Depth Texture**. Reading from a 3x3 neighborhood has been proven to decrease ghosting and improve edge quality.

2. We read the velocity using the newly found coordinates from the **Velocity Texture** block, paying attention to use a linear sampler, as velocity is not just in increments of pixels, but can be in-between pixels.

3. We read the color information from the **History Texture** block. This is basically the last frame's TAA output. We can optionally apply a filter to read the texture to further enhance the quality.

4. We will read the current scene color. In this step, we will also cache information again by reading a neighborhood around the current pixel position to constrain the history color we read previously and guide the final resolve phase.

5. History constraint. We try to limit the previous frame color inside an area of the current color to reject invalid samples coming from occlusion or disocclusion. Without doing that there would be a lot of ghosting.

6. The sixth and final step is **Resolve**. We combine the current color and the constraint history color to generate the final pixel color by applying some additional filters.

The result of the current frame's TAA will be the next frame history texture, so we simply switch the textures (history and TAA result) every frame without the need to copy the results over, as seen in some implementations.

Now that we have seen an overview of the algorithm, we can start by implementing an initial TAA shader.

The simplest TAA implementation

The best way to understand this technique is to build a basic implementation missing some important steps and to have a blurry or jittery rendering as it is easy to do.

The basic ingredients for this technique are simple if done correctly, but each must be done in a precise way. We will first add jittering to the camera so that we can render slightly different points of view of the scene and gather additional data.

We will then add motion vectors so that we can read the previous frame color information in the right place. Finally, we will reproject, or simply put, read the history frame color data and combine it with current frame data.

Let us see the different steps.

Jittering the camera

The objective of this step is to translate the projection camera by a small amount in both the *x* and *y* axes.

We have added some utility code in the `GameCamera` class:

```
void GameCamera::apply_jittering( f32 x, f32 y ) {
    // Reset camera projection
    camera.calculate_projection_matrix();
    // Calculate jittering translation matrix and modify
        projection matrix
    mat4s jittering_matrix = glms_translate_make( { x, y,
                                                    0.0f } );
    camera.projection = glms_mat4_mul( jittering_matrix,
                                       camera.projection );
    camera.calculate_view_projection();
}
```

Every step is important and error prone, so be careful.

We first want to reset the projection matrix, as we will manually modify it. We then build a translation matrix with the jittering values in x and y, and we will see later how to calculate them.

Finally, we multiply the projection matrix by the jittering matrix and calculate the new view-projection matrix. Beware of multiplication order, as if this is wrong you will see a jittery blurry mess even when not moving the camera!

Having this working, we can optimize the code by removing the matrix construction and multiplication, having cleaner and less error-prone code, like so:

```
void GameCamera::apply_jittering( f32 x, f32 y ) {
    camera.calculate_projection_matrix();
    // Perform the same calculations as before, with the
        observation that
    // we modify only 2 elements in the projection matrix:
    camera.projection.m20 += x;
    camera.projection.m21 += y;
    camera.calculate_view_projection();
}
```

Choosing jittering sequences

We will now build a sequence of x and y values to jitter the camera. Normally there are different sequences that are used:

- Halton
- Hammersley
- Martin Robert's R2
- Interleaved gradients

There are all the implementations for the preceding sequences in the code, and each can give a slightly different look to the image, as it changes how we collect samples over time.

There is plenty of material on using the different sequences that we will provide links to at the end of the chapter; right now what is important is to know that we have a sequence of two numbers that we repeat after a few frames to jitter the camera.

Let us say that we choose the Halton sequence. We first want to calculate the values for x and y:

```
f32 jitter_x = halton( jitter_index, 2 );
f32 jitter_y = halton( jitter_index, 3 );
```

These values are in the [0,1] range, but we want to jitter in both directions, so we map it to the [-1.1] range:

```
f32 jitter_offset_x = jitter_x * 2 - 1.0f;
f32 jitter_offset_y = jitter_y * 2 - 1.0f;
```

We now apply them to the apply jitter method, with a caveat: we want to add sub-pixel jittering, thus we need to divide these offsets by the screen resolution:

```
game_camera.apply_jittering( jitter_offset_x / gpu.swapchain_
width, jitter_offset_y / gpu.swapchain_height );
```

Finally, we have a jitter period to choose after how many frames we repeat the jittering numbers, updated like this:

```
jitter_index = ( jitter_index + 1 ) % jitter_period;
```

A good period is normally four frames, but in the accompanying code, there is the possibility to change this number and see the effect on the rendering image.

Another fundamental thing to do is to cache previous and current jittering values and send them to the GPU, so that motion vectors take into consideration the full movement.

We've added `jitter_xy` and `previous_jitter_xy` as variables in the scene uniforms to be accessed in all shaders.

Adding motion vectors

Now that we correctly jittered the camera and saved the offsets, it is time to add motion vectors to properly read the color data from the previous frame. There are two sources of motion: camera motion and dynamic object motion.

We added a velocity texture with R16G16 format to store the per-pixel velocity. For each frame, we clear that to (0,0) and we calculate the different motions. For camera motion, we will calculate the current and previous screen space position, considering the jitter and the motion vector.

We will perform this in a compute shader:

```
layout (local_size_x = 8, local_size_y = 8, local_size_z =
    1) in;
void main() {
    ivec3 pos = ivec3(gl_GlobalInvocationID.xyz);
    // Read the raw depth and reconstruct NDC coordinates.
    const float raw_depth = texelFetch(global_textures[
        nonuniformEXT(depth_texture_index)], pos.xy, 0).r;
    const vec2 screen_uv = uv_nearest(pos.xy, resolution);
    vec4 current_position_ndc = vec4(
        ndc_from_uv_raw_depth( screen_uv, raw_depth ), 1.0f
    );

    // Reconstruct world position and previous NDC position
    const vec3 pixel_world_position =
        world_position_from_depth
            (screen_uv, raw_depth, inverse_view_projection);
    vec4 previous_position_ndc = previous_view_projection *
        vec4(pixel_world_position, 1.0f);
    previous_position_ndc.xyz /= previous_position_ndc.w;
    // Calculate the jittering difference.
    vec2 jitter_difference = (jitter_xy -
                             previous_jitter_xy)* 0.5f;
    // Pixel velocity is given by the NDC [-1,1] difference
        in X and Y axis
```

```
    vec2 velocity = current_position_ndc.xy -
                    previous_position_ndc.xy;
    // Take in account jittering
    velocity -= jitter_difference;
    imageStore( motion_vectors, pos.xy, vec4(velocity, 0,
                                             0) );
```

Dynamic meshes need an additional output to be written in the vertex or mesh shaders, with similar calculations done in the camera motion shader:

```
// Mesh shader version
gl_MeshVerticesNV[ i ].gl_Position = view_projection *
    (model * vec4(position, 1));
vec4 world_position = model * vec4(position, 1.0);
vec4 previous_position_ndc = previous_view_projection *
    vec4(world_position, 1.0f);
previous_position_ndc.xyz /= previous_position_ndc.w;
vec2 jitter_difference = (jitter_xy - previous_jitter_xy) *
                         0.5f;
vec2 velocity = gl_MeshVerticesNV[ i ].gl_Position.xy -
    previous_position_ndc.xy - jitter_difference;
vTexcoord_Velocity[i] = velocity;
```

And after this, just writing the velocity to its own render target will be all that is needed.

Now that we have the motion vectors, we can finally see the implementation of an extremely basic TAA shader.

First implementation code

We again run a compute shader to calculate TAA. The implementation of the simplest possible shader is the following:

```
vec3 taa_simplest( ivec2 pos ) {
    const vec2 velocity = sample_motion_vector( pos );
    const vec2 screen_uv = uv_nearest(pos, resolution);
    const vec2 reprojected_uv = screen_uv - velocity;

    vec3 current_color = sample_color(screen_uv.xy).rgb;
    vec3 history_color =
```

```
            sample_history_color(reprojected_uv).rgb;
    // source_weight is normally around 0.9.
    return mix(current_color, previous_color,
            source_weight);
}
```

Going through the code, the steps are simple:

1. Sample the velocity at the pixel position.
2. Sample the current color at the pixel position.
3. Sample the history color at the previous pixel position, calculated using the motion vectors.
4. Mix the colors, taking something like 10% of the current frame colors.

Before moving on to any improvement it is paramount to have this working perfectly.

You should see a blurrier image with a big problem: ghosting when moving the camera or an object. If the camera and the scene are static, there should be no pixel movement. This is fundamental to knowing that jittering and reprojection are working properly.

With this implementation working, we are now ready to see the different improvement areas to have a more solid TAA.

Improving TAA

There are five areas to improve TAA: reprojection, history sampling, scene sampling, history constraint, and resolve.

Each one has different parameters to be tweaked that can suit the rendering needs of a project – TAA is not exact or perfect, thus some extra care from a visual perspective needs to be taken into account.

Let's see the different areas in detail so that the accompanying code will be clearer.

Reprojection

The first thing to do is to improve reprojection and thus calculate the coordinates to read the velocity to drive the *History sampling* section.

To calculate the history texture pixel coordinates, the most common solution is to get the closest pixel in a 3x3 square around the current pixel, as an idea by Brian Karis. We will read the depth texture and use the depth value as a way to determine the closest pixel, and cache the x and y position of that pixel:

```
void find_closest_fragment_3x3(ivec2 pixel, out ivec2
                            closest_position, out
```

```
                         float closest_depth) {
    closest_depth = 1.0f;
    closest_position = ivec2(0,0);

    for (int x = -1; x <= 1; ++x ) {
        for (int y = -1; y <= 1; ++y ) {
            ivec2 pixel_position = pixel + ivec2(x, y);
            pixel_position = clamp(pixel_position,
                ivec2(0), ivec2(resolution.x - 1,
                    resolution.y - 1));
            float current_depth =
                texelFetch(global_textures[
                    nonuniformEXT(depth_texture_index)],
                    pixel_position, 0).r;
            if ( current_depth < closest_depth ) {
                closest_depth = current_depth;
                closest_position = pixel_position;
            }
        }
    }
}
```

By just using the found pixel position as the read coordinate for the motion vectors, ghosting will be much less visible, and edges will be smoother:

```
            float closest_depth = 1.0f;
            ivec2 closest_position = ivec2(0,0);
            find_closest_fragment_3x3( pos.xy,
                                        closest_position,
                                        closest_depth );
            const vec2 velocity = sample_motion_vector
                (closest_position.xy);
            // rest of the TAA shader
```

There can be other ways of reading the velocity, but this has proven to be the best trade-off between quality and performance. Another way to experiment would be to use the maximum velocity in a similar 3x3 neighborhood of pixels.

There is no perfect solution, and thus experimentation and parametrization of the rendering technique are highly encouraged. After we have calculated the pixel position of the history texture to read, we can finally sample it.

History sampling

In this case, the simplest thing to do is to just read the history texture at the calculated position. The reality is that we can apply a filter to enhance the visual quality of the read as well.

In the code, we've added options to try different filters, and the standard choice here is to use a Catmull-Rom filter to enhance the sampling:

```
// Sample motion vectors.
  const vec2 velocity = sample_motion_vector_point(
                    closest_position );
  const vec2 screen_uv = uv_nearest(pos.xy, resolution);
  const vec2 reprojected_uv = screen_uv - velocity;


// History sampling: read previous frame samples and
    optionally apply a filter to it.
vec3 history_color = vec3(0);
history_color = sample_history_color(
             reprojected_uv ).rgb;
switch (history_sampling_filter) {
   case HistorySamplingFilterSingle:
        history_color = sample_history_color(
                    reprojected_uv ).rgb;
        break;


   case HistorySamplingFilterCatmullRom:
        history_color = sample_texture_catmull_rom(
                    reprojected_uv,
                    history_color_texture_index );
        break;
 }
```

After we have the history color, we will sample the current scene color and cache information needed for both the history constraint and the final resolve phase.

Using the history color without further processing would result in ghosting.

Scene sampling

At this point, ghosting is less noticeable but still present, so with a similar mentality to searching for the closest pixel, we can search around the current pixel to calculate color information and apply a filter to it.

Basically, we are treating a pixel like a signal instead of a simple color. The subject can be quite long and interesting and at the end of the chapter, there will be resources to dive deeper into this. Also, in this step, we will cache information used for the history boundaries used to constrain the color coming from the previous frames.

What we need to know is that we sample another 3x3 area around the current pixel and calculate the information necessary for the constraint to happen. The most valuable information is the minimum and maximum color in this area, and Variance Clipping (which we will look at later on) also requires mean color and square mean color (known as **moments**) to be calculated to aid history constraint. Finally, we will also apply some filtering to the sampling of the color.

Let's see the code:

```
// Current sampling: read a 3x3 neighborhood and cache
   color and other data to process history and final
   resolve.
   // Accumulate current sample and weights.
   vec3 current_sample_total = vec3(0);
   float current_sample_weight = 0.0f;
   // Min and Max used for history clipping
   vec3 neighborhood_min = vec3(10000);
   vec3 neighborhood_max = vec3(-10000);
   // Cache of moments used in the constraint phase
   vec3 m1 = vec3(0);
   vec3 m2 = vec3(0);

   for (int x = -1; x <= 1; ++x ) {
       for (int y = -1; y <= 1; ++y ) {

           ivec2 pixel_position = pos + ivec2(x, y);
           pixel_position = clamp(pixel_position,
               ivec2(0), ivec2(resolution.x - 1,
                   resolution.y - 1));
```

```
                vec3 current_sample =
                sample_current_color_point(pixel_position).rgb;
                vec2 subsample_position = vec2(x * 1.f, y *
                                               1.f);
                float subsample_distance = length(
                                          subsample_position
                                          );
                float subsample_weight = subsample_filter(
                                         subsample_distance );

                current_sample_total += current_sample *
                                        subsample_weight;
                current_sample_weight += subsample_weight;

                neighborhood_min = min( neighborhood_min,
                                        current_sample );
                neighborhood_max = max( neighborhood_max,
                                        current_sample );

                m1 += current_sample;
                m2 += current_sample * current_sample;
            }
        }
    vec3 current_sample = current_sample_total /
                          current_sample_weight;
```

What all this code does is sample color, filter it, and cache information for the history constraint, and thus we are ready to move on to the next phase.

The history constraint

Finally, we arrived at the constraint of the history sampled color. Based on previous steps we have created a range of possible color values that we consider valid. If we think of each color channel as a value, we basically created an area of valid colors that we will constraint against.

A constraint is a way of accepting or discarding color information coming from the history texture, reducing ghosting to almost nothing. Over time, different ways to constrain history sampled color were developed in search of better criteria to discard colors.

Some implementations also tried relying on depth or velocity differences, but this seems to be the more robust solution.

We have added four constraints to test:

- RGB clamp
- RGB clip
- Variance clip
- Variance clip with clamped RGB

The best quality is given by variance clip with the clamped RGB, but it is interesting to see the other ones, as they are the ones that were employed in the first implementations.

Here is the code:

```
    switch (history_clipping_mode) {

        // This is the most complete and robust history
           clipping mode:
        case HistoryClippingModeVarianceClipClamp:
        default: {
            // Calculate color AABB using color moments m1
               and m2
            float rcp_sample_count = 1.0f / 9.0f;
            float gamma = 1.0f;
            vec3 mu = m1 * rcp_sample_count;
            vec3 sigma = sqrt(abs((m2 * rcp_sample_count) -
                        (mu * mu)));
            vec3 minc = mu - gamma * sigma;
            vec3 maxc = mu + gamma * sigma;
            // Clamp to new AABB
            vec3 clamped_history_color = clamp(
                                    history_color.rgb,
                                    neighborhood_min,
                                    neighborhood_max
                                    );
            history_color.rgb = clip_aabb(minc, maxc,
                            vec4(clamped_history_color,
```

```
                             1), 1.0f).rgb;

            break;
        }
    }
```

The `clip_aabb` function is the method that constrains the sampled history color within minimum and maximum color values.

In brief, we are trying to build an AABB in colorspace to limit the history color to be within that range, so that the final color is more plausible compared to the current one.

The last step in the TAA shader is resolve, or combining current and history colors and applying some filters to generate the final pixel color.

Resolve

Once again, we will apply some additional filters to decide whether the previous pixel is usable or not and by how much.

By default, we start with using just 10% of the current frame pixel and rely on history, so without any of those filters the image will be quite blurry:

```
// Resolve: combine history and current colors for final
    pixel color
    vec3 current_weight = vec3(0.1f);
    vec3 history_weight = vec3(1.0 - current_weight);
```

The first filter we will see is the temporal one, which uses the cached neighborhood minimum and maximum colors to calculate how much to blend the current and previous colors:

```
        // Temporal filtering
        if (use_temporal_filtering() ) {
            vec3 temporal_weight = clamp(abs(neighborhood_max -
                                    neighborhood_min) /
                                    current_sample,
                                    vec3(0), vec3(1));
            history_weight = clamp(mix(vec3(0.25), vec3(0.85),
                                    temporal_weight), vec3(0),
                                    vec3(1));
```

```
            current_weight = 1.0f - history_weight;
    }
```

The next two filters are linked; thus, we have them together.

They both work with luminance, with one used to suppress so-called **fireflies**, or very bright single pixels that can exist in images when there is a strong source of light, while the second uses the difference in luminance to further steer the weight toward either the current or previous colors:

```
    // Inverse luminance filtering
    if (use_inverse_luminance_filtering() ||
        use_luminance_difference_filtering() ) {
        // Calculate compressed colors and luminances
        vec3 compressed_source = current_sample /
            (max(max(current_sample.r, current_sample.g),
                current_sample.b) + 1.0f);
        vec3 compressed_history = history_color /
            (max(max(history_color.r, history_color.g),
                history_color.b) + 1.0f);
        float luminance_source = use_ycocg() ?
            compressed_source.r :
                luminance(compressed_source);
        float luminance_history = use_ycocg() ?
            compressed_history.r :
                luminance(compressed_history);

        if ( use_luminance_difference_filtering() ) {
            float unbiased_diff = abs(luminance_source -
            luminance_history) / max(luminance_source,
            max(luminance_history, 0.2));
            float unbiased_weight = 1.0 - unbiased_diff;
            float unbiased_weight_sqr = unbiased_weight *
                                        unbiased_weight;
            float k_feedback = mix(0.0f, 1.0f,
                                    unbiased_weight_sqr);

            history_weight = vec3(1.0 - k_feedback);
            current_weight = vec3(k_feedback);
```

```
            }

            current_weight *= 1.0 / (1.0 + luminance_source);
            history_weight *= 1.0 / (1.0 + luminance_history);
        }
```

We combine the result using the newly calculated weights, and finally, we output the color:

```
        vec3 result = ( current_sample * current_weight +
                        history_color * history_weight ) /
                      max( current_weight + history_weight,
                      0.00001 );
        return result;
```

At this point, the shader is complete and ready to be used. In the accompanying demo, there will be many tweaking parameters to learn the differences between the different filters and steps involved.

One of the most common complaints about TAA is the blurriness of the image. We will see a couple of ways to improve that next.

Sharpening the image

One thing that can be noticed in the most basic implementation, and a problem often linked to TAA, is a decrease in the sharpness of the image.

We have already improved it by using a filter when sampling the scene, but we can work on the final image appearance outside of TAA in different ways. We will briefly discuss three different ways to improve the sharpening of the image.

Sharpness post-processing

One of the ways to improve the sharpness of the image is to add a simple sharpening shader in the post-process chain.

The code is simple, and it is luminance based:

```
        vec4 color = texture(global_textures[
                     nonuniformEXT(texture_id)], vTexCoord.xy);
        float input_luminance = luminance(color.rgb);
        float average_luminance = 0.f;

        // Sharpen
```

```
    for (int x = -1; x <= 1; ++x ) {
        for (int y = -1; y <= 1; ++y ) {
            vec3 sampled_color = texture(global_textures[
                nonuniformEXT(texture_id)], vTexCoord.xy +
                    vec2( x / resolution.x, y /
                        resolution.y )).rgb;
            average_luminance += luminance( sampled_color
                                                        );
        }
    }
    average_luminance /= 9.0f;

    float sharpened_luminance = input_luminance -
                                average_luminance;
    float final_luminance = input_luminance +
                            sharpened_luminance *
                            sharpening_amount;
    color.rgb = color.rgb * (final_luminance /
            input_luminance);
```

Based on this code, when the sharpening amount is 0 the image is not sharpened. The standard value is 1.

Negative mip bias

A global way to reduce blurriness is to modify the `mipLodBias` field in the `VkSamplerCreateInfo` structure to be a negative number, such as -0.25, thus shifting the texture **mip,** the pyramid of progressively smaller images of a texture to higher values.

This should be done by considering the performance difference, as we are sampling at a higher MIP level, and if the level is too high, we could re-introduce aliasing.

A global engine option to tweak would be a great solution to this.

Unjitter texture UVs

Another possible fix to sample sharper textures is to calculate the UVs as the camera was without any jittering, like so:

```
vec2 unjitter_uv(float uv, vec2 jitter) {
    return uv - dFdxFine(uv) * jitter.x + dFdyFine(uv) *
```

```
        jitter.y;
}
```

I personally did not try this method but found it interesting and something to experiment with. It was written about by Emilio Lopez in his TAA article, linked in the *Reference* section, also citing a colleague named Martin Sobek who came up with the idea.

The combination of TAA and sharpening drastically improves the edges of the image while retaining the details inside the objects.

We need to look at one last aspect of the image: banding.

Improving banding

Banding is a problem affecting various steps in the rendering of a frame. It affects Volumetric Fog and lighting calculations, for example.

Figure 11.5 – Banding problem detail in Volumetric Fog

We can see in *Figure 11.5* how this can be present in Volumetric Fog if no solution is implemented. A solution to remove banding in visuals is to add some dithering to various passes of the frame, but that also adds visual noise to the image.

Dithering is defined as the intentional addition of noise specifically to remove banding. Different type of noises can be used, as we will see in the accompanying code. Adding temporal reprojection smoothens the noise added, thus becoming one of the best ways to improve the visual quality of the image.

In *Chapter 10*, *Adding Volumetric Fog*, we saw a very simple temporal reprojection scheme, and we have also added noise to various steps of the algorithm. We have now seen a more complex implementation of a temporal reprojection scheme to enhance the image, and it should be clearer on reasoning behind animated dithering: animating dithering gives effectively more samples, and thanks to temporal reprojection, uses them effectively. Dithering is linked to its own temporal reprojection, thus in the Volumetric Fog steps, the dithering scale can be too large to be cleaned up by TAA.

When applying Volumetric Fog to the scene though, we can add a small, animated dithering that increases the fog visuals while being cleaned up by TAA. Another dithering application is in the lighting shader, again at the per-pixel level and thus eligible to be cleaned up by TAA.

> **Note**
> Trying to get a noise-free image is hard as the temporal reprojection uses more than one frame, thus it is not possible to show here in an image what appears banding-free in the accompanying application.

Summary

In this chapter, we introduced the TAA rendering technique.

We gave an overview of the algorithm by trying to highlight the different shader steps involved. We then moved on to create the simplest possible TAA shader: an exercise to give us a deeper understanding of the technique itself.

Following that, we started enhancing the various steps using filters and information taken from the current scene. We encourage you to add custom filters and tweak parameters and different scenes to understand and develop the technique further.

An idea to experiment with could also be to apply the history constraint to the temporal reprojection phase of the Volumetric Fog, as suggested by my friend Marco Vallario a few months ago.

In the next chapter, we will add support for ray tracing to the Raptor Engine, a recent technological advancement that unlocks high-quality illumination techniques, which we will cover in the following chapters.

Further reading

We touched on several topics in this chapter, from the history of post-process anti-aliasing to implementations of TAA, to banding and noise.

Thanks to the graphics community, which shares a lot of information on their findings, it is possible to sharpen our knowledge on this subject.

The following are some links to read:

- For an index of the evolution of Post-Process Anti-Aliasing techniques: http://www.iryoku.com/research-impact-retrospective-mlaa-from-2009-to-2017.
- The first MLAA paper: https://www.intel.com/content/dam/develop/external/us/en/documents/z-shape-arm-785403.pdf.
- An MLAA GPU implementation: http://www.iryoku.com/mlaa/.
- SMAA, an evolution of MLAA: http://www.iryoku.com/smaa/.
- The best article on signal processing and anti-aliasing by Matt Pettineo: https://therealmjp.github.io/posts/msaa-resolve-filters/.
- Temporal Reprojection Anti-Aliasing in Inside, containing the first full documentation of a TAA technique. Includes information about history constraints and AABB clipping: http://s3.amazonaws.com/arena-attachments/655504/c5c71c5507f0f8bf344252958254fb7d.pdf?1468341463.
- High-Quality Temporal Supersampling, Unreal Engine TAA implementation: https://de45xmedrsdbp.cloudfront.net/Resources/files/TemporalAA_small-59732822.pdf.
- An excursion in temporal super-sampling, introducing variance clipping: https://developer.download.nvidia.com/gameworks/events/GDC2016/msalvi_temporal_supersampling.pdf.
- A TAA article, with tips, such as UV unjittering and Mip bias: https://www.elopezr.com/temporal-aa-and-the-quest-for-the-holy-trail/.
- Another great TAA article with a full implementation: https://alextardif.com/TAA.html.
- Banding in games: https://loopit.dk/banding_in_games.pdf.

12
Getting Started with Ray Tracing

In this chapter, we are introducing ray tracing into our rendering pipeline. Thanks to the addition of hardware support for ray tracing in modern GPUs, it's now possible to integrate ray tracing techniques into real-time rendering.

Ray tracing requires a different setup compared to the traditional rendering pipeline, which is why we are dedicating a whole chapter to setting up a ray tracing pipeline. We are going to cover in detail how to set up a shader binding table to tell the API which shaders to invoke when an intersection test for a given ray succeeds or fails.

Next, we are going to explain how to create the **Bottom Level Acceleration Structure** (**BLAS**) and **Top Level Acceleration Structure** (**TLAS**). These **Acceleration Structures** (**AS**) are needed to speed up scene ray traversal and ensure that ray tracing can be performed at an interactive rate.

In this chapter, we'll cover the following main topics:

- Introduction to ray tracing in Vulkan
- Building the BLAS and TLAS
- Defining and creating a ray tracing pipeline

Technical requirements

The code for this chapter can be found at the following URL: `https://github.com/PacktPublishing/Mastering-Graphics-Programming-with-Vulkan/tree/main/source/chapter12`.

Introduction to ray tracing in Vulkan

Ray tracing support in hardware was first introduced in 2018 with the NVidia RTX series. Originally, ray tracing support in Vulkan was only available through an NVidia extension, but later, the functionality was ratified through a Khronos extension to allow multiple vendors to support the ray tracing API in Vulkan. We are dedicating a full chapter just to the setup of a ray tracing pipeline, as it requires new constructs that are specific to ray tracing.

The first departure from the traditional rendering pipeline is the need to organize our scene into Acceleration Structures. These structures are needed to speed up scene traversal, as they allow us to skip entire meshes that the ray has no chance to intersect with.

These Acceleration Structures are usually implemented as a **Bounded Volume Hierarchy** (**BVH**). A BVH subdivides the scene and individual meshes into bounding boxes and then organizes them into a tree. Leaf nodes of this tree are the only nodes containing geometry data, while parent nodes define the position and extent of the volume that encompasses the children.

A simple scene and its BVH representation is illustrated by the following image:

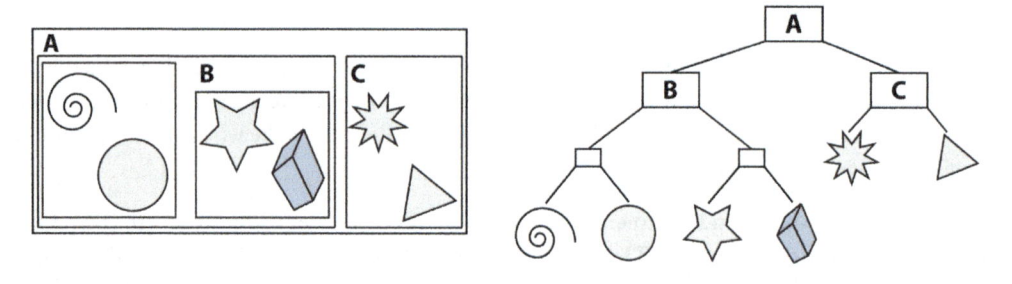

Figure 12.1 – A scene example on the left and its BVH representation on the right (source: Wikipedia)

The Vulkan API makes a further distinction between a TLAS and BLAS. A BLAS contains individual mesh definitions. These can then be grouped into a TLAS, where multiple instances of the same mesh can be placed in the scene by defining their transform matrices.

This organization is pictured in the following figure:

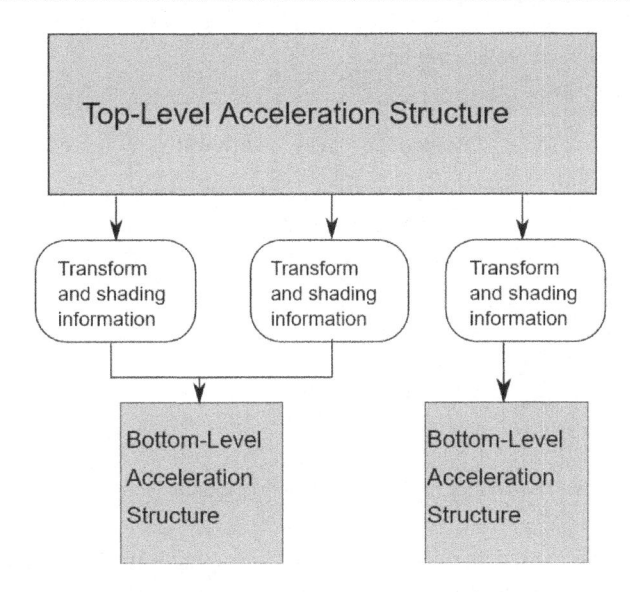

Figure 12.2 – Each BLAS can be added multiple times to a TLAS with different shading and transform details (source: Vulkan spec)

Now that we have defined our Acceleration Structures, we can turn our attention to the ray tracing pipeline. The major change introduced with ray tracing pipelines is the ability to call other shaders within a shader. This is achieved by defining shader binding tables. Each slot in these tables defines one of the following shader types:

- **Ray generation**: In a traditional ray tracing pipeline, this is the entry point from which rays are generated. As we will see in later chapters, rays can also be spawned from fragments and compute shaders.
- **Intersection**: This shader allows the application to implement custom geometry primitives. In Vulkan, we can only define triangles and **Axis-Aligned Bounding Boxes (AABB)**.
- **Any-hit**: This is executed after an intersection shader is triggered. Its main use is to determine whether the hit should be processed further or ignored.
- **Closest hit**: This shader is triggered the first time a ray hits a primitive.
- **Miss**: This shader is triggered if the ray doesn't hit any primitive.
- **Callable**: These are shaders that can be called from within an existing shader.

The flow is summarized in the following figure:

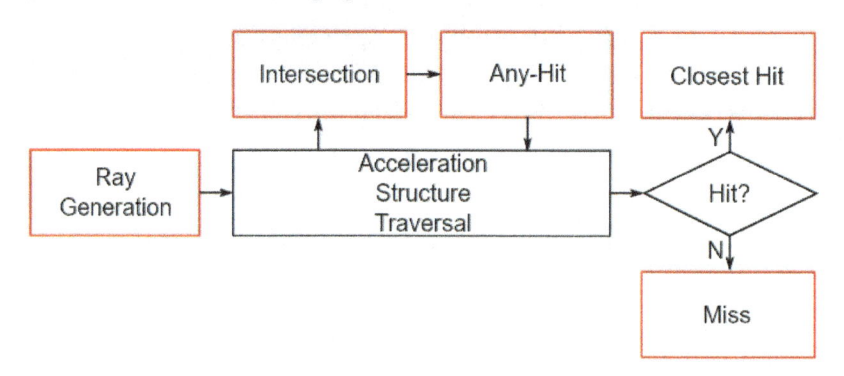

Figure 12.3 – The shader flow of a ray tracing pipeline (source: Vulkan spec)

In this section, we have provided an overview of how ray tracing is implemented in the Vulkan API. In the next section, we are going to have a better look at how to create Acceleration Structures.

Building the BLAS and TLAS

As we mentioned in the previous section, ray tracing pipelines require geometry to be organized into Acceleration Structures to speed up the ray traversal of the scene. In this section, we are going to explain how to accomplish this in Vulkan.

We start by creating a list of `VkAccelerationStructureGeometryKHR` when parsing our scene. For each mesh, this data structure is defined as follows:

```
VkAccelerationStructureGeometryKHR geometry{
    VK_STRUCTURE_TYPE_ACCELERATION_STRUCTURE_GEOMETRY_KHR };
geometry.geometryType = VK_GEOMETRY_TYPE_TRIANGLES_KHR;
geometry.flags =  mesh.is_transparent() ? 0 :
    VK_GEOMETRY_OPAQUE_BIT_KHR;
```

Each geometry structure can define three types of entries: triangles, AABBs, and instances. We are going to use triangles here, as that's how our meshes are defined. We are going to use instances later when defining the TLAS.

The following code demonstrates how the `triangles` structure is used:

```
geometry.geometry.triangles.sType =
    VK_STRUCTURE_TYPE_ACCELERATION_STRUCTURE_GEOMETRY
        _TRIANGLES_DATA_KHR;
```

```
geometry.geometry.triangles.vertexFormat =
    VK_FORMAT_R32G32B32_SFLOAT;
geometry.geometry.triangles.vertexData.deviceAddress =
    renderer->gpu->get_buffer_device_address(
        mesh.position_buffer ) + mesh.position_offset;
geometry.geometry.triangles.vertexStride = sizeof( float )
    * 3;
geometry.geometry.triangles.maxVertex = vertex_count;
geometry.geometry.triangles.indexType = mesh.index_type;
geometry.geometry.triangles.indexData.deviceAddress =
    renderer->gpu->get_buffer_device_address(
        mesh.index_buffer );
```

Geometry data is defined as it normally would be for traditional draws: we need to provide a vertex and index buffer, a vertex stride, and a vertex format. The primitive count is defined in the next structure.

Finally, we also need to fill a VkAccelerationStructureBuildRangeInfoKHR structure to store the primitive definition for our mesh:

```
VkAccelerationStructureBuildRangeInfoKHR build_range_info{ };
build_range_info.primitiveCount = vertex_count;
build_range_info.primitiveOffset = mesh.index_offset;
```

Now that we have the details for our meshes, we can start building the BLAS. This is a two-step process. First, we need to query how much memory our AS requires. We do so by defining a VkAccelerationStructureBuildGeometryInfoKHR structure:

```
VkAccelerationStructureBuildGeometryInfoKHR as_info{
    VK_STRUCTURE_TYPE_ACCELERATION_STRUCTURE_BUILD
        _GEOMETRY_INFO_KHR };
as_info.type =
    VK_ACCELERATION_STRUCTURE_TYPE_BOTTOM_LEVEL_KHR;
as_info.mode =
    VK_BUILD_ACCELERATION_STRUCTURE_MODE_BUILD_KHR;
as_info.geometryCount = scene->geometries.size;
as_info.pGeometries = scene->geometries.data;
```

These flags tell the Vulkan API that this BLAS could be updated or compacted in the future:

```
as_info.flags =
    VK_BUILD_ACCELERATION_STRUCTURE_ALLOW_UPDATE_BIT_KHR |
        VK_BUILD_ACCELERATION_STRUCTURE_ALLOW
            _COMPACTION_BIT_KHR;
```

When querying the size of the AS, we need to provide a list with the maximum number of primitives for each geometry entry:

```
for ( u32 range_index = 0; range_index < scene->
    geometries.size; range_index++ ) {
        max_primitives_count[ range_index ] = scene->
            build_range_infos[ range_index ].primitiveCount;
}
```

We are now ready to query the size of our AS:

```
VkAccelerationStructureBuildSizesInfoKHR as_size_info{
    VK_STRUCTURE_TYPE_ACCELERATION_STRUCTURE_BUILD
        _SIZES_INFO_KHR };
vkGetAccelerationStructureBuildSizesKHR( gpu.vulkan_device,
    VK_ACCELERATION_STRUCTURE_BUILD_TYPE_DEVICE_KHR,
        &as_info, max_primitives_count.data, &as_size_info );
```

When building an AS, we need to provide two buffers: one for the actual AS data, and one for a scratch buffer that is used in the building process. The two buffers are created as follows:

```
as_buffer_creation.set(
    VK_BUFFER_USAGE_ACCELERATION_STRUCTURE_STORAGE_BIT_KHR,
        ResourceUsageType::Immutable,
            as_size_info.accelerationStructureSize )
                .set_device_only( true )
                    .set_name( "blas_buffer" );
scene->blas_buffer = gpu.create_buffer(
    as_buffer_creation );
as_buffer_creation.set(
VK_BUFFER_USAGE_STORAGE_BUFFER_BIT |
    VK_BUFFER_USAGE_SHADER_DEVICE_ADDRESS_BIT_KHR,
        ResourceUsageType::Immutable,
```

```
                    as_size_info.buildScratchSize )
                .set_device_only( true )
                    .set_name( "blas_scratch_buffer" );
BufferHandle blas_scratch_buffer_handle =
    gpu.create_buffer( as_buffer_creation );
```

This is similar to the code for creating buffers that we have used many times before, but there are two key differences that we want to highlight:

- The AS buffer needs to be created with the VK_BUFFER_USAGE_ACCELERATION_STRUCTURE_STORAGE_BIT_KHR usage flag
- The scratch buffer needs to be created with VK_BUFFER_USAGE_SHADER_DEVICE_ADDRESS_BIT_KHR. The ray tracing extension also requires the VK_KHR_buffer_device_address extension. This allows us to query the GPU virtual address for a given buffer, but it has to be created with this usage flag.

Now we have everything we need to create our BLAS. First, we retrieve a handle for our AS:

```
VkAccelerationStructureCreateInfoKHR as_create_info{
    VK_STRUCTURE_TYPE_ACCELERATION_STRUCTURE
        _CREATE_INFO_KHR };
as_create_info.buffer = blas_buffer->vk_buffer;
as_create_info.offset = 0;
as_create_info.size =
    as_size_info.accelerationStructureSize;
as_create_info.type =
    VK_ACCELERATION_STRUCTURE_TYPE_BOTTOM_LEVEL_KHR;

vkCreateAccelerationStructureKHR( gpu.vulkan_device,
    &as_create_info, gpu.vulkan_allocation_callbacks,
        &scene->blas );
```

At this point, scene->blas is only a handle. To build our acceleration, we populate the remaining fields of our VkAccelerationStructureBuildGeometryInfoKHR structure:

```
as_info.dstAccelerationStructure = scene->blas;
as_info.scratchData.deviceAddress =
    gpu.get_buffer_device_address(
        blas_scratch_buffer_handle );
VkAccelerationStructureBuildRangeInfoKHR* blas_ranges[] = {
```

```
        scene->build_range_infos.data
};
```

Finally, we record the command to build the AS:

```
vkCmdBuildAccelerationStructuresKHR( gpu_commands->
    vk_command_buffer, 1, &as_info, blas_ranges );
gpu.submit_immediate( gpu_commands );
```

Notice that we submit this command immediately. This is required because it's not possible to build a BLAS and TLAS on the same submission, as the TLAS depends on a fully constructed BLAS.

The next and final step it to build the TLAS. The process is similar to the one we just described for the BLAS and we are going to highlight the differences. The TLAS is defined by specifying instances to multiple BLASes, where each BLAS can have its own transform. This is very similar to traditional instancing: we define our geometry once and it can be rendered multiple times by simply changing its transform.

We start by defining a VkAccelerationStructureInstanceKHR structure:

```
VkAccelerationStructureInstanceKHR tlas_structure{ };
tlas_structure.transform.matrix[ 0 ][ 0 ] = 1.0f;
tlas_structure.transform.matrix[ 1 ][ 1 ] = 1.0f;
tlas_structure.transform.matrix[ 2 ][ 2 ] = 1.0f;
tlas_structure.mask = 0xff;
tlas_structure.flags = VK_GEOMETRY_INSTANCE_TRIANGLE_FACING_CULL_DISABLE_BIT_KHR;
tlas_structure.accelerationStructureReference =
    blas_address;
```

As mentioned previously, we provide a BLAS reference and its transform. We then need to create a buffer to hold this data:

```
as_buffer_creation.reset().set(
    VK_BUFFER_USAGE_ACCELERATION_STRUCTURE
    _BUILD_INPUT_READ_ONLY_BIT_KHR | VK_BUFFER_USAGE_
    SHADER_DEVICE_ADDRESS_BIT,
    ResourceUsageType::Immutable, sizeof(
    VkAccelerationStructureInstanceKHR ) )
    .set_data( &tlas_structure )
    .set_name( "tlas_instance_buffer" );
```

```
BufferHandle tlas_instance_buffer_handle =
    gpu.create_buffer( as_buffer_creation );
```

Notice the `VK_BUFFER_USAGE_ACCELERATION_STRUCTURE_BUILD_INPUT_READ_ONLY_BIT_KHR` usage flag, which is required for buffers that are going to be used during the AS build.

Next, we define a `VkAccelerationStructureGeometryKHR` structure:

```
VkAccelerationStructureGeometryKHR tlas_geometry{
    VK_STRUCTURE_TYPE_ACCELERATION_STRUCTURE_GEOMETRY_KHR };
tlas_geometry.geometryType =
    VK_GEOMETRY_TYPE_INSTANCES_KHR;
tlas_geometry.geometry.instances.sType =
    VK_STRUCTURE_TYPE_ACCELERATION_STRUCTURE
        _GEOMETRY_INSTANCES_DATA_KHR;
tlas_geometry.geometry.instances.arrayOfPointers = false;
tlas_geometry.geometry.instances.data.deviceAddress =
    gpu.get_buffer_device_address(
        tlas_instance_buffer_handle );
```

Now that we have defined the structure of our TLAS, we need to query its size. We won't repeat the full code, but here are the differences in the `VkAccelerationStructureBuildGeometryInfoKHR` structure compared to when creating a BLAS:

```
as_info.type =
    VK_ACCELERATION_STRUCTURE_TYPE_TOP_LEVEL_KHR;
as_info.geometryCount = 1;
as_info.pGeometries = &tlas_geometry;
```

After creating the data and scratch buffer for the TLAS, we are ready to get the TLAS handle:

```
as_create_info.buffer = tlas_buffer->vk_buffer;
as_create_info.offset = 0;
as_create_info.size =
    as_size_info.accelerationStructureSize;
as_create_info.type =
    VK_ACCELERATION_STRUCTURE_TYPE_TOP_LEVEL_KHR;

vkCreateAccelerationStructureKHR( gpu.vulkan_device,
                                  &as_create_info,
```

```
                              gpu.vulkan_allocation_
                                  callbacks,
                                  &scene->tlas );
```

Finally, we can build our TLAS:

```
as_info.dstAccelerationStructure = scene->tlas;
as_info.scratchData.deviceAddress =
    gpu.get_buffer_device_address(
        tlas_scratch_buffer_handle );

VkAccelerationStructureBuildRangeInfoKHR tlas_range_info{ };
    tlas_range_info.primitiveCount = 1;

VkAccelerationStructureBuildRangeInfoKHR* tlas_ranges[] = {
    &tlas_range_info
};
vkCmdBuildAccelerationStructuresKHR( gpu_commands->
    vk_command_buffer, 1, &as_info, tlas_ranges );
```

As before, we submit this command immediately so that the TLAS is ready when we start rendering. While it's not possible to build BLAS and TLAS in the same submission, it is possible to create multiple BLAS and TLAS in parallel.

Our Acceleration Structures are now ready to be used for ray tracing!

In this section, we have detailed the steps required to create BLASes and TLASes. We started by recording the triangle primitives for our geometry. We then used this data to create a BLAS instance, which was then used as part of a TLAS.

In the next section, we are going to define a ray tracing pipeline that makes use of these Acceleration Structures.

Defining and creating a ray tracing pipeline

Now that we have defined our Acceleration Structures, we can turn our attention to ray tracing pipelines. As we mentioned previously, ray tracing shaders work differently compared to traditional graphics and compute shaders. Ray tracing shaders are setup to call other shaders according to the shader binding table setup.

If you are familiar with C++, you can think of this setup as a simple form of polymorphism: the interface of a ray tracing pipeline is always the same, but we can dynamically override which shaders (methods) get called at runtime. We don't have to define all the entry points though.

In this example, for instance, we are going to define only a ray generation, the closest hit, and the miss shader. We are ignoring any-hit and intersection shaders for now.

As the name implies, the shader binding table can be represented in table form. This is the binding table we are going to build in our example:

Ray Generation
Closest Hit
Miss

The order in the table is important, as that's the order used by the driver to tell the GPU which shader to invoke according to the stage that has been triggered.

Before we start building our pipeline, let's have a look at three example shaders we are going to use. We start with the ray generation shader, which is responsible for spawning the rays to traverse our scene. First, we have to enable the GLSL extension for ray tracing:

```
#extension GL_EXT_ray_tracing : enable
```

Next, we have to define a variable that is going to be populated by other shaders:

```
layout( location = 0 ) rayPayloadEXT vec4 payload;
```

We then define a uniform variable that will contain a reference to our AS:

```
layout( binding = 1, set = MATERIAL_SET ) uniform
    accelerationStructureEXT as;
```

Finally, we define the parameters for our ray generation call:

```
layout( binding = 2, set = MATERIAL_SET ) uniform rayParams
{
    uint sbt_offset;
    uint sbt_stride;
    uint miss_index;
    uint out_image_index;
};
```

`sbt_offset` is the offset into our shader binding table, which can be used in case multiple shaders of the same type are defined within a shader binding table. In our case, this will be 0, as we only have one entry for each shader.

`sbt_stride` is the size of each entry in the binding table. This value has to be queried for each device by passing a `VkPhysicalDeviceRayTracingPipelinePropertiesKHR` structure to `vkGetPhysicalDeviceProperties2`.

`miss_index` is used to compute the index of the miss shader. This can be used if multiple miss shaders are present within a binding table. It will be 0 in our use case.

Finally, `out_image_index` is the index of the image in our bindless image array to which we are going to write.

Now that we have defined the inputs and outputs of our ray generation shader, we can invoke the function to trace rays into the scene!

```
traceRayEXT( as, // top level acceleration structure
             gl_RayFlagsOpaqueEXT, // rayFlags
             0xff, // cullMask
             sbt_offset,
             sbt_stride,
             miss_index,
             camera_position.xyz, // origin
             0.0, // Tmin
             compute_ray_dir( gl_LaunchIDEXT,
             gl_LaunchSizeEXT ),
             100.0, // Tmax
             0 // payload
           );
```

The first parameter is the TLAS we want to traverse. Since this is a parameter to the `traceRayEXT` function, we could cast rays into multiple Acceleration Structures in the same shader.

`rayFlags` is a bit mask that determines which geometry is going to trigger a callback to our shaders. In this case, we are only interested in geometry that has the opaque flag.

`cullMask` is used to match only the entries in the AS that have the same mask value defined. This allows us to define a single AS that can be used for multiple purposes.

Finally, the payload determines the location index of the ray tracing payload we have defined here. This allows us to invoke `traceRayEXT` multiple times, with each invocation using a different payload variable.

The other fields are self-explanatory or have been explained previously. Next, we are going to have a better look at how ray directions are computed:

```
vec3 compute_ray_dir( uvec3 launchID, uvec3 launchSize) {
```

Ray tracing shaders are very similar to compute shaders, and, like compute shaders, each invocation has an ID. For a ray tracing shader this is defined in the `gl_LaunchIDEXT` variable. Likewise, `gl_LaunchSizeEXT` defines the total invocation size. This is akin to the workgroup size for compute shaders.

In our case, we have one invocation per pixel in the image. We compute x and y in **normalized device coordinates** (**NDCs**) as follows:

```
float x = ( 2 * ( float( launchID.x ) + 0.5 ) / float(
    launchSize.x ) - 1.0 );
float y = ( 1.0 - 2 * ( float( launchID.y ) + 0.5 ) /
    float( launchSize.y ) );
```

Notice that we have to invert y, as otherwise, our final image will be upside-down.

Finally, we compute our world space direction by multiplying the coordinates by the `inverse_view_projection` matrix:

```
vec4 dir = inverse_view_projection * vec4( x, y, 1, 1 );
dir = normalize( dir );

return dir.xyz;
}
```

Once `traceRayEXT` returns, the payload variable will contain the value computed through the other shaders. The final step of the ray generation is to save the color for this pixel:

```
imageStore( global_images_2d[ out_image_index ], ivec2(
    gl_LaunchIDEXT.xy ), payload );
```

We are now going to have a look at an example of a closest hit shader:

```
layout( location = 0 ) rayPayloadInEXT vec4 payload;

void main() {
    payload = vec4( 1.0, 0.0, 0.0, 1.0 );
}
```

The main difference from the ray generation shader is that the payload is now defined with the `rayPayloadInEXT` qualifier. It's also important that the location matches the one defined in the ray generation shader.

The miss shader is identical, except we use a different color to distinguish between the two.

Now that we have defined our shader code, we can start building our pipeline. Compiling ray tracing shader modules works in the same way as other shaders. The main difference is the shader type. For ray tracing, these enumerations have been added:

- `VK_SHADER_STAGE_RAYGEN_BIT_KHR`
- `VK_SHADER_STAGE_ANY_HIT_BIT_KHR`
- `VK_SHADER_STAGE_CLOSEST_HIT_BIT_KHR`
- `VK_SHADER_STAGE_MISS_BIT_KHR`
- `VK_SHADER_STAGE_INTERSECTION_BIT_KHR`
- `VK_SHADER_STAGE_CALLABLE_BIT_KHR`

For a ray tracing pipeline, we have to populate a new `VkRayTracingShaderGroupCreateInfoKHR` structure:

```
shader_group_info.sType =
    VK_STRUCTURE_TYPE_RAY_TRACING_SHADER
        _GROUP_CREATE_INFO_KHR;
shader_group_info.type =
    VK_RAY_TRACING_SHADER_GROUP_TYPE_GENERAL_KHR;
shader_group_info.generalShader = stage index;
shader_group_info.closestHitShader = VK_SHADER_UNUSED_KHR;
shader_group_info.anyHitShader = VK_SHADER_UNUSED_KHR;
shader_group_info.intersectionShader =
    VK_SHADER_UNUSED_KHR;
```

In this example, we are defining a general shader, which can be a generation, miss, or callable shader. In our case, we are defining our ray generation shader. As you can see, it's also possible to define other shaders within the same group entry. We have decided to have individual entries for each shader type as it allows us more flexibility in building our shader binding table.

Other shader types are defined similarly, and we are not going to repeat them here. As a quick example, here is how we define a closest hit shader:

```
shader_group_info.type =
    VK_RAY_TRACING_SHADER_GROUP_TYPE
        _TRIANGLES_HIT_GROUP_KHR;
shader_group_info.closestHitShader = stage_index;
```

Now that we have our shader groups defined, we can create our pipeline object:

```
VkRayTracingPipelineCreateInfoKHR pipeline_info{
    VK_STRUCTURE_TYPE_RAY_TRACING_PIPELINE_CREATE_INFO_KHR };
pipeline_info.stageCount = shader_state_data->
    active_shaders;
pipeline_info.pStages = shader_state_data->
    shader_stage_info;
pipeline_info.groupCount = shader_state_data->
    active_shaders;
pipeline_info.pGroups = shader_state_data->
    shader_group_info;
pipeline_info.maxPipelineRayRecursionDepth = 1;
pipeline_info.layout = pipeline_layout;

vkCreateRayTracingPipelinesKHR( vulkan_device,
    VK_NULL_HANDLE, pipeline_cache, 1, &pipeline_info,
        vulkan_allocation_callbacks, &pipeline->vk_pipeline );
pipeline->vk_bind_point =
    VkPipelineBindPoint::VK_PIPELINE
        _BIND_POINT_RAY_TRACING_KHR;
```

Notice the `maxPipelineRayRecursionDepth` field. It determines the maximum number of call stacks in case we have a recursive call to the `rayTraceEXT` function. This is needed by the compiler to determine how much memory could be used by this pipeline at runtime.

We have omitted the `pLibraryInfo` and `pLibraryInterface` fields, as we are not using them. Multiple ray tracing pipelines can be combined to create a larger program, similar to how you link multiple objects in C++. This can help reduce compile times for ray tracing pipelines, as individual components need to be compiled only once.

The last step is to create our shader binding table. We start by computing the size required for our table:

```
u32 group_handle_size =
    ray_tracing_pipeline_properties.shaderGroupHandleSize;
sizet shader_binding_table_size = group_handle_size *
    shader_state_data->active_shaders;
```

We simply multiply the handle size by the number of entries in our table.

Next, we call `vkGetRayTracingShaderGroupHandlesKHR` to get the handles of the groups in the ray tracing pipeline:

```
Array<u8> shader_binding_table_data{ };
shader_binding_table_data.init( allocator,
    shader_binding_table_size, shader_binding_table_size );

vkGetRayTracingShaderGroupHandlesKHR( vulkan_device,
    pipeline->vk_pipeline, 0, shader_state_data->
        active_shaders, shader_binding_table_size,
            shader_binding_table_data.data );
```

Once we have the shader group handles, we can combine them to create individual tables for each shader type. They are stored in separate buffers:

```
BufferCreation shader_binding_table_creation{ };
shader_binding_table_creation.set(
    VK_BUFFER_USAGE_SHADER_BINDING_TABLE_BIT_KHR |
    VK_BUFFER_USAGE_SHADER_DEVICE_ADDRESS_BIT_KHR,
    ResourceUsageType::Immutable, group_handle_size
    ).set_data( shader_binding_table_data.data
    ).set_name( "shader_binding_table_raygen" );
pipeline->shader_binding_table_raygen = create_buffer(
    shader_binding_table_creation );

shader_binding_table_creation.set_data(
    shader_binding_table_data.data + group_handle_size )
        .set_name( "shader_binding_table_hit" );
pipeline->shader_binding_table_hit = create_buffer(
    shader_binding_table_creation );

shader_binding_table_creation.set_data(
    shader_binding_table_data.data + ( group_handle_size *
        2 ) ).set_name( "shader_binding_table_miss" );
pipeline->shader_binding_table_miss = create_buffer(
    shader_binding_table_creation );
```

Defining and creating a ray tracing pipeline 283

We only have one entry per table, so we simply copy each group handle into its buffer. Notice that the buffer has to be created with the VK_BUFFER_USAGE_SHADER_BINDING_TABLE_BIT_KHR usage flag.

This completes our ray tracing pipeline creation. All that's left is to actually use it to generate an image! This is accomplished by the following code:

```
u32 shader_group_handle_size = gpu_device->
    ray_tracing_pipeline_properties.shaderGroupHandleSize;

VkStridedDeviceAddressRegionKHR raygen_table{ };
raygen_table.deviceAddress = gpu_device->
    get_buffer_device_address( pipeline->
        shader_binding_table_raygen );
raygen_table.stride = shader_group_handle_size;
raygen_table.size = shader_group_handle_size;

VkStridedDeviceAddressRegionKHR hit_table{ };
hit_table.deviceAddress = gpu_device->
    get_buffer_device_address( pipeline->
        shader_binding_table_hit );

VkStridedDeviceAddressRegionKHR miss_table{ };
miss_table.deviceAddress = gpu_device->
    get_buffer_device_address( pipeline->
        shader_binding_table_miss );

VkStridedDeviceAddressRegionKHR callable_table{ };

vkCmdTraceRaysKHR( vk_command_buffer, &raygen_table,
    &miss_table, &hit_table, &callable_table, width,
        height, depth );
```

We define VkStridedDeviceAddressRegionKHR for each shader binding table. We use the table buffers we previously created. Notice that we still need to define a table for callable shaders, even if we are not using them. The width, height, and depth parameters determine the invocation size of our ray tracing shader.

In this section, we have illustrated how to create and use a ray tracing pipeline. We started by defining the organization of our shader binding table. Next, we looked at a basic ray generation and closest hit shader. We then showed how to create a ray tracing pipeline object and how to retrieve shader group handles.

These handles were then used to populate the buffers of our shader binding tables. Finally, we demonstrated how to combine all these components to invoke our ray tracing pipeline.

Summary

In this chapter, we have provided the details on how to use ray tracing in Vulkan. We started by explaining two fundamental concepts:

- **Acceleration Structures**: These are needed to speed up scene traversal. This is essential to achieve real-time results.
- **Shader binding tables**: Ray tracing pipelines can invoke multiple shaders, and these tables are used to tell the API which shaders to use for which stage.

In the next section, we provided the implementation details to create TLASes and BLASes. We first record the list of geometries that compose our mesh. Next, we use this list to create a BLAS. Each BLAS can then be instanced multiple times within a TLAS, as each BLAS instance defines its own transform. With this data, we can then create our TLAS.

In the third and final section, we explained how to create a ray tracing pipeline. We started with the creation of individual shader types. Next, we demonstrated how to combine these individual shaders into a ray tracing pipeline and how to generate a shader binding table from a given pipeline.

Next, we have shown how to write a simple ray generation shader used in combination with a closest hit shader and a miss shader. Finally, we demonstrate how to combine all these pieces to trace rays in our scene.

In the next chapter, we are going to leverage all the knowledge from this chapter to implement ray-traced shadows!

Further reading

As always, we have only provided the most relevant details on how to use the Vulkan API. We recommend you read the Vulkan specification for more details. Here is the list of the most relevant sections:

- `https://registry.khronos.org/vulkan/specs/1.3-extensions/html/vkspec.html#pipelines-ray-tracing`
- `https://registry.khronos.org/vulkan/specs/1.3-extensions/html/vkspec.html#interfaces-raypipeline`

- `https://registry.khronos.org/vulkan/specs/1.3-extensions/html/vkspec.html#acceleration-structure`
- `https://registry.khronos.org/vulkan/specs/1.3-extensions/html/vkspec.html#ray-tracing`

This website provides more details on Acceleration Structures: `https://www.scratchapixel.com/lessons/3d-basic-rendering/introduction-acceleration-structure/introduction`.

There are plenty of resources online about real-time ray tracing. It's still a novel field and subject to ongoing research. A good starting point is provided by these two freely available books:

- `http://www.realtimerendering.com/raytracinggems/rtg/index.html`
- `http://www.realtimerendering.com/raytracinggems/rtg2/index.html`

13
Revisiting Shadows with Ray Tracing

In this chapter, we are going to implement shadows using **ray tracing**. In *Chapter 8, Adding Shadows Using Mesh Shaders*, we used traditional shadow mapping techniques to get the visibility from each light and use that information to compute the shadow term for the final image. Using ray tracing for shadows allows us to get more detailed results and to have finer-grained control over the quality of results based on the distance and intensity of each light.

We are going to implement two techniques: the first one is similar to the one used in offline rendering, where we shoot rays to each light to determine visibility. While this approach gives us the best results, it can be quite expensive depending on the number of lights in the scene.

The second technique is based on a recent article from **Ray Tracing Gems**. We use some heuristics to determine how many rays we need to cast per light, and we combine the results with spatial and temporal filters to make the result stable.

In this chapter, we'll cover the following main topics:

- Implementing simple ray-traced shadows
- Implementing an advanced technique for ray-traced shadows

Technical requirements

By the end of this chapter you will learn how to implement basic ray-traced shadows. You will also become familiar with a more advanced technique that is capable of rendering multiple lights with soft shadows.

The code for this chapter can be found at the following URL: `https://github.com/PacktPublishing/Mastering-Graphics-Programming-with-Vulkan/tree/main/source/chapter13`.

Implementing simple ray-traced shadows

As we mentioned in the introduction, shadow mapping techniques have been a staple of real-time rendering for many years. Before the introduction of ray tracing capabilities in GPUs, using other techniques was simply too expensive.

This hasn't prevented the graphics community from coming up with clever solutions to increase the quality of results while maintaining a low cost. The main issue with traditional techniques is that they are based on capturing depth buffers from the point of view of each light. This works well for objects that are near the light and camera, but as we move further away, depth discontinuities lead to artefacts in the final result.

Solutions to this problem include filtering the result – for instance, using **Percentage Closer Filtering** (**PCF**) or **Cascade Shadow Maps** (**CSM**). This technique requires capturing multiple depth *slices* – the cascades to maintain enough resolution as we move further away from the light. This is usually employed only for sunlight, as it can require a lot of memory and time to re-render the scene multiple times. It can also be quite difficult to get good results on the boundaries between cascades.

The other main issue with shadow mapping is that it can be difficult to get hard shadows because of the resolution of the depth buffer and the discontinuities it introduces. We can alleviate these issues with ray tracing. Offline rendering has used ray and path tracing for many years to achieve photo-realistic effects, including shadows.

They, of course, have the luxury of being able to wait for hours or days for a single frame to complete, but we can get similar results in real time. In the previous chapter, we used the `vkCmdTraceRaysKHR` command to cast rays into a scene.

For this implementation, we are introducing ray queries, which allow us to traverse the Acceleration Structures we set up from a fragment and compute shaders.

We are going to modify the `calculate_point_light_contribution` method of our lighting pass to determine which lights each fragment can see and determine the final shadow term.

First, we need to enable the `VK_KHR_ray_query` device extension. We also need to enable the related shader extension:

```
#extension GL_EXT_ray_query : enable
```

Then, instead of computing the cube map from each light point of view, we simply cast a ray from the fragment world position to each light.

We start by initializing a `rayQueryEXT` object:

```
rayQueryEXT rayQuery;
rayQueryInitializeEXT(rayQuery, as, gl_RayFlagsOpaqueEXT |
```

```
        gl_RayFlagsTerminateOnFirstHitEXT, 0xff,
            world_position, 0.001, l, d);
```

Notice the `gl_RayFlagsTerminateOnFirstHitEXT` parameter, as we are only interested in the first hit for this ray. `l` is the direction from `world_position` to the light and we use a small offset from the ray origin to avoid self-intersection.

The last parameter, d, is the distance from `world_position` to the light position. It's important to specify this value, as the ray query could report intersections past the light position otherwise, and we could incorrectly mark a fragment to be in shadow.

Now that we have initialized the ray query object, we call the following method to start scene traversal:

```
    rayQueryProceedEXT( rayQuery );
```

This will return either when a hit is found or when the ray terminates. When using ray queries, we don't have to specify a shader binding table. To determine the result of ray traversal, there are several methods we can use to query the outcome. In our case, we only want to know whether the ray hit any geometry:

```
if ( rayQueryGetIntersectionTypeEXT( rayQuery, true ) ==
    gl_RayQueryCommittedIntersectionNoneEXT ) {
        shadow = 1.0;
}
```

If not, it means we can see the light we are processing from this fragment, and we can account for this light contribution in the final computation. We repeat this for each light to obtain the overall shadow term.

While this implementation is really simple, it mainly works for point lights. For other types of light – area lights, for instance – we would need to cast multiple rays to determine the visibility. As the number of lights increases, it can become too expensive to use this simple technique.

In this section, we have demonstrated a simple implementation to get started with real-time ray-traced shadows. In the next section, we are going to introduce a new technique that scales better and can support multiple types of light.

Improving ray-traced shadows

In the previous section, we described a simple algorithm that can be used to compute the visibility term in our scene. As we mentioned, this doesn't scale well for a large number of lights and can require a large number of samples for different types of light.

In this section, we are going to implement a different algorithm inspired by the article *Ray Traced Shadows* in the *Ray Tracing Gems* book. As will be common in this chapter and upcoming chapters, the main idea is to spread the computation cost over time.

This can still lead to noisy results, as we are still using a low number of samples. To achieve the quality we are looking for, we are going to make use of spatial and temporal filtering, similar to what we did in *Chapter 11, Temporal Anti-Aliasing*.

The technique is implemented over three passes, and we are also going to leverage motion vectors. We are now going to explain each pass in detail.

Motion vectors

As we saw in *Chapter 11, Temporal Anti-Aliasing*, motion vectors are needed to determine how far an object at a given fragment has moved between frames. We need this information to determine which information to keep and which to discard for our computation. This helps us avoid ghosting artifacts in the final image.

For the technique in this chapter, we need to compute motion vectors differently compared to **Temporal Anti-Aliasing (TAA)**. We first compute the proportional difference of depth between the two frames:

```
float depth_diff = abs( 1.0 - ( previous_position_ndc.z /
    current_position_ndc.z ) );
```

Next, we compute an epsilon value that will be used to determine acceptable changes in depth:

```
float c1 = 0.003;
float c2 = 0.017;
float eps = c1 + c2 * abs( view_normal.z );
```

Finally, we use these two values to decide whether the reprojection was successful:

```
vec2 visibility_motion = depth_diff < eps ? vec2(
    current_position_ndc.xy - previous_position_ndc.xy ) :
        vec2( -1, -1 );
```

The following figure shows the result of this computation:

Figure 13.1 – The motion vector's texture

We are going to store this value in a texture for later use. The next step is to compute the variation in visibility for the past four frames.

Computing visibility variance

This technique uses data from the past four frames to determine how many samples are needed for each light for each fragment. We store the `visibility` values in a 3D RGBA16 texture, where each channel is the `visibility` value of the previous frames. Each layer stores the visibility history for individual lights.

This is one of the first compute shaders where we use a 3D dispatch size. It's worth highlighting the `dispatch` call:

```
gpu_commands->dispatch( x, y, render_scene->active_lights );
```

In this pass, we simply compute the difference between the minimum and maximum value over the past four frames:

```
vec4 last_visibility_values = texelFetch(
    global_textures_3d[ visibility_cache_texture_index ],
        tex_coord, 0 );

float max_v = max( max( max( last_visibility_values.x,
```

```
            last_visibility_values.y ), last_visibility_values.z ),
        last_visibility_values.w );
float min_v = min( min( min( last_visibility_values.x,
    last_visibility_values.y ), last_visibility_values.z ),
        last_visibility_values.w );

float delta = max_v - min_v;
```

The historical values are set to 0 during the first frame. We store the delta in another 3D texture to be used in the next pass. The following figure shows the result of this pass:

Figure 13.2 – The visibility variation for the past four frames

Computing visibility

This pass is responsible for computing how many rays to shoot for each light depending on the variance across the past four frames.

This pass needs to read a lot of data from different textures. We are going to use **local data storage** (**LDS**) to cache the values across all threads within a shader invocation:

```
local_image_data[ local_index.y ][ local_index.x ] =
    texelFetch( global_textures_3d[ variation_texture_index
        ], global_index, 0 ).r;
```

As we explained in *Chapter 9, Implementing Variable Rate Shading*, we need to be careful about synchronizing these writes by placing a `barrier()` call before accessing the data stored in `local_image_data`. Likewise, we need to populate values around the edges of the matrix. The code is the same as before and we won't replicate it here.

Next, we are going to filter this data to make it more temporally stable. The first step is to compute the maximum value in a 5x5 region and store the result in another LDS matrix:

```
local_max_image_data[ local_index.y ][ local_index.x ] =
    max_filter( local_index );
```

`max_filter` is implemented as follows:

```
for ( int y = -2; y <= 2; ++y ) {
    for ( int x = -2; x <= 2; ++x ) {
        ivec2 xy = index.xy + ivec2( x, y );

        float v = local_image_data[ xy.y ][ xy.x ];
        max_v = max( max_v, v );
    }
}
```

After computing the max values, we pass them through a 13x13 tent filter:

```
float spatial_filtered_value = 0.0;
for ( int y = -6; y <= 6; ++y ) {
    for ( int x = -6; x <= 6; ++x ) {
        ivec2 index = local_index.xy + ivec2( x, y );
        float v = local_max_image_data[ index.y ][ index.x
        ];
        float f = tent_kernel[ y + 6 ][ x + 6 ];

        spatial_filtered_value += v * f;
    }
}
```

This is done to smooth out differences between adjacent fragments while still giving more weight to the fragment we are processing. We then combine this value with temporal data:

```
vec4 last_variation_values = texelFetch(
    global_textures_3d[ variation_cache_texture_index ],
```

```
                global_index, 0 );

float filtered_value = 0.5 * ( spatial_filtered_value +
    0.25 * ( last_variation_values.x +
        last_variation_values.y +
        last_variation_values.z +
        last_variation_values.w ) );
```

Before moving on, we update the variation cache for the next frame:

```
last_variation_values.w = last_variation_values.z;
last_variation_values.z = last_variation_values.y;
last_variation_values.y = last_variation_values.x;
last_variation_values.x = texelFetch( global_textures_3d[
    variation_texture_index ], global_index, 0 ).r;
```

We now leverage the data we just obtained to compute the visibility term. First, we need to determine the sample count. If the reprojection in the previous pass has failed, we simply use the maximum sample count:

```
uint sample_count = MAX_SHADOW_VISIBILITY_SAMPLE_COUNT;
if ( motion_vectors_value.r != -1.0 ) {
```

If the reprojection was successful, we get the sample count for the last frame and determine whether the sample count has been stable over the past four frames:

```
    sample_count = sample_count_history.x;

    bool stable_sample_count =
        ( sample_count_history.x == sample_count_history.y ) &&
        ( sample_count_history.x == sample_count_history.z ) &&
        ( sample_count_history.x == sample_count_history.w );
```

We then combine this information with the filtered value we computed previously to determine the sample count for this frame:

```
    float delta = 0.2;
    if ( filtered_value > delta && sample_count <
        MAX_SHADOW_VISIBILITY_SAMPLE_COUNT ) {
            sample_count += 1;
    } else if ( stable_sample_count &&
```

```
            sample_count >= 1 ) {
                sample_count -= 1;
        }
```

If the filtered value surpasses a given threshold, we are going to increase the sample count. This means we identified a high-variance value across the past four frames and we'd need more samples to converge to a better result.

If, on the other hand, the sample count has been stable across the past four frames, we decrease the sample count.

While this works well in practice, it could reach a sample count of 0 if the scene is stable – for instance, when the camera is not moving. This would lead to an unlit scene. For this reason, we force the sample count to 1 if the past four frames also had a sample count of 0:

```
        bvec4 hasSampleHistory = lessThan(
            sample_count_history, uvec4( 1 ) );
        bool zeroSampleHistory = all( hasSampleHistory );
        if ( sample_count == 0 && zeroSampleHistory ) {
            sample_count = 1;
        }
    }
```

Here is an example of the sample count cache texture:

Figure 13.3 – The sample count cache texture

Notice that fragments that *see* the light tend to require more samples, as expected.

Now that we know how many samples we need, we can move on to computing the `visibility` value:

```
float visibility = 0.0;
if ( sample_count > 0 ) {
    // world position and normal are computed the same as
        before
    visibility = get_light_visibility(
        gl_GlobalInvocationID.z, sample_count,
        pixel_world_position, normal, frame_index );
}
```

`get_light_visibility` is the method that traces rays through the scene. It's implemented as follows:

```
const vec3 position_to_light = light.world_position -
    world_position;
const vec3 l = normalize( position_to_light );
const float NoL = clamp(dot(normal, l), 0.0, 1.0);
float d = sqrt( dot( position_to_light, position_to_light ) );
```

We first compute a few parameters as we have done before for our lighting implementation. In addition, we compute d, the distance between the world position of this fragment and the light we are processing.

Next, we trace rays through the scene only if this light is close enough and it's not behind geometry at this fragment. This is achieved using the following code:

```
float visiblity = 0.0;
float attenuation =
    attenuation_square_falloff(position_to_light,
        1.0f / light.radius);
const float scaled_distance = r / d;

if ( ( NoL > 0.001f ) && ( d <= r ) && ( attenuation >
    0.001f ) ) {
```

We then trace one ray per sample. To make sure the results converge over time, we compute the ray direction by using a pre-computed Poisson disk:

```
        for ( uint s = 0; s < sample_count; ++s ) {
            vec2 poisson_sample = POISSON_SAMPLES[ s *
                FRAME_HISTORY_COUNT + frame_index ];
```

```
            vec3 random_dir = normalize( vec3( l.x +
                poisson_sample.x, l.y + poisson_sample.y, l.z )
                );
            vec3 random_x = x_axis * poisson_sample.x *
                (scaled_distance) * 0.01;
            vec3 random_y = y_axis * poisson_sample.y *
                (scaled_distance) * 0.01;
            vec3 random_dir = normalize(l + random_x +
                random_y);
```

Now that we have computed our ray direction, we can start ray traversal:

```
            rayQueryEXT rayQuery;
            rayQueryInitializeEXT(rayQuery, as,
                gl_RayFlagsOpaqueEXT |
                gl_RayFlagsTerminateOnFirstHitEXT,
                0xff, world_position, 0.001,
                random_dir, d);
            rayQueryProceedEXT( rayQuery );
```

This code is very similar to the code we presented in the first section, but in this case, we accumulate the `visibility` value for each direction the light is visible from:

```
            if (rayQueryGetIntersectionTypeEXT(rayQuery, true)
                != gl_RayQueryCommittedIntersectionNoneEXT) {
                    visibility +=
                        rayQueryGetIntersectionTEXT(rayQuery,
                            true) < d ? 0.0f : 1.0f;
            }
            else {
                visiblity += 1.0f;
            }
        }
    }
```

Finally, we return the average of the computed `visibility` value:

```
    return visiblity / float( sample_count );
```

Now that we have the `visibility` value for this frame, we need to update our visibility history cache. If the reprojection was successful, we simply add the new value:

```
vec4 last_visibility_values = vec4(0);
if ( motion_vectors_value.r != -1.0 ) {
    last_visibility_values = texelFetch(
        global_textures_3d[ visibility_cache_texture_index
            ], global_index, 0 );

    last_visibility_values.w = last_visibility_values.z;
    last_visibility_values.z = last_visibility_values.y;
    last_visibility_values.y = last_visibility_values.x;
```

If, on the other hand, the reprojection failed, we overwrite all `history` entries with the new `visibility` value:

```
} else {
    last_visibility_values.w = visibility;
    last_visibility_values.z = visibility;
    last_visibility_values.y = visibility;
}
last_visibility_values.x = visibility;
```

The last step is to also update the sample count cache:

```
sample_count_history.w = sample_count_history.z;
sample_count_history.z = sample_count_history.y;
sample_count_history.y = sample_count_history.x;
sample_count_history.x = sample_count;
```

Now that we have updated the visibility term for this frame and updated all the caches, we can move to the last pass and compute the filtered visibility that will be used in our lighting computation.

Computing filtered visibility

If we were to use the `visibility` value as computed in the previous section, the output would be very noisy. For each frame, we might have a different sample count and sample positions, especially if the camera or objects are moving.

Improving ray-traced shadows

For this reason, we need to *clean up* the result before we can use it. One common approach is to use a denoiser. A denoiser is usually implemented as a series of compute passes that, as the name implies, will reduce the noise as much as possible. Denoisers can take a significant amount of time, especially as the resolution increases.

In our case, we are going to use a simple temporal and spatial filter to reduce the amount of time this technique takes. As with the previous pass, we need to read data into LDS first. This is accomplished by following two lines:

```
local_image_data[ local_index.y ][ local_index.x ] =
    visibility_temporal_filter( global_index );
local_normal_data[ local_index.y ][ local_index.x ] =
    get_normal( global_index );
```

`visibility_temporal_filter` is implemented as follows:

```
vec4 last_visibility_values = texelFetch(
    global_textures_3d[ visibility_cache_texture_index ],
        ivec3( xy, index.z ), 0 );

float filtered_visibility = 0.25 * (
    last_visibility_values.x + last_visibility_values.y +
    last_visibility_values.z + last_visibility_values.w );
```

We first read the historical visibility data at this fragment for the given light and simply compute the average. This is our temporal filter. Depending on your use case, you might use a different weighting function, giving more emphasis to more recent values.

For spatial filtering, we are going to use a Gaussian kernel. The original article uses variable-sized kernels according to visibility variance. In our implementation, we decided to use a fixed 5x5 Gaussian kernel, as it provides good enough results.

The loop to compute the filtered value is implemented as follows:

```
vec3 p_normal = local_normal_data[ local_index.y ][
    local_index.x ];
```

First, we store the normal in our fragment location. We then iterate over the kernel size to compute the final term:

```
for ( int y = -2; y <= 2; ++y ) {
    for ( int x = -2; x <= 2; ++x ) {
```

```
            ivec2 index = local_index.xy + ivec2( x, y );

            vec3 q_normal = local_normal_data[ local_index.y +
                y ][ local_index.x + x ];

            if ( dot( p_normal, q_normal ) <= 0.9 ) {
                continue;
            }
```

As described in the article, if the normals of adjacent fragments diverge, we ignore this data point. This is done to prevent shadow leaking.

Finally, we combine the value that has already gone through the temporal filter with the kernel value:

```
            float v = local_image_data[ index.y ][ index.x ];
            float k = gaussian_kernel[ y + 2 ][ x + 2 ];

            spatial_filtered_value += v * k;
        }
    }
```

The following figure illustrates the content of the filtered visibility texture:

Figure 13.4 – The filtered visibility texture

This concludes the computation of the `visibility` value for each light. We can now use this information during our lighting pass, as described in the next section.

Using the filtered visibility

Using our `visibility` term is really simple. In the `calculate_point_light_contribution` method, we simply have to read the visibility we have computed in the previous passes:

```
float shadow = texelFetch( global_textures_3d[
    shadow_visibility_texture_index ], ivec3( screen_uv,
        shadow_light_index ), 0 ).r;
float attenuation =
    attenuation_square_falloff(position_to_light, 1.0f /
        light.radius) * shadow;
if ( attenuation > 0.0001f && NoL > 0.0001f ) {
// same code as before
```

It could be possible to combine traditional shadow maps with a ray tracing implementation similar to the one we described here. It all depends on the frame budget for the technique, the type of lights in the scene, and the desired quality.

In this section, we have presented a different implementation for ray-traced shadows. The first step is to compute and store the visibility variance across the past four frames. Next, we computed the sample count for each fragment and each light using a `max` filter followed by a tent filter.

We then used this sample count to trace rays into the scene to determine a raw `visibility` value. In the last pass, we passed this `visibility` value through a temporal and spatial filter to reduce noise. Finally, we used this filtered value in our lighting computation.

Summary

In this chapter, we have presented two implementations for ray-traced shadows. In the first section, we provided a simple implementation similar to what you might find in an offline renderer. We simply shoot one ray per fragment to each light to determine whether it's visible or not from that position.

While this works well for point lights, it would require many rays to support other light types and render soft shadows. For this reason, we also provided an alternative that makes use of spatial and temporal information to determine how many samples to use per light.

We start by computing the visibility variance of the past four frames. We then filter this value to determine how many rays to shoot for each fragment for each light. We use this count to traverse the scene and determine the `visibility` value for each fragment. Finally, we filter the visibility we obtained to reduce the noise. The filtered visibility is then used in the lighting computation to determine the final shadow term.

In the next chapter, we continue our ray tracing journey by implementing global illumination!

Further reading

The technique we have implemented in this chapter is detailed in *Chapter 13, Revisiting Shadows with Ray Tracing,* of the book *Ray Tracing Gems*. It is freely available here: http://www.realtimerendering.com/raytracinggems/rtg/index.html.

We have only used a limited set of the GLSL APIs available for ray tracing. We recommend reading the GLSL extension specification to see all the options available:

- https://github.com/KhronosGroup/GLSL/blob/master/extensions/ext/GLSL_EXT_ray_tracing.txt
- https://github.com/KhronosGroup/GLSL/blob/master/extensions/ext/GLSL_EXT_ray_query.txt

We used a few filters in this chapter. Signal processing is a vast and wonderful field that has more implications in graphics programming than people realize. To get you started, we recommend this article by Bart Wronski: https://bartwronski.com/2021/02/15/bilinear-down-upsampling-pixel-grids-and-that-half-pixel-offset/.

14
Adding Dynamic Diffuse Global Illumination with Ray Tracing

So far in this book, illumination has been based on direct lighting coming from point lights. In this chapter, we will enhance lighting by adding indirect lighting, often referred to as global illumination in the context of video games.

This type of illumination comes from emulating the behavior of light. Without going into quantum physics and optics, the information we need to consider is that light bounces off surfaces a few times until its energy becomes zero.

Throughout movies and video games, global illumination has always been an important aspect of lighting, but often impossible to perform in real time.

With movies, it often took minutes (if not hours) to render a single frame, until global illumination was pioneered. Video games were inspired by this and now include it in their lighting.

In this chapter, we will discover how to implement real-time global illumination by covering these topics:

- Introduction to indirect lighting
- Introduction to **Dynamic Diffuse Global Illumination (DDGI)**
- Implementing DDGI

Each topic will contain subsections so that you can expand upon the knowledge provided.

The following figure shows how the code from this chapter helps contribute to indirect lighting:

Figure 14.1 – Indirect lighting output

In *Figure 14.1*, the scene has a point light on the left. We can see the green color from the light bouncing off the left curtain onto the floor and the right pillars and curtains.

On the floor in the distance, we can see the color of the sky tinting the walls. The occlusion given by its visibility provides a very low light contribution to the arches.

Technical requirements

The code for this chapter can be found at the following URL: `https://github.com/PacktPublishing/Mastering-Graphics-Programming-with-Vulkan/tree/main/source/chapter14`.

Introduction to indirect lighting

Going back to direct and indirect lighting, direct lighting just shows the first interaction between light and matter, but light continues to travel in space, bouncing at times.

From a rendering perspective, we use the G-buffer information to calculate the first light interaction with surfaces that are visible from our point of view, but we have little data on what is outside of our view.

The following diagram shows direct lighting:

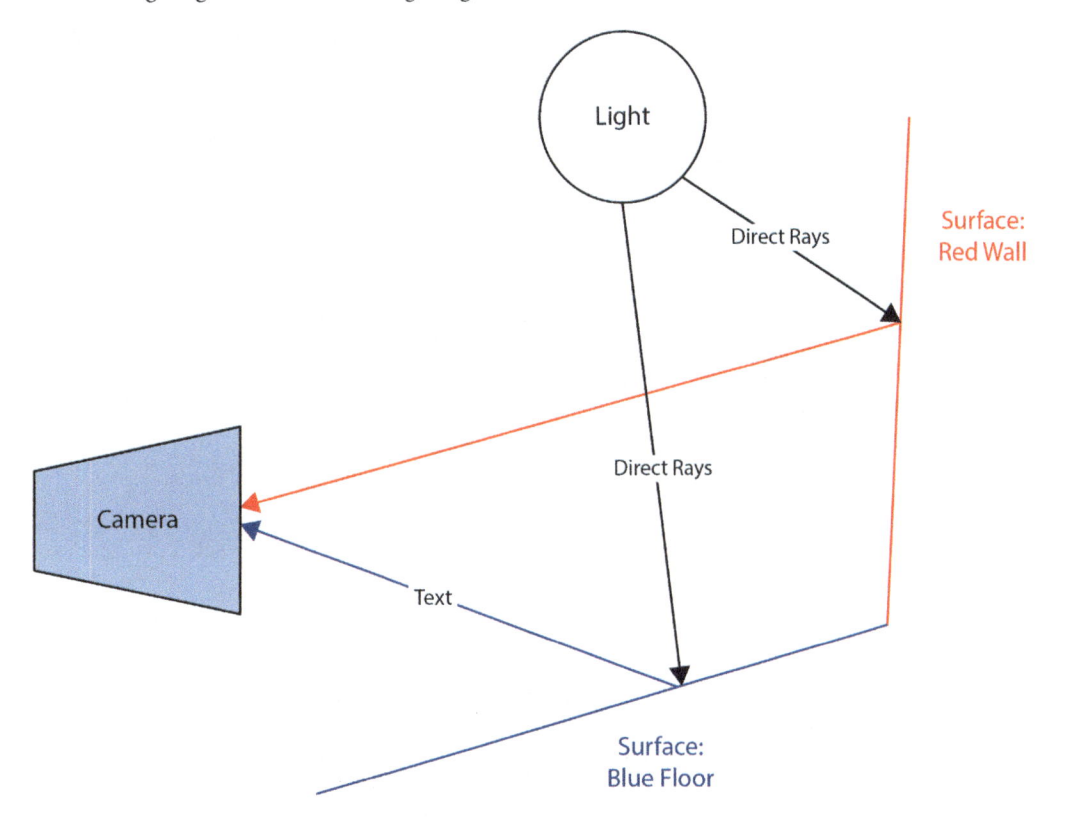

Figure 14.2 – Direct lighting

Figure 14.2 describes the current lighting setup. There are light-emitting rays, and those rays interact with surfaces. Light bounces off these surfaces and is captured by the camera, becoming the pixel color. This is an extremely simplified vision of the phenomena, but it contains all the basics we need.

For indirect lighting, relying only on the camera's point of view is insufficient as we need to calculate how other lights and geometries can contribute and still affect the visible part of the scene but are outside of the view, as well as the visible surfaces.

For this matter, **ray tracing** is the best tool: it's a way to query the scene spacially as we can use it to calculate how different bounces of light contribute to the final value of a given fragment.

Here is a diagram showing indirect lighting:

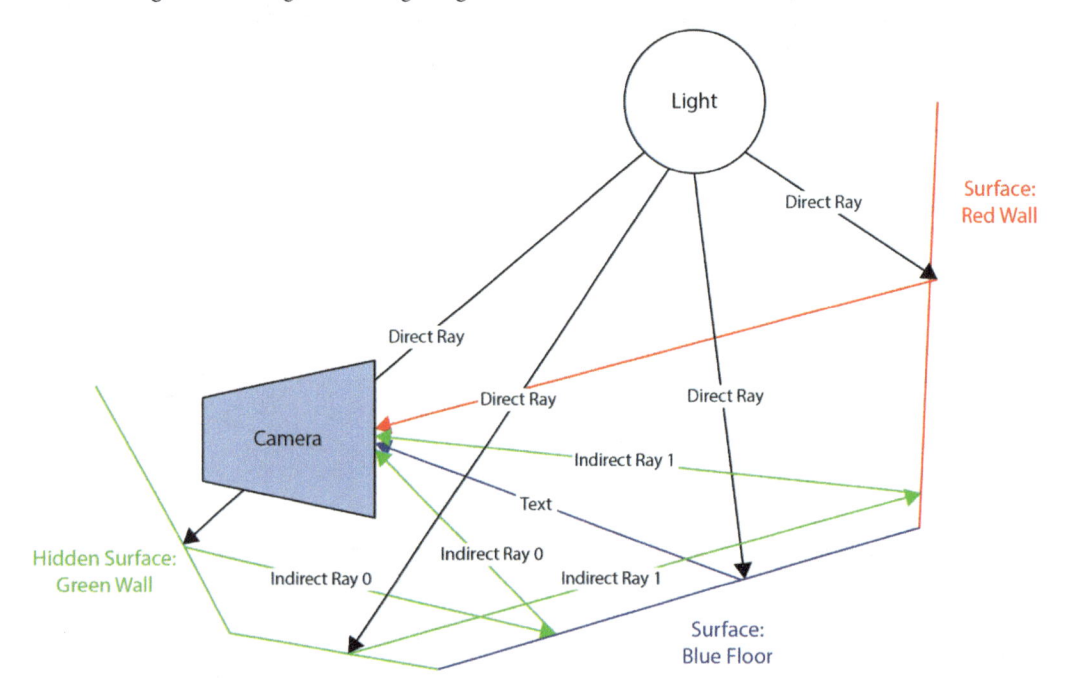

Figure 14.3 – Indirect lighting

Figure 14.3 shows indirect rays bouncing off surfaces until they hit the camera again.

There are two rays highlighted in this figure:

- **Indirect Ray 0**, bouncing off a hidden surface onto the blue floor and finally into the camera
- **Indirect Ray 0**, bouncing off another surface and bouncing off the red wall, and finally into the camera

With indirect illumination, we want to capture the phenomena of rays of light bouncing off surfaces, both hidden and not.

For example, in this setup, there are some rays between the red and blue surfaces that will bounce within each other, tinting the closer parts of the surfaces of the respective colors.

Adding indirect illumination to lighting enhances the realism and visual quality of the image, but how can we achieve that?

In the next section, we will talk about the implementation that we chose: **Dynamic Diffuse Global Illumination**, or **DDGI**, which was developed mainly by researchers at Nvidia but is rapidly becoming one of the most used solutions in AAA games.

Introduction to Dynamic Diffuse Global Illumination (DDGI)

In this section, we will explain the algorithm behind DDGI. DDGI is based on two main tools: light probes and irradiance volumes:

- **Light probes** are points in space, represented as spheres, that encode light information
- **Irradiance volumes** are defined as spaces that contain three-dimensional grids of light probes with fixed spacing between them

Sampling is easier when the layout is regular, even though we will see some improvements to placements later. Probes are encoded using octahedral mapping, a convenient way to map a square to a sphere. Links to the math behind octahedral mapping have been provided in the *Further reading* section.

The core idea behind DDGI is to dynamically update probes using ray tracing: for each probe, we will cast some rays and calculate the radiance at the triangle intersection. Radiance is calculated with the dynamic lights present in the engine, reacting in real time to any light or geometry changes.

Given the low resolution of the grid compared to the pixels on the screen, the only lighting phenomenon possible is diffuse lighting. The following diagram provides an overview of the algorithm, showing the relationships and the sequences between shaders (green rectangles) and textures (yellow ellipses):

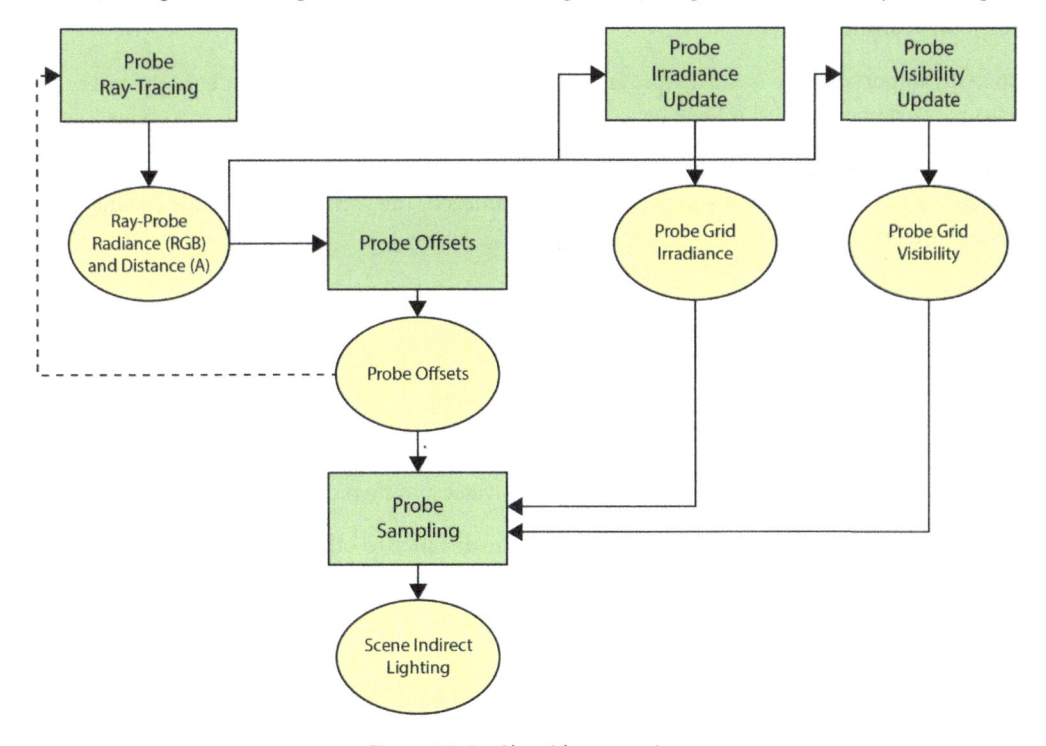

Figure 14.4 – Algorithm overview

Let's provide a quick overview of the algorithm before looking at each step in detail:

1. Perform ray tracing for each probe and calculate the radiance and distance.
2. Update the irradiance of all probes with the radiance calculated while applying some hysteresis.
3. Update the visibility data of all probes with the distance calculated in the ray tracing pass, again with some hysteresis.
4. (Optional) Calculate the per-probe offset position using the ray tracing distance.
5. Calculate indirect lighting by reading the updated irradiance, visibility, and probe offsets.

In the following subsections, we will cover each step of the algorithm.

Ray tracing for each probe

This is the first step of the algorithm. For each ray of each probe that needs an update, we must ray trace the scene using dynamic lighting.

In the ray tracing hit shader, we calculate the world position and normal of the hit triangle and perform a simplified diffuse lighting calculation. Optionally, but more expensive, we can read the other irradiance probes to add an infinite number of bounces to the lighting calculation, giving it an even more realistic look.

Especially important here is the texture layout: each row represents the rays for a single probe. So, if we have 128 rays per probe, we will have a row of 128 texels, while each column represents a probe.

Thus, a configuration with 128 rays and 24 probes will result in a 128x24 texture dimension. We store the lighting calculation as radiance in the RGB channels of the texture, and the hit distance in the Alpha channel.

Hit distance will be used to help with light leaks and calculating probe offsets.

Probes offsetting

Probes offsetting is a step that's done when an irradiance volume is loaded into the world, or its properties are changed (such as spacing or position). Using the hit distances from the ray tracing step, we can calculate if a probe is placed straight into a surface and then create an offset for it.

The offsetting amount cannot be bigger than half the distance to other probes so that the grid still maintains some coherency between the grid indices and their position. This step is only done a few times (normally, around five is a suitable number) as having it run continuously will indefinitely move the probes, thus causing light flickering.

Once the offsets have been calculated, every probe will have the final world position, drastically increasing the visual quality of indirect lighting.

Here, we can see the improvement after calculating these offsets:

Figure 14.5 – Global illumination with (left) and without (right) probe offsets

As you can see, the probes that are inside a geometry not only give no lighting contribution to the sampling but can create visual artifacts.

Thanks to probe offsetting, we can place probes in a better position.

Probes irradiance and visibility updates

We now have the result of each ray that's been traced for each probe with dynamic lighting applied. How can we encode this information? As seen in the *Introduction to Dynamic Diffuse Global Illumination (DDGI)* section, one of the ways is to use octahedral mapping, which unwraps a sphere into a rectangle.

Given that we are storing each probe's radiance as a 3D volume, we need a texture that contains a rectangle for each probe. We will choose to create a single texture with a row that contains a *layer* of probes as MxN, while the height contains the other layers.

For example, if we have a grid of 3x2x4 probes, each row will contain 6 probes (3x2) and the final texture will have 4 rows. We will execute this step two times, one to update the irradiance from the radiance, and the other to update the visibility from the distance of each probe.

Visibility is crucial for minimizing light leaks, and irradiance and visibility are stored in different textures and can have different sizes.

One thing to be aware of is that to add support for bilinear filtering, we need to store an additional 1-pixel border around each rectangle; this will be updated here as well.

The shader will read the new radiance and distances calculated and the previous frame's irradiance and visibility textures to blend the values to avoid flickering, as Volumetric Fog does with temporal reprojection, using a simple hysteresis.

Hysteresis can be changed dynamically if the lighting conditions change drastically to counteract slow updates using hysteresis. The results will normally be slower to react to light movements, but it is a drawback needed to avoid flickering.

The last part of the shader involves updating the borders for bilinear filtering. Bilinear filtering requires samples to be read in a specific order, as highlighted in the following diagram:

6,6	6,1	5,1	4,1	3,1	2,1	1,1	1,6
1,6	1,1	2,1	3,1	4,1	5,1	6,1	6,6
1,5	1,2	2,2	3,2	4,2	5,2	6,2	6,5
1,4	1,3	2,3	3,3	4,3	5,3	6,3	6,4
1,3	1,4	2,4	3,4	4,4	5,4	6,4	6,3
1,2	1,5	2,5	3,5	4,5	5,5	6,5	6,2
1,1	1,6	6,6	3,6	4,6	5,6	6,6	6,1
6,1	6,6	5,6	4,6	3,6	1,6	1,6	1,1

Figure 14.6 – Bilinear filtering samples. The outer grid copies pixels from the written pixel positions inside each rectangle

Figure 14.6 shows the coordinate calculations for copying pixels: the center area is the one that did the full irradiance/visibility update, while the borders copy the values from the pixels at the specified coordinates.

We will run two different shaders – one to update probe irradiance and one to update probe visibility.

In the shader code, we will see the actual code to do this. We are now ready to sample the irradiance of the probes, as seen in the next subsection.

Probes sampling

This step involves reading the irradiance probes and calculating the indirect lighting contribution. We will render from the main camera's point of view, and we will sample the eight closest probes given a world position and direction. The visibility texture is used to minimize leakage and soften the lighting results.

Given the soft lighting nature of diffuse indirect components and to obtain better performance, we have opted to sample this at a quarter resolution, so we need to take extra care of where we sample to avoid pixel inaccuracies.

While looking at probe ray tracing, irradiance updates, visibility updates, probe offsetting, and probe sampling, we described all the basic steps necessary to have a working DDGI implementation.

Other steps can be included to make the rendering even faster, such as using the distances to calculate inactive probes. Other extensions can also be included, such as those that contain a cascade of volumes and hand-placed volumes that give DDGI the best flexibility needed to be used in video games, where different hardware configurations can dictate algorithmic choices.

In the next section, we will learn how to implement DDGI.

Implementing DDGI

The first shaders we will read are the ray tracing shaders. These, as we saw in *Chapter 12*, *Getting Started with Ray Tracing*, come as a bundle that includes the ray-generation, ray-hit, and ray-miss shaders.

There are a set of different methods that convert from world space into grid indices and vice versa that will be used here; they are included with the code.

First, we want to define the ray payload – that is, the information that's cached after the ray tracing query is performed:

```
struct RayPayload {
    vec3 radiance;
    float distance;
};
```

Ray-generation shader

The first shader is called ray-generation. It spawns rays from the probe's position using random directions on a sphere using spherical Fibonacci sequences.

Like dithering for TAA and Volumetric Fog, using random directions and temporal accumulation (which happens in the Probe Update shader) allows us to have more information about the scene, thus enhancing the visuals:

```
layout( location = 0 ) rayPayloadEXT RayPayload payload;
void main() {
const ivec2 pixel_coord = ivec2(gl_LaunchIDEXT.xy);
    const int probe_index = pixel_coord.y;
```

```
const int ray_index = pixel_coord.x;
// Convert from linear probe index to grid probe
    indices and then position:
ivec3 probe_grid_indices = probe_index_to_grid_indices(
    probe_index );
vec3 ray_origin = grid_indices_to_world(
    probe_grid_indices probe_index );
vec3 direction = normalize( mat3(random_rotation) *
    spherical_fibonacci(ray_index, probe_rays) );
payload.radiance = vec3(0);
payload.distance = 0;
traceRayEXT(as, gl_RayFlagsOpaqueEXT, 0xff, 0, 0, 0,
    ray_origin, 0.0, direction, 100.0, 0);

// Store the result coming from Hit or Miss shaders
imageStore(global_images_2d[ radiance_output_index ],
    pixel_coord, vec4(payload.radiance, payload.distance));
}
```

Ray-hit shader

This is where all the heavy lifting happens.

First, we must declare the payload and the barycentric coordinates to calculate the correct triangle data:

```
layout( location = 0 ) rayPayloadInEXT RayPayload payload;
hitAttributeEXT vec2 barycentric_weights;
```

Then, check for back-facing triangles, storing only the distance as lighting is not needed:

```
void main() {
    vec3 radiance = vec3(0);
    float distance = 0.0f;
    if (gl_HitKindEXT == gl_HitKindBackFacingTriangleEXT) {
        // Track backfacing rays with negative distance
        distance = gl_RayTminEXT + gl_HitTEXT;
        distance *= -0.2;
    }
```

Otherwise, calculate the triangle data and perform lighting:

```
else {
```

Next, read the mesh instance data and read the index buffer:

```
uint mesh_index = mesh_instance_draws[
  gl_GeometryIndexEXT ].mesh_draw_index;
MeshDraw mesh = mesh_draws[ mesh_index ];

int_array_type index_buffer = int_array_type(
  mesh.index_buffer );
int i0 = index_buffer[ gl_PrimitiveID * 3 ].v;
int i1 = index_buffer[ gl_PrimitiveID * 3 + 1 ].v;
int i2 = index_buffer[ gl_PrimitiveID * 3 + 2 ].v;
```

Now, we can read the vertices from the mesh buffer and calculate the world space position:

```
float_array_type vertex_buffer = float_array_type(
  mesh.position_buffer );
vec4 p0 = vec4(vertex_buffer[ i0 * 3 + 0 ].v,
  vertex_buffer[ i0 * 3 + 1 ].v,
  vertex_buffer[ i0 * 3 + 2 ].v, 1.0 );
// Calculate p1 and p2 using i1 and i2 in the same
   way.
```

Calculate the world position:

```
const mat4 transform = mesh_instance_draws[
  gl_GeometryIndexEXT ].model;
vec4 p0_world = transform * p0;
// calculate as well p1_world and p2_world
```

As we did for the vertex positions, read the UV buffer and calculate the final UVs of the triangle:

```
float_array_type uv_buffer = float_array_type(
  mesh.uv_buffer );
vec2 uv0 = vec2(uv_buffer[ i0 * 2 ].v, uv_buffer[
  i0 * 2 + 1].v);
// Read uv1 and uv2 using i1 and i2
```

```
            float b = barycentric_weights.x;
            float c = barycentric_weights.y;
            float a = 1 - b - c;

            vec2 uv = ( a * uv0 + b * uv1 + c * uv2 );
```

Read the diffuse texture. We can also read a lower MIP to improve performance:

```
            vec3 diffuse = texture( global_textures[
              nonuniformEXT( mesh.textures.x ) ], uv ).rgb;
```

Read the triangle normals and calculate the final normal. You don't need to read the normal texture as the cached result is so small that those details are lost:

```
            float_array_type normals_buffer =
              float_array_type( mesh.normals_buffer );
            vec3 n0 = vec3(normals_buffer[ i0 * 3 + 0 ].v,
              normals_buffer[ i0 * 3 + 1 ].v,
              normals_buffer[ i0 * 3 + 2 ].v );
            // Similar calculations for n1 and n2 using i1 and
              i2
            vec3 normal = a * n0 + b * n1 + c * n2;
            const mat3 normal_transform = mat3(mesh_instance_draws
              [gl_GeometryIndexEXT ].model_inverse);
            normal = normal_transform * normal;
```

We can calculate the world position and the normal, and then calculate the direct lighting:

```
            const vec3 world_position = a * p0_world.xyz + b *
              p1_world.xyz + c * p2_world.xyz;
            vec3 diffuse = albedo * direct_lighting(world_position,
              normal);
            // Optional: infinite bounces by samplying previous
              frame Irradiance:
            diffuse += albedo * sample_irradiance( world_position,
              normal, camera_position.xyz ) *
              infinite_bounces_multiplier;
```

Finally, we can cache the radiance and the distance:

```
    radiance = diffuse;
    distance = gl_RayTminEXT + gl_HitTEXT;
}
```

Now, let's write the results to the payload:

```
    payload.radiance = radiance;
    payload.distance = distance;
}
```

Ray-miss shader

In this shader, we simply return the sky color. Alternatively, if present, an environment cube map can be added:

```
layout( location = 0 ) rayPayloadInEXT RayPayload payload;
void main() {
payload.radiance = vec3( 0.529, 0.807, 0.921 );
payload.distance = 1000.0f;
}
```

Updating probes irradiance and visibility shaders

This compute shader will read the previous frame's irradiance/visibility and the current frame's radiance/distance and update the octahedral representation of each probe. This shader will be executed twice – once to update the irradiance and once to update the visibility. It will also update the borders to add support for bilinear filtering.

First, we must check if the current pixel is a border. If so, we must change modes:

```
layout (local_size_x = 8, local_size_y = 8, local_size_z =
        1) in;
void main() {
    ivec3 coords = ivec3(gl_GlobalInvocationID.xyz);
    const uint probe_with_border_side = probe_side_length +
                                     2;
    const uint probe_last_pixel = probe_side_length + 1;
    int probe_index = get_probe_index_from_pixels
      (coords.xy, int(probe_with_border_side),
```

```
            probe_texture_width);
    // Check if thread is a border pixel
    bool border_pixel = ((gl_GlobalInvocationID.x %
        probe_with_border_side) == 0) ||
        ((gl_GlobalInvocationID.x % probe_with_border_side )
        == probe_last_pixel );
    border_pixel = border_pixel ||
        ((gl_GlobalInvocationID.y % probe_with_border_side)
        == 0) || ((gl_GlobalInvocationID.y %
        probe_with_border_side ) == probe_last_pixel );
```

For non-border pixels, calculate a weight based on ray direction and the direction of the sphere encoded with octahedral coordinates, and calculate the irradiance as the summed weight of the radiances:

```
    if ( !border_pixel ) {
        vec4 result = vec4(0);
        uint backfaces = 0;
        uint max_backfaces = uint(probe_rays * 0.1f);
```

Add the contribution from each ray:

```
            for ( int ray_index = 0; ray_index < probe_rays;
                ++ray_index ) {
                ivec2 sample_position = ivec2( ray_index,
                    probe_index );
                vec3 ray_direction = normalize(
                    mat3(random_rotation) *
                    spherical_fibonacci(ray_index, probe_rays) );
                vec3 texel_direction = oct_decode
                    (normalized_oct_coord(coords.xy));
                float weight = max(0.0, dot(texel_direction,
                    ray_direction));
```

Read the distance for this ray and early out if there are too many back faces:

```
                float distance = texelFetch(global_textures
                    [nonuniformEXT(radiance_output_index)],
                    sample_position,
                    0).w;
```

```
            if ( distance < 0.0f &&
                use_backfacing_blending() ) {
            ++backfaces;
            // Early out: only blend ray radiance into
                the probe if the backface threshold
                hasn't been exceeded
            if (backfaces >= max_backfaces) {
                return;
            }
            continue;
            }
```

At this point, depending on if we are updating the irradiance or the visibility, we perform different calculations.

For **irradiance**, we must do the following:

```
            if (weight >= EPSILON) {
                vec3 radiance = texelFetch(global_textures
                    [nonuniformEXT(radiance_output_index)],
                    sample_position, 0).rgb;
                radiance.rgb *= energy_conservation;

                // Storing the sum of the weights in alpha
                    temporarily
                result += vec4(radiance * weight, weight);
            }
```

For **visibility**, we must read and limit the distance:

```
            float probe_max_ray_distance = 1.0f * 1.5f;
            if (weight >= EPSILON) {
                float distance = texelFetch(global_textures
                    [nonuniformEXT(radiance_output_index)],
                    sample_position, 0).w;
                // Limit distance
                distance = min(abs(distance),
                  probe_max_ray_distance);
```

```
                        vec3 value = vec3(distance, distance *
                          distance, 0);
                        // Storing the sum of the weights in alpha
                          temporarily
                        result += vec4(value * weight, weight);
                }
        }
```

Finally, apply the weight:

```
        if (result.w > EPSILON) {
            result.xyz /= result.w;
            result.w = 1.0f;
        }
```

Now, we can read the previous frame's irradiance or visibility and blend it using hysteresis.

For **irradiance**, we must do the following:

```
        vec4 previous_value = imageLoad( irradiance_image,
          coords.xy );
        result = mix( result, previous_value, hysteresis );
        imageStore(irradiance_image, coords.xy, result);
```

For **visibility**, we must do the following:

```
        vec2 previous_value = imageLoad( visibility_image,
          coords.xy ).rg;
        result.rg = mix( result.rg, previous_value,
          hysteresis );
        imageStore(visibility_image, coords.xy,
          vec4(result.rg, 0, 1));
```

At this point, we end the shader for non-border pixels. We will wait for the local group to finish and copy the pixels to the borders:

```
        // NOTE: returning here.
        return;
    }
```

Next, we must operate on the border pixels.

Given that we are working on a local thread group that's as big as each square, when a group is finished, we can copy the border pixels with the currently updated data. This is an optimization process that helps us avoid dispatching two other shaders and adding barriers to wait for the updates to be done.

After implementing the preceding code, we must wait for the group to finish:

```
groupMemoryBarrier();
barrier();
```

Once those barriers are in the shader code, all the groups will be completed.

We have the final irradiance/visibility stored in the texture, so we can copy the border pixels to add bilinear sampling support. As shown in *Figure 14.6*, we need to read the pixels in a specific order to ensure bilinear filtering is working properly.

First, we must calculate the source pixel coordinates:

```
const uint probe_pixel_x = gl_GlobalInvocationID.x %
  probe_with_border_side;
const uint probe_pixel_y = gl_GlobalInvocationID.y %
  probe_with_border_side;
bool corner_pixel = (probe_pixel_x == 0 ||
  probe_pixel_x == probe_last_pixel) && (probe_pixel_y
  == 0 || probe_pixel_y == probe_last_pixel);
bool row_pixel = (probe_pixel_x > 0 && probe_pixel_x <
  probe_last_pixel);
ivec2 source_pixel_coordinate = coords.xy;
if ( corner_pixel ) {
    source_pixel_coordinate.x += probe_pixel_x == 0 ?
      probe_side_length : -probe_side_length;
    source_pixel_coordinate.y += probe_pixel_y == 0 ?
      probe_side_length : -probe_side_length;
}
else if ( row_pixel ) {
    source_pixel_coordinate.x +=
      k_read_table[probe_pixel_x - 1];
    source_pixel_coordinate.y += (probe_pixel_y > 0) ?
      -1 : 1;
}
```

```
    else {
        source_pixel_coordinate.x += (probe_pixel_x > 0) ?
            -1 : 1;
        source_pixel_coordinate.y +=
            k_read_table[probe_pixel_y - 1];
    }
```

Next, we must copy the source pixels to the current border.

For **irradiance**, we must do the following:

```
vec4 copied_data = imageLoad( irradiance_image,
    source_pixel_coordinate );
imageStore( irradiance_image, coords.xy, copied_data );
```

For **visibility**, we must do the following:

```
vec4 copied_data = imageLoad( visibility_image,
    source_pixel_coordinate );
imageStore( visibility_image, coords.xy, copied_data );
}
```

We now have the updated irradiance and visibility ready to be sampled by the scene.

Indirect lighting sampling

This compute shader is responsible for reading the indirect irradiance so that it's ready to be used by the illumination. It uses a utility method called `sample_irradiance`, which is also used inside the ray-hit shader to simulate an infinite bounce.

First, though, let's look at the compute shader. When using the quarter resolution, cycle through a neighborhood of 2x2 pixels and get the closest depth, and save the pixel index:

```
layout (local_size_x = 8, local_size_y = 8, local_size_z =
        1) in;
void main() {
    ivec3 coords = ivec3(gl_GlobalInvocationID.xyz);
    int resolution_divider = output_resolution_half == 1 ?
        2 : 1;
    vec2 screen_uv = uv_nearest(coords.xy, resolution /
```

```
    resolution_divider);

float raw_depth = 1.0f;
int chosen_hiresolution_sample_index = 0;
if (output_resolution_half == 1) {
    float closer_depth = 0.f;
    for ( int i = 0; i < 4; ++i ) {
        float depth = texelFetch(global_textures
          [nonuniformEXT(depth_fullscreen_texture_index)
          ], (coords.xy) * 2 + pixel_offsets[i], 0).r;
        if ( closer_depth < depth ) {
            closer_depth = depth;
            chosen_hiresolution_sample_index = i;
        }
    }

    raw_depth = closer_depth;
}
```

With the cached index of the closest depth, read the normal as well:

```
vec3 normal = vec3(0);
if (output_resolution_half == 1) {
    vec2 encoded_normal = texelFetch(global_textures
        [nonuniformEXT(normal_texture_index)],
        (coords.xy) * 2 + pixel_offsets
        [chosen_hiresolution_sample_index], 0).rg;
    normal = normalize(octahedral_decode(encoded_normal)
        );
}
```

Now that we have calculated the depth and the normal, we can gather the world position and use the normal to sample the irradiance:

```
const vec3 pixel_world_position =
  world_position_from_depth(screen_uv, raw_depth,
  inverse_view_projection)
vec3 irradiance = sample_irradiance(
```

```
            pixel_world_position, normal, camera_position.xyz );
        imageStore(global_images_2d[ indirect_output_index ],
            coords.xy, vec4(irradiance,1));
    }
```

The second part of this shader is about the `sample_irradiance` function, which does the actual heavy lifting.

It starts by calculating a bias vector to move the sampling so that it's a little bit in front of the geometry, to help with leaks:

```
vec3 sample_irradiance( vec3 world_position, vec3 normal,
    vec3 camera_position ) {
        const vec3 V = normalize(camera_position.xyz -
            world_position);
        // Bias vector to offset probe sampling based on normal
            and view vector.
        const float minimum_distance_between_probes = 1.0f;
        vec3 bias_vector = (normal * 0.2f + V * 0.8f) *
            (0.75f  minimum_distance_between_probes) *
            self_shadow_bias;
        vec3 biased_world_position = world_position +
            bias_vector;

        // Sample at world position + probe offset reduces
            shadow leaking.
        ivec3 base_grid_indices =
            world_to_grid_indices(biased_world_position);
        vec3 base_probe_world_position =
            grid_indices_to_world_no_offsets( base_grid_indices
            );
```

We now have the grid world position and indices at the sampling world position (plus the bias).

Now, we must calculate a per-axis value of where the sampling position is within the cell:

```
        // alpha is how far from the floor(currentVertex)
            position. on [0, 1] for each axis.
        vec3 alpha = clamp((biased_world_position -
            base_probe_world_position) , vec3(0.0f), vec3(1.0f));
```

Implementing DDGI

At this point, we can sample the eight adjacent probes to the sampling point:

```
vec3  sum_irradiance = vec3(0.0f);
float sum_weight = 0.0f;
```

For each probe, we must calculate its world space position from the indices:

```
// Iterate over adjacent probe cage
for (int i = 0; i < 8; ++i) {
    // Compute the offset grid coord and clamp to the
       probe grid boundary
    // Offset = 0 or 1 along each axis
    ivec3  offset = ivec3(i, i >> 1, i >> 2) &
      ivec3(1);
    ivec3  probe_grid_coord = clamp(base_grid_indices +
      offset, ivec3(0), probe_counts - ivec3(1));
    int probe_index =
      probe_indices_to_index(probe_grid_coord);
    vec3 probe_pos =
      grid_indices_to_world(probe_grid_coord,
      probe_index);
```

Compute the trilinear weights based on the grid cell vertex to smoothly transition between probes:

```
vec3 trilinear = mix(1.0 - alpha, alpha, offset);
float weight = 1.0;
```

Now, we can see how the visibility texture is used. It stores depth and depth squared values, and helps tremendously with light leaking.

This test is based on variance, such as Variance Shadow Map:

```
vec3 probe_to_biased_point_direction =
  biased_world_position - probe_pos;
float distance_to_biased_point =
  length(probe_to_biased_point_direction);
probe_to_biased_point_direction *= 1.0 /
  distance_to_biased_point;
{
```

```
            vec2 uv = get_probe_uv
              (probe_to_biased_point_direction,
              probe_index, probe_texture_width,
              probe_texture_height,
              probe_side_length );
            vec2 visibility = textureLod(global_textures
            [nonuniformEXT(grid_visibility_texture_index)],
            uv, 0).rg;
            float mean_distance_to_occluder = visibility.x;
            float chebyshev_weight = 1.0;
```

Check if the sampled probe is in "shadow" and calculate the Chebyshev weight:

```
            if (distance_to_biased_point >
               mean_distance_to_occluder) {
               float variance = abs((visibility.x *
                 visibility.x) - visibility.y);
               const float distance_diff =
                 distance_to_biased_point -
                 mean_distance_to_occluder;
               chebyshev_weight = variance / (variance +
                 (distance_diff * distance_diff));
               // Increase contrast in the weight
               chebyshev_weight = max((chebyshev_weight *
                 chebyshev_weight * chebyshev_weight),
                   0.0f);
            }

             // Avoid visibility weights ever going all of
                the way to zero
            chebyshev_weight = max(0.05f, chebyshev_weight);
            weight *= chebyshev_weight;
        }
```

With the weight calculated for this probe, we can apply the trilinear offset, read the irradiance, and calculate its contribution:

```
        vec2 uv = get_probe_uv(normal, probe_index,
          probe_texture_width, probe_texture_height,
          probe_side_length );
        vec3 probe_irradiance =
          textureLod(global_textures
          [nonuniformEXT(grid_irradiance_output_index)],
          uv, 0).rgb;
         // Trilinear weights
        weight *= trilinear.x * trilinear.y * trilinear.z +
          0.001f;
        sum_irradiance += weight * probe_irradiance;
        sum_weight += weight;
}
```

With all the probes sampled, the final irradiance is scaled accordingly and returned:

```
    vec3 irradiance = 0.5f * PI * sum_irradiance /
      sum_weight;
    return irradiance;
}
```

With that, we've finished looking at the irradiance sampling compute shader and utility functions.

More filters can be applied to the sampling to further smooth the image, but this is the most basic version that's enhanced by the visibility data.

Now, let's learn how the `calculate_lighting` method can be modified to add diffuse indirect.

Modifications to the calculate_lighting method

In our `lighting.h` shader file, add the following lines once the direct lighting computations have been done:

```
    vec3 F = fresnel_schlick_roughness(max(dot(normal, V),
      0.0), F0, roughness);
    vec3 kS = F;
    vec3 kD = 1.0 - kS;
    kD *= 1.0 - metallic;
```

```
    vec3 indirect_irradiance = textureLod(global_textures
        [nonuniformEXT(indirect_lighting_texture_index)],
      screen_uv, 0).rgb;
    vec3 indirect_diffuse = indirect_irradiance *
      base_colour.rgb;
    const float ao = 1.0f;
    final_color.rgb += (kD * indirect_diffuse) * ao;
```

Here, `base_colour` is the albedo coming from the G-buffer and `final_color` is the pixel color with all the direct lighting contributions calculated.

The basic algorithm is complete, but there is one last shader to have a look at: the Probe Offset shader. It calculates a per-probe world-space offset to avoid intersecting probes with geometries.

Probe offsets shader

This compute shader cleverly uses the per-ray distances coming from the ray tracing pass to calculate the offset based on backface and frontface counts.

First, we must check for an invalid probe index to avoid writing to the wrong memory:

```
  layout (local_size_x = 32, local_size_y = 1, local_size_z =
        1) in;
void main() {
    ivec3 coords = ivec3(gl_GlobalInvocationID.xyz);
    // Invoke this shader for each probe
    int probe_index = coords.x;
    const int total_probes = probe_counts.x *
        probe_counts.y * probe_counts.z;
    // Early out if index is not valid
    if (probe_index >= total_probes) {
        return;
    }
```

Now, we must search for front and backface hits based on the ray tracing distance that's been calculated.

First, declare all the necessary variables:

```
    int closest_backface_index = -1;
    float closest_backface_distance = 100000000.f;
    int closest_frontface_index = -1;
```

```
    float closest_frontface_distance = 100000000.f;
    int farthest_frontface_index = -1;
    float farthest_frontface_distance = 0;
    int backfaces_count = 0;
```

For each ray of this probe, read the distance and calculate if it is a front or backface. We store negative distances for backfaces in the hit shader:

```
    // For each ray cache front/backfaces index and
       distances.
    for (int ray_index = 0; ray_index < probe_rays;
       ++ray_index) {
      ivec2 ray_tex_coord = ivec2(ray_index,
        probe_index);
      float ray_distance = texelFetch(global_textures
        [nonuniformEXT(radiance_output_index)],
        ray_tex_coord, 0).w;
      // Negative distance is stored for backface hits in
         the Ray Tracing Hit shader.
      if ( ray_distance <= 0.0f ) {
        ++backfaces_count;
        // Distance is a positive value, thus negate
           ray_distance as it is negative already if
        // we are inside this branch.
        if ( (-ray_distance) <
             closest_backface_distance ) {
           closest_backface_distance = ray_distance;
           closest_backface_index = ray_index;
        }
      }
      else {
          // Cache either closest or farther distance and
             indices for this ray.
          if (ray_distance < closest_frontface_distance)
          {
              closest_frontface_distance = ray_distance;
              closest_frontface_index = ray_index;
```

```
            } else if (ray_distance >
                       farthest_frontface_distance) {
            farthest_frontface_distance = ray_distance;
            farthest_frontface_index = ray_index;
        }
    }
}
```

We know the front and backface indices and distances for this probe. Given that we incrementally move the probe, read the previous frame's offset:

```
    vec4 current_offset = vec4(0);
// Read previous offset after the first frame.
if ( first_frame == 0 ) {
    const int probe_counts_xy = probe_counts.x *
      probe_counts.y;
    ivec2 probe_offset_sampling_coordinates =
        ivec2(probe_index % probe_counts_xy, probe_index
        / probe_counts_xy);
    current_offset.rgb = texelFetch(global_textures
      [nonuniformEXT(probe_offset_texture_index)],
      probe_offset_sampling_coordinates, 0).rgb;
}
```

Now, we must check if the probe can be considered inside a geometry and calculate an offset moving away from that direction, but within the probe spacing limit, that we can call a `cell`:

```
vec3 full_offset = vec3(10000.f);
vec3 cell_offset_limit = max_probe_offset *
  probe_spacing;
// Check if a fourth of the rays was a backface, we can
   assume the probe is inside a geometry.
const bool inside_geometry = (float(backfaces_count) /
  probe_rays) > 0.25f;
if (inside_geometry && (closest_backface_index != -1))
{
    // Calculate the backface direction.
    const vec3 closest_backface_direction =
```

```
            closest_backface_distance * normalize(
            mat3(random_rotation) *
            spherical_fibonacci(closest_backface_index,
            probe_rays) );
```

Find the maximum offset inside the cell to move the probe:

```
        const vec3 positive_offset = (current_offset.xyz +
           cell_offset_limit) / closest_backface_direction;
        const vec3 negative_offset = (current_offset.xyz -
           cell_offset_limit) / closest_backface_direction;
        const vec3 maximum_offset = vec3(max
           (positive_offset.x, negative_offset.x),
           max(positive_offset.y, negative_offset.y),
           max(positive_offset.z, negative_offset.z));
        // Get the smallest of the offsets to scale the
           direction
        const float direction_scale_factor = min(min
           (maximum_offset.x, maximum_offset.y),
           maximum_offset.z) - 0.001f;
        // Move the offset in the opposite direction of the
           backface one.
        full_offset = current_offset.xyz -
           closest_backface_direction *
           direction_scale_factor;
    }
```

If we have not hit a backface, we must move the probe slightly to put it in a resting position:

```
    else if (closest_frontface_distance < 0.05f) {
        // In this case we have a very small hit distance.
        // Ensure that we never move through the farthest
           frontface
        // Move minimum distance to ensure not moving on a
           future iteration.
        const vec3 farthest_direction = min(0.2f,
           farthest_frontface_distance) * normalize(
           mat3(random_rotation) *
```

```
                spherical_fibonacci(farthest_frontface_index,
                    probe_rays) );
                const vec3 closest_direction = normalize(mat3
                    (random_rotation) * spherical_fibonacci
                    (closest_frontface_index, probe_rays));
                // The farthest frontface may also be the closest
                    if the probe can only
                // see one surface. If this is the case, don't move
                    the probe.
                if (dot(farthest_direction, closest_direction) <
                    0.5f) {
                    full_offset = current_offset.xyz +
                        farthest_direction;
                }
            }
```

Update the offset only if it is within the spacing or inside the cell limits. Then, store the value in the appropriate texture:

```
        if (all(lessThan(abs(full_offset), cell_offset_limit)))
        {
            current_offset.xyz = full_offset;
        }
        const int probe_counts_xy = probe_counts.x *
            probe_counts.y;
        const int probe_texel_x = (probe_index %
            probe_counts_xy);
        const int probe_texel_y = probe_index /
            probe_counts_xy;
        imageStore(global_images_2d[ probe_offset_texture_index
            ], ivec2(probe_texel_x, probe_texel_y),
            current_offset);
    }
```

With that, we have calculated the probe offsets.

Again, this shader demonstrates how to cleverly use information you already have – in this case, the per-ray probe distances – to move probes outside of intersecting geometries.

We presented a fully funcitonal version of DDGI, but there are some improvements that can be made and the technique can be expanded in different directions. Some examples of improvements are a classification system to disable non contributing probes, or adding a moving grid with cascades of different grid spacing centered around the camera. Combined with hand-placed volumes can create a complete diffuse global-illumination system.

While having a GPU with ray-tracing capabilities is necessary for this technique, we could bake irradiance and visibility for static scene parts and use them on older GPUs. Another improvement can be changing hysteresis based on probe luminance changes, or adding a staggered probe update based on distance and importance.

All these ideas show how powerful and configurable DDGI is and we encourage the reader to experiment and create other improvements.

Summary

In this chapter, we introduced the DDGI technique. We started by talking about global illumination, the lighting phenomena that is implemented by DDGI. Then, we provided an overview of the algorithm, explaining each step in more detail.

Finally, we wrote and commented on all the shaders in the implementation. DDGI already enhances the lighting of the rendered frame, but it can be improved and optimized.

One of the aspects of DDGI that makes it useful is its configurability: you can change the resolution of irradiance and visibility textures and change the number of rays, number of probes, and spacing of probes to support lower-end ray tracing-enabled GPUs.

In the next chapter we are going to add another element that will help us increase the accuracy of our lighting solution: reflections!

Further reading

Global illumination is an incredibly big topic that's covered extensively in all rendering literature, but we wanted to highlight links that are more connected to the implementation of DDGI.

DDGI itself is an idea that mostly came from a team at Nvidia in 2017, with the central ideas described at https://morgan3d.github.io/articles/2019-04-01-ddgi/index.html.

The original articles on DDGI and its evolution are as follows. They also contain supplemental code that was incredibly helpful in implementing the technique:

- https://casual-effects.com/research/McGuire2017LightField/index.html
- https://www.jcgt.org/published/0008/02/01/
- https://jcgt.org/published/0010/02/01/

The following is a great overview of DDGI with Spherical Harmonics support, and the only diagram to copy the border pixels for bilinear interpolation. It also describes other interesting topics: `https://handmade.network/p/75/monter/blog/p/7288-engine_work__global_illumination_with_irradiance_probes`.

The DDGI presentation by Nvidia can be found at `https://developer.download.nvidia.com/video/gputechconf/gtc/2019/presentation/s9900-irradiance-fields-rtx-diffuse-global-illumination-for-local-and-cloud-graphics.pdf`.

The following is an intuitive introduction to global illumination: `https://www.scratchapixel.com/lessons/3d-basic-rendering/global-illumination-path-tracing`.

Global Illumination Compendium: `https://people.cs.kuleuven.be/~philip.dutre/GI/`.

Finally, here is the greatest website for real-time rendering: `https://www.realtimerendering.com/`.

15
Adding Reflections with Ray Tracing

In this chapter, we are going to implement reflections using ray tracing. Before ray tracing hardware was introduced, applications implemented reflections using screen-space techniques. However, this technique has drawbacks as it can only use information from what's visible on the screen. If one of the rays goes outside the visible geometry on the screen, we usually fall back to an environment map. Because of this limitation, the rendered reflections can be inconsistent, depending on the camera position.

By introducing ray tracing hardware, we can overcome this limitation as we now have access to geometry that is not visible on the screen. The downside is that we might need to perform some expensive lighting computations. If the reflected geometry is outside the screen, this means we don't have the data from the G-buffer and we need to compute the color, light, and shadow data from scratch.

To lower the cost of this technique, developers usually trace reflections at half resolution or use ray tracing only if screen-space reflection fails. Another approach is to use lower-resolution geometry in the ray tracing path to lower the cost of ray traversal. In this chapter, we are going to implement a ray tracing-only solution, as this gives the best-quality results. Then, it will be easy to implement the optimizations mentioned previously on top of it.

In this chapter, we'll cover the following main topics:

- How screen-space reflections work
- Implementing ray-traced reflections
- Implementing a denoiser to make the ray-traced output usable

Technical requirements

By the end of the chapter, you will have a good understanding of the different solutions available for reflections. You will also learn how to implement ray-traced reflections and how to improve the final result with the help of a denoiser.

The code for this chapter can be found at the following URL: `https://github.com/PacktPublishing/Mastering-Graphics-Programming-with-Vulkan/tree/main/source/chapter15`.

How screen-space reflections work

Reflections are an important rendering element that can provide a better sense of immersion in the scene. For this reason, developers have developed a few techniques over the years to include this effect, even before ray tracing hardware was available.

One of the most common approaches is to ray-march the scene after the G-buffer data becomes available. Whether a surface will produce reflections is determined by the material's roughness. Only materials with a low roughness will emit a reflection. This also helps reduce the cost of this technique since usually, only a low number of surfaces will satisfy this requirement.

Ray marching is a technique similar to ray tracing and was introduced in *Chapter 10*, *Adding Volumetric Fog*. As a quick reminder, ray marching works similarly to ray tracing. Instead of traversing the scene to determine whether the ray hit any geometry, we move in the ray's direction by small increments for a fixed number of iterations.

This has both advantages and disadvantages. The advantage is that this technique has a fixed cost independent of the scene's complexity as the maximum number of iterations per ray is pre-determined. The downside is that the quality of the results depends on the step size and the number of iterations.

For the best quality, we want a large number of iterations and a small step size, but this would make the technique too expensive. The compromise is to use a step size that gives good enough results and then pass the result through a denoising filter to try and reduce the artifacts introduced by the low-frequency sampling.

As the name implies, this technique works in screen space, similar to other techniques such as **Screen-Space Ambient Occlusion (SSAO)**. For a given fragment, we start by determining whether it produces a reflection or not. If it does, we determine the reflected ray's direction based on the surface normal and view direction.

Next, we move along the reflected ray direction for the given number of iterations and step size. At each step, we check against the depth buffer to determine whether we hit any geometry. Since the depth buffer has a limited resolution, usually, we define a delta value that determines whether we consider a given iteration a hit.

If the difference between the ray depth and the value stored in the depth buffer is under this delta, we can exit the loop; otherwise, we must continue. The size of this delta can vary, depending on the scene's complexity, and is usually tweaked manually.

If the ray marching loop hits visible geometry, we look up the color value at that fragment and use it as the reflected color. Otherwise, we either return black or determine the reflected color using an environment map.

We are skipping over some implementation details here as they are not relevant to this chapter. We have provided resources that go into more detail in the *Further reading* section.

As mentioned previously, this technique is limited to information that is visible on screen. The main drawback is that reflections will disappear as the camera moves if the reflected geometry is no longer rendered on the screen. The other downside comes from ray marching as we have limited resolution in terms of the number and size of steps we can take.

This can introduce holes in the reflection, which is usually addressed through aggressive filtering. This can result in blurry reflections and makes it difficult to obtain crisp reflections, depending on the scene and viewpoint.

In this section, we introduced screen space reflections. We explained the main ideas behind this technique and some of its shortcomings. In the next section, we are going to implement ray-traced reflections, which can reduce some of the limitations of this technique.

Implementing ray-traced reflections

In this section, we are going to leverage the hardware ray tracing capabilities to implement reflections. Before diving into the code, here's an overview of the algorithm:

1. We start with the G-buffer data. We check whether the roughness for a given fragment is below a certain threshold. If it is, we move to the next step. Otherwise, we don't process this fragment any further.
2. To make this technique viable in real time, we cast only one reflection ray per fragment. We will demonstrate two ways to pick the reflection's ray direction: one that simulates a mirror-like surface and another that samples the GGX distribution for a given fragment.
3. If the reflection ray hits some geometry, we need to compute its surface color. We shoot another ray toward a light that has been selected through importance sampling. If the selected light is visible, we compute the color for the surface using our standard lighting model.
4. Since we are using only one sample per fragment, the final output will be noisy, especially since we are randomly selecting the reflected direction at each frame. For this reason, the output of the ray tracing step will be processed by a denoiser. We have implemented a technique called **spatiotemporal variance-guided filtering** (**SVGF**), which has been developed specifically for this use case. The algorithm will make use of spatial and temporal data to produce a result that contains only a small amount of noise.
5. Finally, we use the denoised data during our lighting computation to retrieve the specular color.

Now that you have a good overview of the steps involved, let's dive in! The first step is checking whether the roughness for a given fragment is above a certain threshold:

```
if ( roughness <= 0.3 ) {
```

We have selected 0.3 as it gives us the results we are looking for, though feel free to experiment with other values. If this fragment is contributing to the reflection computation, we initialize our random number generator and compute the two values needed to sample the GGX distribution:

```
rng_state = seed( gl_LaunchIDEXT.xy ) + current_frame;
float U1 = rand_pcg() * rnd_normalizer;
float U2 = rand_pcg() * rnd_normalizer;
```

The two random functions can be implemented as follows:

```
uint seed(uvec2 p) {
    return 19u * p.x + 47u * p.y + 101u;
}
uint rand_pcg() {
    uint state = rng_state;
    rng_state = rng_state * 747796405u + 2891336453u;
    uint word = ((state >> ((state >> 28u) + 4u)) ^ state)
                 277803737u;
    return (word >> 22u) ^ word;
}
```

These two functions have been taken from the wonderful *Hash Functions for GPU Rendering* paper, which we highly recommend. It contains many other functions that you can experiment with. We selected this seed function so that we can use the fragment's position.

Next, we need to pick our reflection vector. As mentioned previously, we have implemented two techniques. For the first technique, we simply reflect the view vector around the surface normal for a mirror-like surface. This can be computed as follows:

```
vec3 reflected_ray = normalize( reflect( incoming, normal ) );
```

When using this method, we get the following output:

Figure 15.1 – Mirror-like reflections

The other method computes the normal by randomly sampling the GGX distribution:

```
vec3 normal = sampleGGXVNDF( incoming, roughness, roughness,
                             U1, U2 );
vec3 reflected_ray = normalize( reflect( incoming, normal ) );
```

The `sampleGGXVNDF` function has been taken from the *Sampling the GGX Distribution of Visible Normals* paper. Its implementation is clearly described in this paper; we suggest you read it for more details.

In brief, this method computes a random normal according to the BRDF of the material and the view direction. This process is needed to make sure the computed reflection is more physically accurate.

Next, we must trace a ray in the scene:

```
traceRayEXT( as, // topLevel
             gl_RayFlagsOpaqueEXT, // rayFlags
             0xff, // cullMask
             sbt_offset, // sbtRecordOffset
             sbt_stride, // sbtRecordStride
             miss_index, // missIndex
             world_pos, // origin
```

```
            0.05, // Tmin
            reflected_ray, // direction
            100.0, // Tmax
            0 // payload index
    );
```

If the ray has a hit, we use importance sampling to select a light for our final color computation. The main idea behind importance sampling is to determine which element, which light in our case, is more likely to be selected based on a given probability distribution.

We have adopted the importance value described in the *Importance Sampling of Many Lights on the GPU* chapter from the book *Ray Tracing Gems*.

We start by looping through all the lights in the scene:

```
for ( uint l = 0; l < active_lights; ++l ) {
    Light light = lights[ l ];
```

Next, we compute the angle between the light and the normal of the triangle that has been hit:

```
    vec3 p_to_light = light.world_position - p_world.xyz;
    float point_light_angle = dot( normalize( p_to_light ),
                                    triangle_normal );
    float theta_i = acos( point_light_angle );
```

Then, we compute the distance between the light and the fragment position in the world space:

```
    float distance_sq = dot( p_to_light, p_to_light );
    float r_sq = light.radius * light.radius;
```

After, we use these two values to determine whether this light should be considered for this fragment:

```
    bool light_active = ( point_light_angle > 1e-4 ) && (
                        distance_sq <= r_sq );
```

The next step involves computing an orientation parameter. This tells us whether the light is shining directly on the fragment or at an angle:

```
    float theta_u = asin( light.radius / sqrt( distance_sq
) );
    float theta_prime = max( 0, theta_i - theta_u );
    float orientation = abs( cos( theta_prime ) );
```

Finally, we must compute the importance value by also taking into account the intensity of the light:

```
float importance = ( light.intensity * orientation ) /
                   distance_sq;
float final_value = light_active ? importance : 0.0;
lights_importance[ l ] = final_value;
```

If the given light is not considered active for this fragment, its importance will have a value of 0. Finally, we must accumulate the importance value for this light:

```
total_importance += final_value;
}
```

Now that we have the importance values, we need to normalize them. Like any other probability distribution function, our values need to sum to 1:

```
for ( uint l = 0; l < active_lights; ++l ) {
    lights_importance[ l ] /= total_importance;
}
```

We can now select the light to be used for this frame. First, we must generate a new random value:

```
float rnd_value = rand_pcg() * rnd_normalizer;
```

Next, we must loop through the lights and accumulate the importance of each light. Once the accumulated value is greater than our random value, we have found the light to use:

```
for ( ; light_index < active_lights; ++light_index ) {
    accum_probability += lights_importance[ light_index ];
      if ( accum_probability > rnd_value ) {
         break;
    }
}
```

Now that we have selected the light, we must cast a ray toward it to determine whether it's visible or not. If it's visible, we compute the final color for the reflected surface using our lighting model.

We compute the shadow factor as described in *Chapter 13, Revisiting Shadows with Ray Tracing*, and the color is calculated in the same way as in *Chapter 14, Adding Dynamic Diffuse Global Illumination with Ray Tracing*.

This is the result:

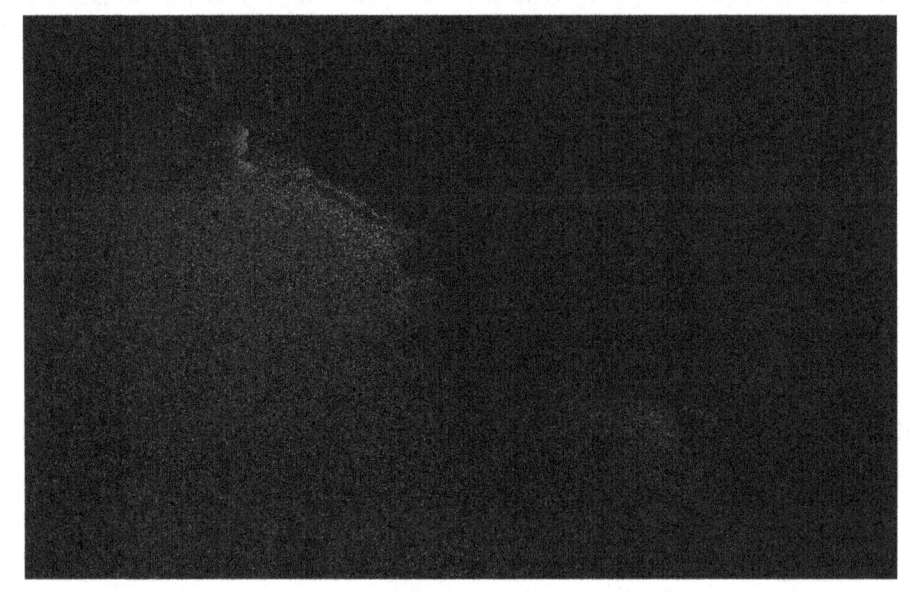

Figure 15.2 – The noisy output of the ray tracing step

In this section, we illustrated our implementation of ray-traced reflections. First, we described two ways to select a ray direction. Then, we demonstrated how to use importance sampling to select the light to use in our computation. Finally, we described how the selected light is used to determine the final color of the reflected surface.

The result of this step will be noisy and cannot be used directly in our lighting computation. In the next section, we will implement a denoiser that will help us remove most of this noise.

Implementing a denoiser

To make the output of our reflection pass usable for lighting computations, we need to pass it through a denoiser. We have implemented an algorithm called SVGF, which has been developed to reconstruct color data for path tracing.

SVGF consists of three main passes:

1. First, we compute the integrated color and moments for luminance. This is the temporal step of the algorithm. We combine the data from the previous frame with the result of the current frame.
2. Next, we compute an estimate for variance. This is done using the first and second moment values we computed in the first step.
3. Finally, we perform five passes of a wavelet filter. This is the spatial step of the algorithm. At each iteration, we apply a 5x5 filter to reduce the remaining noise as much as possible.

Implementing a denoiser

Now that you have an idea of the main algorithm, we can proceed with the code details. We start by computing the moments for the current frame:

```
float u_1 = luminance( reflections_color );
float u_2 = u_1 * u_1;
vec2 moments = vec2( u_1, u_2 );
```

Next, we use the motion vectors value – the same values we computed in *Chapter 11, Temporal Anti-Aliasing* – to determine whether we can combine the data for the current frame with the previous frame.

First, we compute the position on the screen of the previous frame:

```
bool check_temporal_consistency( uvec2 frag_coord ) {
    vec2 frag_coord_center = vec2( frag_coord ) + 0.5;
    vec2 motion_vector = texelFetch( global_textures[
                            motion_vectors_texture_index ],
                            ivec2( frag_coord ), 0 ).rg;
    vec2 prev_frag_coord = frag_coord_center +
                            motion_vector;
```

Next, we check whether the old fragment coordinates are valid:

```
    if ( any( lessThan( prev_frag_coord, vec2( 0 ) ) ) ||
        any( greaterThanEqual( prev_frag_coord,
                            resolution ) ) ) {
            return false;
    }
```

Then, we check whether the mesh ID is consistent with the previous frame:

```
    uint mesh_id = texelFetch( global_utextures[
                        mesh_id_texture_index ],
                        ivec2( frag_coord ), 0 ).r;
    uint prev_mesh_id = texelFetch( global_utextures[
                        history_mesh_id_texture_index ],
                        ivec2( prev_frag_coord ), 0 ).r;

    if ( mesh_id != prev_mesh_id ) {
        return false;
    }
```

Next, we check for large depth discontinuities, which can be caused by disocclusion from the previous frame. We make use of the difference between the current and previous frame's depth, and also of the screen space derivative of the depth for the current frame:

```
float z = texelFetch( global_textures[
                     depth_texture_index ],
                     ivec2( frag_coord ), 0 ).r;
float prev_z = texelFetch( global_textures[
                     history_depth_texture ],
                     ivec2( prev_frag_coord ), 0
                     ).r;

vec2 depth_normal_dd = texelFetch( global_textures[
                     depth_normal_dd_texture_index ],
                     ivec2( frag_coord ), 0 ).rg;
float depth_diff = abs( z - prev_z ) / (
                     depth_normal_dd.x + 1e-2 );

if ( depth_diff > 10 ) {
    return false;
}
```

The last consistency check is done by using the normal value:

```
float normal_diff = distance( normal, prev_normal ) / (
                     depth_normal_dd.y + 1e-2
                     );
if ( normal_diff > 16.0 ) {
    return false;
}
```

If all of these tests pass, this means the values from the previous frame can be used for temporal accumulation:

```
if ( is_consistent ) {
    vec3 history_reflections_color = texelFetch(
    global_textures[ history_reflections_texture_index ],
    ivec2( frag_coord ), 0 ).rgb;
    vec2 history_moments = texelFetch( global_textures[
```

```
                    history_moments_texture_index ],
                    ivec2( frag_coord ), 0 ).rg;

    float alpha = 0.2;
    integrated_color_out = reflections_color * alpha +
    ( 1 - alpha ) * history_reflections_color;
    integrated_moments_out = moments * alpha + ( 1 - alpha
    ) * moments;
```

If the consistency check fails, we will only use the data from the current frame:

```
} else {
    integrated_color_out = reflections_color;
    integrated_moments_out = moments;
}
```

This concludes the accumulation pass. This is the output we obtain:

Figure 15.3 – The color output after the accumulation step

The next step is to compute the variance. This can easily be done as follows:

```
float variance = moments.y - pow( moments.x, 2 );
```

Adding Reflections with Ray Tracing

Now that we have our accumulated value, we can start implementing the wavelet filter. As mentioned previously, this is a 5x5 cross-bilateral filter. We start with the familiar double loop, being careful not to access out-of-bounds values:

```
for ( int y = -2; y <= 2; ++y) {
    for( int x = -2; x <= 2; ++x ) {
        ivec2 offset = ivec2( x, y );
        ivec2 q = frag_coord + offset;

        if ( any( lessThan( q, ivec2( 0 ) ) ) || any(
            greaterThanEqual( q, ivec2( resolution ) ) ) )
        {
            continue;
        }
```

Next, we compute the filter kernel value and weighting value, w:

```
float h_q = h[ x + 2 ] * h[ y + 2 ];
float w_pq = compute_w( frag_coord, q );
float sample_weight = h_q * w_pq;
```

We'll explain the implementation of the weighting function in a moment. Next, we load the integrated color and variance for the given fragment:

```
vec3 c_q = texelFetch( global_textures[
integrated_color_texture_index ], q, 0 ).rgb;
float prev_variance = texelFetch( global_textures[
variance_texture_index ], q, 0 ).r;
```

Lastly, we accumulate the new color and variance values:

```
new_filtered_color += h_q * w_pq * c_q;
color_weight += sample_weight;

new_variance += pow( h_q, 2 ) * pow( w_pq, 2 ) *
                prev_variance;
variance_weight += pow( sample_weight, 2 );
    }
}
```

Before storing the newly computed values, we need to divide them by the accumulated weight:

```
new_filtered_color /= color_weight;
new_variance /= variance_weight;
```

We repeat this process five times. The resulting color output will be used for our lighting computation for the specular color.

As promised, we are now going to look at the weight computation. There are three elements to the weight: normal, depth, and luminance. In the code, we tried to follow the naming from the paper so that it's easier to match with our implementation of the formulas.

We start with the normals:

```
vec2 encoded_normal_p = texelFetch( global_textures[
                        normals_texture_index ], p, 0 ).rg;
vec3 n_p = octahedral_decode( encoded_normal_p );

vec2 encoded_normal_q = texelFetch( global_textures[
                        normals_texture_index ], q, 0 ).rg;
vec3 n_q = octahedral_decode( encoded_normal_q );

float w_n = pow( max( 0, dot( n_p, n_q ) ), sigma_n );
```

We compute the cosine between the normal of the current fragment and the fragment from the filter to determine the weight of the normal component.

We look at depth next:

```
float z_dd = texelFetch( global_textures[ depth_normal_dd_
                         texture_index ], p, 0 ).r;
float z_p = texelFetch( global_textures[ depth_texture_index ],
                        p, 0 ).r;
float z_q = texelFetch( global_textures[ depth_texture_index ],
                        q, 0 ).r;

float w_z = exp( -( abs( z_p - z_q ) / ( sigma_z * abs(
            z_dd ) + 1e-8 ) ) );
```

In a similar fashion to the accumulation step, we make use of the difference between the depth values between two fragments. The screen-space derivative is also included. As before, we want to penalize large depth discontinuities.

The last weight element is luminance. We start by computing the luminance for the fragments we are processing:

```
vec3 c_p = texelFetch( global_textures[ integrated_color_
                      texture_index ], p, 0 ).rgb;
vec3 c_q = texelFetch( global_textures[ integrated_color_
                      texture_index ], q, 0 ).rgb;

float l_p = luminance( c_p );
float l_q = luminance( c_q );
```

Next, we pass the variance value through a Gaussian filter to reduce instabilities:

```
float g = 0.0;
const int radius = 1;
for ( int yy = -radius; yy <= radius; yy++ ) {
    for ( int xx = -radius; xx <= radius; xx++ ) {
        ivec2 s = p + ivec2( xx, yy );
        float k = kernel[ abs( xx ) ][ abs( yy ) ];
        float v = texelFetch( global_textures[
            variance_texture_index ], s, 0 ).r;
        g += v * k;
    }
}
```

Finally, we compute the luminance weight and combine it with the other two weight values:

```
float w_l = exp( -( abs( l_p - l_q ) / ( sigma_l * sqrt
            ( g ) + 1e-8 ) ) );

return w_z * w_n * w_l;
```

This concludes our implementation of the SVGF algorithm. After five passes, we get the following output:

Figure 15.4 – The output at the end of the denoising step

In this section, we described how to implement a common denoising algorithm. The algorithm consists of three passes: an accumulation phase for the color and luminance moments, a step for computing luminance variance, and a step for the wavelet filter, which is repeated five times.

Summary

In this chapter, we described how to implement ray-traced reflections. We started with an overview of screen-space reflection, a technique that was used for many years before ray tracing hardware was available. We explained how it works and some of its limitations.

Next, we described our ray tracing implementation to determine reflection values. We provided two methods to determine the reflected ray direction and explained how the reflected color is computed if a hit is returned.

Since we only use one sample per fragment, the result of this step is noisy. To reduce as much of this noise as possible, we implemented a denoiser based on SVGF. This technique consists of three passes. First, there's a temporal accumulation step to compute color and luminance moments. Then, we compute the luminance variance. Finally, we process the color output by passing it through five iterations of a wavelet filter.

This chapter also concludes our book! We hope you enjoyed reading it as much as we had fun writing it. When it comes to modern graphics techniques, there is only so much that can be covered in a single book. We have included what we thought are some of the most interesting features and techniques when it comes to implementing them in Vulkan. Our goal is to provide you with a starting set of tools that you can build and expand upon. We wish you a wonderful journey on the path to mastering graphics programming!

We very much welcome your feedback and corrections, so please feel free to reach out to us.

Further reading

We have only provided a brief introduction to screen-space reflections. The following articles go into more detail about their implementation, their limitations, and how to improve the final results:

- `https://lettier.github.io/3d-game-shaders-for-beginners/screen-space-reflection.html`
- `https://bartwronski.com/2014/01/25/the-future-of-screenspace-reflections/`
- `https://bartwronski.com/2014/03/23/gdc-follow-up-screenspace-reflections-filtering-and-up-sampling/`

We have only used one of the many hashing techniques presented in the paper *Hash Functions for GPU Rendering*: `https://jcgt.org/published/0009/03/02/`.

This link contains more details about the sampling technique we used to determine the reflection vector by sampling the BRDF – *Sampling the GGX Distribution of Visible Normals*: `https://jcgt.org/published/0007/04/01/`.

For more details about the SVGF algorithm we presented, we recommend reading the original paper and supporting material: `https://research.nvidia.com/publication/2017-07_spatiotemporal-variance-guided-filtering-real-time-reconstruction-path-traced`.

We used importance sampling to determine which light to use at each frame. Another technique that has become popular in the last few years is **Reservoir Spatio-Temporal Importance Resampling** (**ReSTIR**). We highly recommend reading the original paper and looking up the other techniques that have been inspired by it: `https://research.nvidia.com/publication/2020-07_spatiotemporal-reservoir-resampling-real-time-Ray-Tracing-dynamic-direct`.

In this chapter, we implemented the SVGF algorithm from scratch for pedagogical purposes. Our implementation is a good starting point to build upon, but we also recommend looking at production denoisers from AMD and Nvidia to compare results:

- `https://gpuopen.com/fidelityfx-denoiser/`
- `https://developer.nvidia.com/rtx/Ray-Tracing/rt-denoisers`

Index

A

Acceleration Structures (ASes) 268, 276
any-hit shader 269
application layer 16
Array of Structures (AoS) 123
arrays 10
asset baking 11
async compute
 separate queue, adding 114
AsynchronousLoader class
 command pools, creating for transfer queue 69, 70
 file request, processing 72
 finished transfer renderer, signaling 75
 responsibilities 69
 semaphores and fences, creating for GPU synchronization 71, 72
 staging buffer, creating 70, 71
 upload request, processing 72-75
asynchronous loading 61-63
 AsynchronousLoader class 69
 I/O thread and tasks, creating 63, 64
 Vulkan queues 64
Axis Aligned Bounding Boxes (AABBs) 131, 160, 269

B

banding 234
bi-directional distribution function (BRDF) 25
bindless 31
bindless rendering
 descriptor pool, creating 34-36
 descriptor set, updating 36-38
 device supports, checking 32, 33
 implementing 32
 shader code, updating 39, 40
 unlocking 32
Bottom Level Acceleration Structure (BLAS)
 building 270-276
Bounded Volume Hierarchy (BVH) 160, 268

C

calculate_lighting method
 modifying 325, 326
callable shader 269
Cascade Shadow Maps (CSM) 288
closest hit shader 269
cloth simulation
 implementing, with compute shaders 117

clustered lighting
  forward technique, versus deferred technique 157-159
  history 156, 157
code
  application layer 16
  foundation layer 9
  graphics layer 13-15
  layers 8, 9
  structure 7, 8
  testing, on Linux 5-7
  testing, on macOS 7
  testing, on Windows 4
code, foundation layer
  arrays 10
  file operations 11
  hash maps 10
  logging 12
  memory management 10
  process execution 13
  serialization 11
  strings 12
  time management 12
compute shaders
  benefits 117
  overview 118, 119
  used, for GPU culling 146
  used, for implementing cloth simulation 117
  writing 120-125
CPU lights assignment 168-173
cubemap shadows 182, 183

D

data-driven approach 88, 90
data injection 228-230

deferred shading 158
  advantages 158
  disadvantages 158
delta time 12
denoiser
  implementing 340-347
depth-first search (DFS) 96
depth pyramid algorithm 147-149
  used, for occlusion culling 149-152
Depth Texture 249
descriptor pool
  creating 34-36
descriptor set
  updating 36-38
Directed Acyclic Graph (DAG) 85
direct memory access (DMA) 66
Dynamic Diffuse Global Illumination (DDGI) 306, 307
  algorithm overview 308
  calculate_lighting method, modifying 325, 326
  implementing 311
  indirect lighting, sampling 320-324
  probe offsets shader 326-331
  probes irradiance and visibility shaders, updating 315-320
  ray-generation shader 311
  ray-hit shader 312-315
  ray-miss shader 315
  tools 307
Dynamic Diffuse Global Illumination (DDGI), algorithm
  probes irradiance and visibility updates 309, 310
  probes offsetting 308, 309
  probes sampling 310
  ray tracing, for each probe 308

E

enkiTS
  used, for task-based multi-threading 58
  using 59, 61
event ID (EID) 28
extinction 224

F

fiber-based parallelism 59
file operations 11
filtered visibility
  computing 298-301
  using 301
filters
  spatial filters 235, 236
  temporal filters 237, 238
fireflies 261
forward rendering 156
forward technique, versus deferred technique
  light clusters 160
  light tiles 159
frame graphs 82, 85, 86
  building 86, 87
  data-driven approach 88
  implementing 91
  parsing 93, 94
  rendering 102-106
  resources 91, 92
  topological sort, implementing 94-97
frame graphs, properties
  acyclic 87
  directed 86
frustum culling
  performing 142
frustum voxel (froxel) 225

G

G-buffer 156
  implementing 160-167
geometric buffer 156
glTF scene format 16-24
GPU culling
  implementing, with compute shaders 146
GPU debugging 27-29
GPU light
  processing 174, 175
graphics layer 13-15

H

hash maps 10
History Texture block 249

I

image, Temporal Anti-Aliasing (TAA)
  negative mip bias 263
  sharpness post-processing 262, 263
  unjitter texture UVs 263, 264
ImGui
  reference link 16
indirect lighting 304-306
  sampling 320-325
input assembly (IA) 132
intermediate representation (IR) 40
intersection shader 269

J

jittering 248

L

level of detail (LOD) 133
light assignment 157
light clusters
  CPU lights assignment 168-173
  GPU light, processing 174, 175
  implementing 167
Linux
  code, testing on 5-7
local data storage (LDS) 292
logging 12

M

macOS
  code, testing on 7
memory aliasing 85, 98
memory management 10
meshes
  breaking down, into meshlets 132-134
meshlets 131
  bounding spheres example 134
  cone example 135
  generating 135-138
  reference link 135
  subdivision example 133
MeshOptimizer
  reference link 135
mesh shader 193, 194
mesh shaders 131, 138, 139
  implementing 143-146
miss shader 269
Morphological Anti-Aliasing (MLAA) 245
motion vectors 290
Multim In Parvo (MIP) 263
multiple fences
  replacing, with timeline semaphore 107-109

multiple threads
  used, for recording commands 76
multiple threads, used for recording commands 76
  allocation strategy 76
  command buffer recycling 77
  multiple tasks, spawning to record command buffers 81
  primary command buffers, used for drawing 78, 79
  primary, versus secondary command buffers 77
  secondary command buffers, used for drawing 79-81
Multi Sampled Anti-Aliasing (MSAA) 157, 245
multi-threading rendering 57
multiview rendering 184

N

node variables
  inputs 89
  name 89
  outputs 89
normalized device coordinates (NDCs) 279

O

occlusion algorithm 147
occlusion culling
  depth pyramid algorithm, using 149-152
OpenGL Shading Language (GLSL) 39
  compiling, to SPIR-V 41, 42

Index 353

P

Percentage Closer Filtering (PCF) 288
per-light shadow memory
  usage, selecting 200-203
phase function 224
physically based rendering (PBR) 16, 25-27
pinned-task 63
pipeline layout generation
  automating 40, 41
  GLSL, compiling to SPIR-V 41, 42
  SPIR-V output, examining 42-44
Post-Process Anti-Aliasing 245
primitive assembly (PA) 132
probe offsets shader 326-331
probes irradiance and visibility shaders
  updating 315-320
probes offsetting 308, 309
process execution 13

R

ray generation 269
ray-generation shader 311
ray-hit shader 312-315
ray-miss shader 315
ray-traced reflections
  implementing 335-340
ray-traced shadows, improving
    techniques 289
  filtered visibility, computing 298-301
  motion vectors, using 290
  visibility, computing 292-298
  visibility variance, computing 291
ray tracing 268, 287, 305
  for probe 308
  in Vulkan 268-270

Ray Tracing Gems 287
ray tracing pipeline
  creating 276-284
  defining 276-284
resources 91
resources, input/output node
  name 92
  output_handle 91
  producer 91
  ref_count 91
  resource_info 91
  type 91
resource types
  attachment 89
  buffer 90
  reference 90
  texture 89

S

Screen-Space Ambient Occlusion
    (SSAO) 334
screen-space reflections
  working 334, 335
separate queue
  adding, for async compute 114
  work, submitting 115-117
serialization 11
shader code
  updating 39, 40
Shader Storage Buffer Object (SSBO) 187
shadow cubemap face 188, 189
shadow map memory
  improving, with Vulkans
    sparse resources 197

shadow mapping, with mesh shaders
   cubemap shadows 182, 183
   implementing 181
   indirect draw commands
      generation 187, 188
   mesh shader 193, 194
   multiview rendering 184
   overview 181, 182
   per-light mesh instance culling 184-187
   shadow cubemap face culling 188, 189
   shadow map sampling 194-196
   task shader 190-192
shadow techniques
   history 180
   mapping 180
   raytraced shadows 181
   volumes 180
Sharp Morphological Anti-Aliasing (SMAA) 246
simple ray-traced shadows
   implementing 288, 289
Single Instruction, Multiple Data (SIMD) 118
Single Instruction, Multiple Threads (SIMT) 118
sparse shadow map
   rendering into 203-206
sparse textures
   allocating 197-199
   creating 197-199
spatial filters 235, 236
spatiotemporal variance-guided filtering (SVGF) 335
specialization constants
   advantage 216-219
SPIR-V output 42-44
Standard Library (std) 10
Streaming SIMD Extensions (SSE) 245

strings 12
Structure of Arrays (SoA) 123
Synergisic Processing Unit (SPUs) 245

T

TAA, implementation 249
   camera, jittering 250
   implementation code 253, 254
   jittering sequences, selecting 251
   motion vectors, adding 252, 253
TAA, rendering technique
   algorithm overview 247-249
task-based multi-threading
   enkiTS, using 58
task-based parallelism 59
   need for 58, 59
task shader 190-192
task shaders 138, 139
   implementing 140-143
Temporal Anti-Aliasing (TAA) 158, 227, 290
   banding 264, 265
   history constraint 258-260
   history sampling 256
   image, sharpening 262
   improving 254
   reprojection 254, 255
   resolve 260-262
   scene sampling 257, 258
temporal filters 237, 238
threads 58
timeline semaphore
   creating 111
   extension, enabling 109, 110
   used, for replacing multiple fences 107-109
   using, on CPU 111, 112
   using, on GPU 112-114
time management 12

Index   355

Top Level Acceleration Structure (TLAS)
building 270-276
topological sort
implementing 94, 95
resource alias, computing 98-102
transmittance 224

V

variable rate shading (VRS) 209, 210
integrating, with Vulkan 212-216
shading rate, determining 210-212
Velocity Coordinates block 249
Velocity Texture block 249
Virtual Memory Allocator (VMA) 15
virtual textures 197
visibility
computing 292-298
variance, computing 291
Volumetric Fog 224-226
data injection 226
light integration 227
light scattering 226
scene application in Clustered Lighting 227
spatial filtering 227
temporal filtering 227
Volumetric Fog Rendering 222
applying 234
blue noise 239, 240
data injection 228-230
filters, adding 235
implementing 228
lighting contribution, calculating 230, 231
scattering and extinction, integrating 232, 234
volumetric noise generation 238

Volumetric Rendering 222
absorption 223
extinction 224
in-scattering 223
out-scattering 223
phase function 224
transmittance 224
Vulkan
ray tracing 268-270
used, for integrating variable rate shading (VRS) 212-216
Vulkan Memory Allocator (VMA) 199
Vulkan queues 64- 69
Vulkans sparse resources
used, for improving shadow map memory 197
Vulkans sparse resources, with shadow map memory
per-light shadow memory usage, selecting 200-203
rendering, into sparse shadow map 203-206
sparse textures, allocating 197-199
sparse textures, creating 197-199

W

Windows
code, testing on 4
work-stealing queue 59

‹packt›

www.packtpub.com

Subscribe to our online digital library for full access to over 7,000 books and videos, as well as industry leading tools to help you plan your personal development and advance your career. For more information, please visit our website.

Why subscribe?

- Spend less time learning and more time coding with practical eBooks and Videos from over 4,000 industry professionals
- Improve your learning with Skill Plans built especially for you
- Get a free eBook or video every month
- Fully searchable for easy access to vital information
- Copy and paste, print, and bookmark content

Did you know that Packt offers eBook versions of every book published, with PDF and ePub files available? You can upgrade to the eBook version at packtpub.com and as a print book customer, you are entitled to a discount on the eBook copy. Get in touch with us at customercare@packtpub.com for more details.

At www.packtpub.com, you can also read a collection of free technical articles, sign up for a range of free newsletters, and receive exclusive discounts and offers on Packt books and eBooks.

Other Books You May Enjoy

If you enjoyed this book, you may be interested in these other books by Packt:

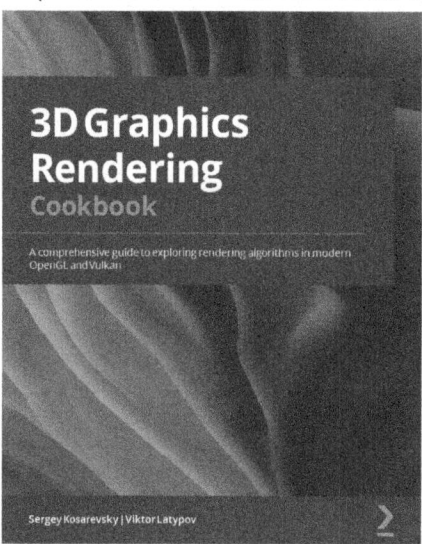

3D Graphics Rendering Cookbook

Sergey Kosarevsky, Viktor Latypov

ISBN: 978-1-83898-619-3

- Improve the performance of legacy OpenGL applications
- Manage a substantial amount of content in real-time 3D rendering engines
- Discover how to debug and profile graphics applications
- Understand how to use the Approaching Zero Driver Overhead (AZDO) philosophy in OpenGL
- Integrate various rendering techniques into a single application
- Find out how to develop Vulkan applications
- Implement a physically based rendering pipeline from scratch
- Integrate a physics library with your rendering engine

Vulkan Cookbook

Pawel Lapinski

ISBN: 978-1-78646-815-4

- Work with Swapchain to present images on screen
- Create, submit, and synchronize operations processed by the hardware
- Create buffers and images, manage their memory, and upload data to them from CPU
- Explore descriptor sets and set up an interface between application and shaders
- Organize drawing operations into a set of render passes and subpasses
- Prepare graphics pipelines to draw 3D scenes and compute pipelines to perform mathematical calculations
- Implement geometry projection and tessellation, texturing, lighting, and post-processing techniques
- Write shaders in GLSL and convert them into SPIR-V assemblies
- Find out about and implement a collection of popular, advanced rendering techniques found in games and benchmarks

Packt is searching for authors like you

If you're interested in becoming an author for Packt, please visit `authors.packtpub.com` and apply today. We have worked with thousands of developers and tech professionals, just like you, to help them share their insight with the global tech community. You can make a general application, apply for a specific hot topic that we are recruiting an author for, or submit your own idea.

Share Your Thoughts

Now you've finished *Mastering Graphics Programming with Vulkan*, we'd love to hear your thoughts! Scan the QR code below to go straight to the Amazon review page for this book and share your feedback or leave a review on the site that you purchased it from.

`https://www.amazon.com/review/create-review/error?asin=1803244798`

Your review is important to us and the tech community and will help us make sure we're delivering excellent quality content.

Download a free PDF copy of this book

Thanks for purchasing this book!

Do you like to read on the go but are unable to carry your print books everywhere?

Is your eBook purchase not compatible with the device of your choice?

Don't worry, now with every Packt book you get a DRM-free PDF version of that book at no cost.

Read anywhere, any place, on any device. Search, copy, and paste code from your favorite technical books directly into your application.

The perks don't stop there, you can get exclusive access to discounts, newsletters, and great free content in your inbox daily

Follow these simple steps to get the benefits:

1. Scan the QR code or visit the link below

   `https://packt.link/free-ebook/9781803244792`

2. Submit your proof of purchase
3. That's it! We'll send your free PDF and other benefits to your email directly